PASTA INTERNATIONAL

BY GERTRUDE HARRIS

ILLUSTRATED BY
VERNON KOSKI

101 PRODUCTIONS
SAN FRANCISCO

Note Measurements in this book are not straight conversions from U.S. measurements to metric, but have been adapted into metric for each individual recipe.

Printed and bound in the United States of America.

Distributed to the book trade in the United States by Charles Scribner's Sons, New York.

Published by 101 Productions
834 Mission Street
San Francisco, California 94103

Library of Congress Cataloging in Publication Data

Harris, Gertrude
    Pasta international.

    Includes index.
    1. Cookery (Macaroni)   I. Title.
TX809.M17H36   641.8'22   78-11295

ISBN 0-89286-143-6 pbk.

CONTENTS

There is a mystique in *pasta* as there is in all familiar growing things: rising bread, the crazy ballooning of cakes, the ripening of fruit on kitchen shelves, trees blooming in spring and the blooming of young cooks. All these inspire a sense of wonder, a hint of witchcraft in the sensitive young of all ages.

The mystique in *pasta* evolves from the enigma of its origin and from its universality. For no matter what kind of flour is milled for its use or what grain it is milled from, *pasta* is always supple, gay and viable. And this, too, we know: The history of *pasta* parallels the history of man and his civilization.

Not only is *pasta* a universal food staple, but it can be served very simply or so elaborately that it has been included in the grandest of gourmet dining. On 15 January 1817, for example, that most distinguished chef, Marie-Antoine Carême, prepared a banquet at the extraordinary Royal Pavilion in Brighton for Britain's Prince Regent, later King George IV. It began with four soups, four fish dishes, four *pièces de résistances* and thirty-six *entrées*, among them *La Timbale de Macaroni à la Napolitaine* (macaroni and grated cheese, layered with forcemeat and steamed in a large mold). It was followed by five *assietes volante* (flying saucers) and all those made up only the first course!

My own interest in *pasta* dates from a childish wonder at its magical properties: A bit of ivory-colored dough became, under the swift and deft manipulation of my mother's hands, a nest of beautiful ribbons, a promenade of little, flour-dusted pillows called *kreplach* or *vareniki*, or *varnishkes*, little bow ties or butterflies in which I participated in the making, for when my mother had cut little rectangles, I was invited to pinch them together in the middle.

Of course, when talking or thinking about *pasta,* it is only natural that one's first thoughts turn to Italy, since of all the European and Oriental cultures that use it, none bestows as fanciful, as humorous or as affectionate attention on it (or any other food) as Italians do. Poems have been written about it, and national honors have been bestowed on *pasta* manufacturers and on chefs who have prepared outstanding *pasta* dishes.

Orientals certainly eat almost as much *pasta* as Italians do, yet it is rice that is usually associated with Orientals. The Jewish people of Eastern Europe also eat it regularly, and many of the dishes eaten in religious and social rituals include some form of noodles, both sweet and savory. What culture does not include some form of *pasta*? Yet it is the Italians who glorify it and indulge in fantasies about it. Gioacchino Rossini is as famous for his culinary skills as for the operas he composed. When traveling to "foreign countries" he had his *pasta* sent to him from Naples. In March of 1859, he wrote to a friend, mourning the absence of good *pasta* in Paris and poignantly signed the letter, "Rossini *Senzamaccheroni*" (Rossini without macaroni). One recipe for which he is famous is a complicated fantasy that requires a syringe to force the filling into large macaroni. He had the syringe made of silver and ivory and the filling was of truffles, *pâté de foie gras* and beef marrow. Those who later ate it called it a "symphony by Rossini." It was Rossini who wrote: "You need intelligence to cook, mix and serve *pasta.*"

Gertrude Harris

HISTORY OF PASTA

In October 1929, a curious "story" appeared in *The Macaroni Journal,* the trade magazine of American *pasta* manufacturers. It was entitled "A Saga of Cathay" and related the story of a simple sailor on a ship that also carried Signore Marco Polo, the great Venetian merchant-traveler of the 13th century. They had been traveling for some time and fresh water was running low. As they passed a small Chinese island, they dropped anchor and the sailor was sent ashore with a cask to fill. He walked, apparently undisturbed, for some time before he spied a well in the courtyard of a large house. He also saw a young Chinese girl cooking strange long strings that struck him as being a form of food, for she tasted them from time to time. He entered the courtyard and communicated not only his need for water but his interest in the long strings, which our heroine invited him to taste. They were, he later explained, delicious, and he asked how they were made and how eaten. He got his "recipe," had his cask refilled and returned to the ship.

When the curious rich young traveler, our Marco Polo, tasted the "strings," he was nonplussed: They were hard and tasteless. "No, no," cried the sailor, "they must be tenderized in boiling water before being eaten," and he showed how he saw the girl do it. He splashed a little oil on the cooked "strings," then some salt and pepper and again Marco tried it. They were indeed delicious! So Marco persuaded the sailor to lead him to the house and there he was entertained with a demonstration of how the flour-and-water dough was made and the strings shaped. Satisfied, Marco returned to the ship with the fresh samples. There he called the ship's captain and cook and repeated the demonstration, making a new batch with enough to dry some for another meal—as he had been told to do. All were convinced that the "strings" were indeed an extraordinary treasure and promptly named them after the lucky sailor, whose name, oddly enough, was Spaghetti!

Now, this is the stuff that dreams are made of, and in barely the time it took to write that rather obvious, though good-humored joke, the word had spread and the incredible story was accepted as fact. Not only by Americans and Italo-Americans, but by Italians in Italy, who should have known better. (It now occurs to me to wonder if the Chinese believe that Marco Polo brought *spaghetti* to China from Italy!)

In reality, Marco Polo's part in the matter of discovering *pasta* was rather greater, and at the same time less, than he deserved. Undoubtedly, he was the most noted traveler and adventurer-merchant-explorer from Europe to the Far East during the Middle Ages. His voyages were indeed vitally important, but what brought him fame was a fortunate series of events that initiated the publication of his story of 24 years (1271 to 1295) in Asia. He was not, by any means, the first European to bridge the Muslim gap that separated the Eastern and Western civilizations, but while other voices were known to very small audiences, Marco Polo's memoirs were almost an overnight sensation. Three factors were responsible: They opened up new possibilities for international trade, created new vistas for learning in intellectual circles, and since so many of the details appeared utterly fantastic to the medieval mind, they seemed, even to the learned, an enjoyable work of romantic fiction not to be taken seriously. (Time has, however, vindicated Marco Polo, proving him to be a remarkably observant and reliable historian.)

The facts of Marco Polo's life are too well known to be detailed here. Suffice it to say that he was born in 1254 in Venice, then one of the greatest trading ports in Europe, and died there in 1324. He came from a long line of rich and influential traveling merchants, and it was quite natural that the young Marco went off with his father Niccolò and his uncle Maffeo, both experienced travelers, when he came of age. The tale of their dramatic return from Asia, unrecognized by family, is now part of the Marco Polo lore. Upon his return, he joined the Venetian navy and took part in a skirmish with the Genoese. He was captured and landed in a Genoese prison, where he met a man from Pisa named Rustichello or Rusticiano, a writer of romantic fiction and an authority on chivalry. Marco, strangely, was not very literate, so the great traveler and the chivalrous literary prisoner put their heads together and wrote Marco's memoirs, what later became known as *Il Milione*.

The original title was *Divisamente Dou Monde* ("Description of the World"), and so impressive was the reception, that by the early 16th century a geographer, Giovanni Batista Ramusio, who had made a well-known copy of the work, wrote that *"Tutta Italia in pochi mesa ne fu piena."* ("In a few months, all of Italy was full of it.") Not, however, as it was meant to be read, but as a fantasy, a romance, in which Kublai Khan was portrayed as a sort of King of Chivalry and Cathay a city of dreamy romance. The Round Table of King Arthur knew no greater glory!

The question as to whether Marco Polo introduced *pasta* into Italy can perhaps be traced to a few paragraphs found only in Ramusio's copy of *Il Milione*: "They do not use bread, these people, but ... wheat with them does not give such increase but what they reap they eat only in strips of macaroni *(lasagne)* and other kinds of paste...." And in his description of the island of Fanfur (Sumatra), he details the use of the heart of the sago palm (others say it was the breadfruit tree) mixed with water and used as flour to make cakes, bread and also *"lasagne,* which are very good and which I often ate."

Would Marco (or any scribe making a copy at that time) thus make so casual a reference or comparison unless the subject to which he alluded was popularly known and would be generally understood? The truth is that *pasta* was commonplace in *both* Italy and China long before the book was written.

I, too, feel that I have the right to my own theory, which I call the "Theory of Spontaneous Discovery." I feel, and hope to demonstrate here, that *pasta* appeared in many places and during many periods, as it was needed.

Obviously, the history of *pasta* echoes the fury and the fiery cultural competition between races and continents. Whether the Chinese, the Egyptians, the Greeks or the Romans were first to make and eat *pasta* is a small matter compared to the development of the first convenience food.

In days of slow travel, by horse or camel, animal-drawn wagons or carriages, by sailing ship or on foot, food had somehow to be transported without spoiling. It was inevitable that someone—or many people quite independently—would discover a staple like *pasta,* a ribbon like noodle, a rod like *spaghetti,* a tube like macaroni and tiny bits like *couscous, spaetzle, gnocchi, malfattini.* Once dried, it is lightweight and easily stowed in the hold of a ship, in the pocket of a saddle or in a case on top of a carriage. Imagine the advantage of a food that not only remains edible for several years, but can also be reconstituted for ingestion (and even swells by some degrees) by the simple procedure of dropping it into boiling water and cooking

briefly. Moreover, it mates well with any other available food, dried or fresh, or may be eaten simply with a little oil and salt. The advantages of such a food are obvious. How the nomadic people of the world would cherish such a treasure.

To discover the history of *pasta* during the earliest times is to follow the development of a wheat culture. The oldest statements presumably referring to wheat include the discovery of "corn" (a common designation for all grains at one time) in China in 2307 B.C. We also know for a certainty that wheat served as human food throughout the history of the Nile River civilization. The annual floods of the river not only restored the surrounding soil, but also made favorable conditions for growing wheat by drowning out competing grasses.

There are many indications that *pasta* did indeed exist on the Italian peninsula even before the "ancient Romans." In the fourth century B.C., Etruscans inhabited western-central Italy. In the port city of Caere, not far from Rome, is a tomb famous for its magnificent bas-reliefs. Within it are two columns that depict familiar kitchen utensils of the time. One column is of particular interest to us as it shows the utensils for making *pasta*: a rolling pin, a working surface with a raised rim (to keep flour and water from oozing over the side), a pastry cutter, a knife, a water pitcher and ladle, and a bag of flour. They are easily recognizable because, with some modern innovations, they are not too different from those we use today.

Not long after (as centuries go), we find that the Greeks had a well-loved food staple called *laganon,* which they brought to southern Italy and which became the *laganum* of the Romans and eventually *lasagne* in Italian. Even today in the Neapolitan dialect, a *laganatura* is a rolling pin.

Further evidence of the long history of *pasta* in Italy lies in the writings of her great philosophers and poets. Cicero, who lived from 106 B.C. until 43 B.C., mentions it enthusiastically in his writing. And Horace, in one of his famed satires, scolds a friend for being unable to leave his home without five servants following him. He, on the other hand, freely moves about wherever and whenever he pleases: "I wander through the streets ... then I go home to my supper of a bowl of leeks, chickpeas and *lasagne.*"

Soon after the time of Horace, we find a cookbook written by an equally famous, though hardly as abstemious, Roman, Marius Gabius Apicius, a wealthy self-indulgent man but a *gourmand* of the first water. After years of prodigious feasting, he discovered he had almost gone through his fortune; he could not face the lean days ahead and took his own life. The cookbook, entitled *De Re Coquinaria* ("On Cookery"), is quite lost, but so many subsequent authors borrowed from it that we have a good idea what it contained. In one recipe, Apicius refers to strips of dough fried and sauced with honey and pepper. Another describes cooking *pasta* in oil and serving it with a sauce of pepper and *garum* (that incredible condiment that Romans splashed on everything, made of aged fish entrails).

As Rome ate and ate and burned and ate, its vast empire was slowly being undermined and usurped by enemies. From the east came the Arabs, who had been unified in the seventh century by the prophet Muhammad. Under the banner of Islam, the Arabs had taken over the Persian Empire and built their capital in fabled Baghdad, that extraordinary pocket of Eastern wealth and fantasy. The Arabs, forgetting their sparse and lean years as desert nomads, took enthusiastically to the sumptuous comfort and rich elegance in the scented gardens of Baghdad. Soon they moved outward and swept along the Mediterranean coast, learning from each culture and bringing the best of their own lands. They introduced citrus trees to Sicily and Spain and brought exotic spices and other fruits from the oases of North Africa's deserts. These ingredients were used in the exquisite sauces on *couscous,* which they brought to the Sicilians. (There is some controversy on this point of whether the Arabs introduced *couscous* to the Sicilians, or it was known to them before the Arabs arrived. Regardless, the Arabs left an indelible mark on Sicilian culture.)

The Arab conquest came to an end with the Norman invasion in A.D. 1090. King Roger ruled Sicily from 1093 to 1154, and it was he who commissioned an Arab geographer, Al-Adrisi, to write about his explorations there. Al-Adrisi describes a scene in the town of Trabia near Palermo, where he watched people manipulating a flour-and-water mixture into the shape of strings, which he called by the Arab word for string, *itriyah.* This word later became *tria,* and to this day, *trii* is what *spaghetti* is called in some southern parts of Italy and in Sicily.

During the ensuing years—which brings us to the time of Marco Polo—there appeared a curious and subsequently much publicized document (in books on *pasta,* of course) in the archives of Genoa—the notarized will of one Ponzio Bastone dated 1279, some years before Marco Polo returned from the East. It includes a *"bariscella piena de macaronis"* (a basket full of macaroni) and may well be the earliest reference to what we must assume was dried *pasta*. That such an item was listed in a notarized will would indicate that at that time *pasta* was a rather luxurious and expensive article.

In the 14th century, Boccaccio wrote his *Decameron,* a collection of stories told by a group that had hurriedly left plague-ridden Florence for a country villa and are passing the time as pleasantly as possible. One story tells of a simple man named Calandrino, whose friends play endless tricks on him. They tell him of some magic stones he must collect and that they are easy to find in a particular country where there is a mountain of grated Parmesan cheese on which live people who do nothing all day but make macaroni and *ravioli,* boil them in capon broth and toss them down to the folks below.

At about the same time, during the Renaissance in Italy, a cookbook was published that included many recipes for making *pasta.* It was written by the head librarian at the Vatican, one Bartolomeo Sacchi, and was entitled *De Honesta Voluptate Ac Valetudine* ("Of Honest Pleasure and Health").

A most extraordinary event—and one that was to have far-reaching results—occurred in the 16th century. It was the marriage of Catherine de Medici, daughter of Lorenzo, to the French heir to the throne, who was to be Henry II. Catherine took with her to Paris a vast entourage of cooks, and it is recorded that they often prepared their native *pasta* and sauces for the entire court. Should you wonder why the French did not take more

enthusiastically to these tender and richly sauced dishes, you have only to remember Catherine's reputation for poisoning those she disliked.

But while France was not completely won over by *pasta,* its importance in Italy continued to grow. The earliest manufacturers had appeared around 1400, but at that time *pasta* was still an expensive item, as the prices were regulated by the guilds and by law, and it was served mainly on special occasions. Until the 17th century, the Sicilians were the *mangia-maccherone* (macaroni lovers), and then quite suddenly *pasta* became almost synonymous with Naples, along, of course, with erupting Mt. Vesuvius. The city became the center for the manufacture of *spaghetti,* and everywhere in the streets *spaghetti* was being hung from poles or strings to dry. Everyone was making *pasta.* By the end of the 18th century, however, the machinery for making *pasta* had been improved enormously and the manufacture of it became big business. (For details of this growth of the industry, I heartily recommend Anna Del Conte's book, *Portrait of Pasta.*)

Now, we come to the United States, which, even with its comparatively brief history, can boast a vital role in the modern history of *pasta.* When Thomas Jefferson returned from his stint in Paris (1784 to 1789) as ambassador to France, he brought with him the first *pasta* machine in the New World and a box of dried macaroni. Although a small but steady stream of Italians emigrated to the United States in the ensuing years, the first *pasta* factory in America was started by a Frenchman, Antoine Zerega, in Brooklyn, New York, in 1848. (The factory is still in existence in Fair Lawn, New Jersey, and is being run by descendants of the original owners.)

It was not until much later, from about 1880 until the war put a stop to it in 1914, that an incredibly vast number of Italians entered America. They came again briefly after the war until 1920, when the first law to limit immigration was passed. Because of the large Italian population, the manufacture of *pasta* accelerated during the 1920s.

An American agronomist, Mark Carleton, is an important part of the story of *pasta.* In the late 19th century, a disease called "rust" did great damage to the American wheat crop. Carleton, an employee of the United States Department of Agriculture, had done research on this disease, and in 1898, he traveled to Russia in search of a rust-resistant and drought-resistant strain of wheat. He found one, *kubanka,* and returned with a large quantity of seed that he had planted in North Dakota. There, after two arid summers, he was sure he had been right about his selection. With missionary zeal, Carleton set out to convince every wheat farmer, manufacturer and distributor in the long chain from planting the seed to selling the end-product of the excellence of his wheat. He published two papers on the subject and was tireless in his efforts in the cause of durum wheat and semolina *pasta.* He had books of recipes printed and gave them to hotel and restaurant chefs, and was responsible for the success of the growing of durum wheat in the Dakotas and in Manitoba in Canada. When in 1921 and 1922 and later again in 1932 and 1933, disaster struck the wheat fields in the Ukraine, the *pasta* industries in Italy and the United States turned to the wheat that Mark Carleton had provided.

A final story in the long history of *pasta* is one that has as comic a side to it as the one we started with, that of Marco Polo. In the Italy of the 1920s and 1930s, every activity was politically motivated, instigated or in some way connected with Mussolini and Fascism. After a number of *sub rosa* warnings that sent shudders through the entire population of Italy, the Fascist poet Marinetti, who had founded the Futuristic movement, gave a banquet on 15 November 1930, at the Restaurant d'Oca in Milan. At the banquet he officially proclaimed a campaign not only against all established forms of cooking, but especially against *pastasciutta* (*pasta* with sauce). His speech was a long harangue, an all-out attack on "the absurd Italian gastronomic religion." He favored instead what he called "Futurist cooking," which he said would liberate Italy from the "ancient obsession of weight and volume and ... *pastasciutta* ... (which) is an obsolete food, heavy, brutalizing and gross ... (that) induces scepticism, sloth and pessimism."

The national uproar that followed was led by the press with the entire population behind it. Doctors were naturally rather timid when asked their opinion of the nutritional value of *pasta*. The mayor of Naples, The Duke of Bovina, was a happy participant in the denunciation, and was reported in the press as stating that "the angels in Paradise eat nothing but *vermicelli al pomodoro*," to which Marinetti replied that it confirmed his suspicions that Paradise and the life of angels were, at best, monotonous.

In 1932, Marinetti and his friends published *La Cucina Futurista*, which carried a message from Mussolini himself, praising Marinetti. The book suggested recipes that combined the outrageous with the exotic, resulting in such revolting and hilarious dishes as *salame* in a bath of hot black coffee flavored with *eau de cologne,* and *mortadella* sausage with nougat candy. It also suggested meals be served with warmed perfumes sprayed over the guests (warmed so the bald-headed would not suffer from the cold), who were to hold forks in their left hands as they stroked "erogenous textures"—silk, sandpaper or velvet—with their right.

These foolish capers were, however, only a cover-up for the sinister Fascist mania for nationalism, and the obsession with the imminent war. Growing more serious, Marinetti damned expensive imports of wheat and foreign habits of the snobbish aristocracy and the *haute bourgeoisie,* who were infatuated with American customs, cocktail parties, French food, all of which he damned as *esterofil* ("pro-foreign") and anti-Italian.

It is of interest, however, that Marinetti's pronouncements were not all foolishness and bad advice. The suggestion that meals as well as methods of cookery be varied carried a grain of good sense. But the sinister threat of completely abolishing *pastasciutta* was terrifying, though it did little to minimize the eating of the beloved *pasta*.

PASTA VARIETIES AND EQUIPMENT

PASTA VARIETIES

So large is the body of material relating to that international form of food staple generally called *pasta* and sometimes labeled "alimentary paste," that I have had to make a precise decision on what to include here and what to omit. I stopped several times to redefine the word *pasta,* and finally settled on this: *Pasta,* in essence, is the generic term for that vast body of fresh and dried flour-and-egg or flour-and-water mixtures. The flour may be the end product of milling grains of hard or soft wheat, buckwheat, rice, tapioca, sago, soybean and many other grains and roots.

But what, you may well ask, distinguishes *pasta* from mixtures and doughs that are not precisely *pasta,* but similar? *Pasta International* deals only with a flour paste that will hold a recognizable shape even after cooking in boiling liquid or steaming. "But what about *tortillas, bistilla, phyllo* or the gorgeous Navajo Indian blue bread?" my friends asked. They are either pastry dough with so much fat that they will disintegrate when boiled, or they are so delicate they must be baked with melted fat drizzled over them.

Once it was generally believed that *pasta* was only Italian, and the only thing eaten in Italy at that. This is probably because the Italians have elevated *pasta* to such an honored position. In Italy, there is even a small museum devoted to *pasta*—its history, legends, myths, position in the world of arts, the famous people who have written or been quoted on the subject. Each region of Italy has its own traditional *pasta,* and every Italian takes great pleasure in pointing out that there is no ingredient anywhere that cannot somehow be used in it, over it or with it. Finally, the history of *pasta* in Italy can be traced because her early writers mentioned it in poems, satires, dramas and stories, and historians, even scientists, have devoted themselves to its study. Where else in the world has a food been so honored?

Despite such assiduous interest on the part of Italians, it must be understood that many other cultures have used some form of *pasta* throughout their own histories. Recently, I saw a magnificent exhibition of Chinese artifacts dating from prehistoric times. In one of the cases was a fossilized dumpling, easily identifiable as *har gow,* one of my favorites of all the *dim sum* delicacies. The dumpling has not, through tens of thousands of years, changed its shape.

There are also the cultures that have adopted *pasta* into their cuisines once it has been introduced. Not long ago, I met a young Peruvian man. On a hunch I asked him if Peruvians eat *pasta.* Smiling broadly, he said, "Like *spaghetti* and macaroni? Sure. All the time. It's cheap and good and many Italians now live in Peru. We call *spaghetti* '*tallarines*' and we love it." When I asked him if it was served with Peruvian sauces rather than Italian ones, he replied, "Sure. With chicken, beef, fish and hot, very hot with pepper." *Pasta* and Peru? Perhaps an odd combination, but why not?

The most popular and best-known *pasta* shapes can be most easily dealt with here if divided into two categories: those that are homemade and those that are manufactured and sold dried. Many of the ribbon noodles and some of the dumplings may also be purchased fresh or frozen, depending on where you live. Since Italian names are used by *pasta* manufacturers everywhere, I, too, have used them for the most part. I have made a separate category for the Oriental noodles, since they differ markedly.

Homemade Noodles

Homemade noodles, made by hand or with small machines (manual or electric), are usually limited to flat ribbons of various widths. The narrowest ribbons are *capellini* or *capelli d'angelo* (angel's hair). They are not, however, easily made, and are often purchased in dried form. These "hair-fine" noodles are sometimes called *vermicelli* in the Middle East and in India, and are even thinner than the Italian variety. In Spain and South America they are called *fideos* or *fidellos,* names also used by the Sephardic Jews in the Middle East for their very fine noodles.

Tagliatelle are the long, narrow noodles of Emilia-Romagna, where few buy commercial *pasta.* So important are they to the people of the area, that in Bologna, at the Chamber of Commerce, a solid gold replica of one is on display. It is the ideal width and thickness as set by the *Accademia Italiana della Cucina:* one millimeter thick and six millimeters wide (a little more than one thirty-second of an inch thick and a little less than one-quarter inch wide).

Fettuccine are the Roman version of *tagliatelle. Trenette* are very close in size to them both and is the preferred name in Genoa. *Linguine,* slightly thicker and narrower (rather like a square noodle), are the Tuscan favorite, while *tagliolini* is a thinner version of *linguine.*

Pappardelle are about five-eighths inch (12 mm) wide and cut with a fluted pastry cutter to give them their characteristic curly or wavy edges. *Lasagnette* is slightly broader, while the broadest noodle is *lasagna,* about two inches (5 cm) wide with either smooth or wavy edges.

An interesting "noodle" shape is *maltagliati,* which means "poorly cut" or "badly cut." But the name is rather inappropriate, since these noodles are deliberately and carefully cut. The *pasta* sheet is formed into a four-inch (10 cm) flattened roll and first one corner is cut off on the diagonal and then the other is cut off. Now the point is cut off and you again have a straight edge. The process is repeated until the roll is completely cut and then the "noodles" are separated and sprinkled with flour. These noodles are generally used in thick soups and especially when *pasta* and beans are combined.

Other homemade varieties include *maccheroni alla chitarra,* of which an Abruzzi version, *tondarelli,* is given on page 44, and *bigoli,* a slender, whole wheat rod that is made with a special instrument called a *bigolaro,* a small, manual hand press I have not seen in the United States. There are also three varieties that are not strictly noodles, but are easily made at home. The first are *quadrucci,* tiny squares made by making *tagliatelle,* laying the ribbons on top of each other and cutting into squares. These

are primarily used in delicate clear broths. The second is *orecchiette* or "little ears," for which a recipe is given on page 43. The third is a ridged, tubular form, *garganelli,* which is made by cutting out squares of dough, rolling them around a pencil or dowel and pressing against the teeth of a comb or of a specially designed wooden frame (see illustration, this page).

Although the above noodles have Italian names for the most part, the same type of flat *pasta* is used in most other cuisines with much less fuss as to specific names or exact width or thickness. Recipes of these other cuisines, such as German, French and Hungarian, generally direct that

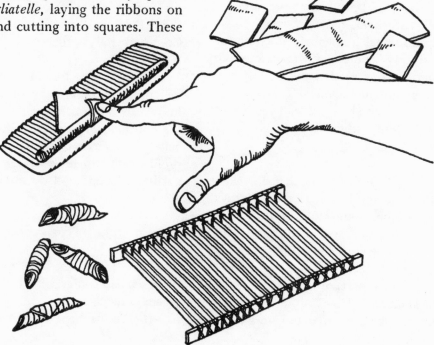

the dough be rolled as thinly as possible or "rather thicker than usual" and cut approximately one-quarter inch (6 mm) wide.

Homemade Dumplings

There are two types of homemade dumplings: dumplings made from small pieces of dough and filled dumplings. The former may be *spaetzle* (Hungary, Germany), *ignoc* (Provence), *gnocchi* (Italy), *nockerl* (Austria, Hungary), *knaidlach* (Jewish), etc. The latter, which are made by cutting sheets of dough into circles, squares, rectangles or triangles, filling the shapes with meats, poultry, fish and vegetables or a combination and sealing to enclose the filling, include *won ton* (China), *pelmeni* (Russia), *vareniki* (Russia), *mandoo* (Korea), etc., and, of course, those of Italy, which are endless: *tortellini, cappelletti, ravioli, agnoletti,* etc.

There are additional homemade filled forms that are not strictly dumplings, but are more appropriately part of this section than any other. These include *manicotti* and *cannelloni,* which are generally four- to six-inch (10 to 15 cm) squares of dough that are rolled into tubes with filling.

Commercial Pasta

We now come to the types of *pasta* that are made in factories, both large and small. To date, *pasta* is being manufactured on some scale in Italy, the United States, Switzerland, Great Britain (who makes certain forms not available in Italy), India, China, Japan, several countries of Southeast Asia, Australia, and even some parts of Africa, where, of course, *couscous* is made.

It must be clear by now that to give a complete and final listing of *pasta* names—either Italian or international—would require a book larger than this entire volume. Therefore, the list that follows is not only incomplete, but barely skims the subject. It will, however, give the reader some idea of the great variety of commercial *pasta* forms and shapes available. You must also add to this list the types mentioned in the homemade noodle section, for they, too, are readily available in dried form, and I have not repeated them in this list.

At this point, I should also point out that there were at one time a great many more varieties of Italian *pasta* than there are now. The difficulties and loss of time involved in changing the die that forms the *pasta* shapes on the great machines has motivated most manufacturers to eliminate many forms from their lists. The following forms are, on the whole, still available from such firms as De Cecco of Italy, Agnesi of Italy and Ronzoni of New York.

A final note to add to the confusion: It must be admitted that many of these pasta forms are known by various other names. Manufacturers prefer one name to another, either because it was so called in their native region or the firm's designer preferred it. So look before you decide to buy a particular shape and do not judge it by its name alone.

Acini di pepe "Peppercorns"; used most often in soups.
Anellini "Little rings," used in soups, but sometimes available in green and red, to be served with a cream sauce.
Bavette Oval *spaghetti,* thinner than usually seen.

Bocconcini "Small mouthfuls," which may have been someone's idea of a joke, because they are grooved tubes about a half inch in diameter and an inch and a half long.

Bucatini Slightly thicker than *spaghetti* and hollow; also known as *perciatelli*.

Cappelli di prete "Priests' hats."

Cavatelli Short, curled forms, rather like a particular kind of shell.

Conchiglie "Conch shells"; ridged forms excellent for trapping sauces. *Conchiglette* are a smaller version used in soup. There are also jumbo shells available for stuffing.

Couscous Tiny, grainlike *pasta*; popular in North Africa and Sicily.

Cravatte "Bow ties."

Creste di gallo "Cockscombs"; pretty and popular form.

Dischi volanti "Flying saucers."

Ditali "Thimbles"; short, ridged tubes. *Ditalini* are a smaller version.

Elbow macaroni Ridged or smooth tubes of varying sizes in the shape of a "lazy" half circle.

Farfalle "Butterflies"; available in several sizes.

Fedelini "The faithful"; a thin form of *spaghetti* usually shaped into a "nest."

Fusilli Noodles in a corkscrew pattern; in Sicily they are made at home by wrapping ribbons of dough around knitting needles and letting them dry.

Gemelli "Twins" formed with two strands of *spaghetti*, one curled around the other.

Gnocchetti sardi A long, narrow shell of Sardinia.

Lingue di Passeri "Sparrows' tongues"; flat, narrow, squarish noodles.

Lumache "Snails"; large, ridged form for stuffing.

Macaroni General term for hollow tubes; available in a large variety of lengths and diameters. Also general term for all *pasta* in some regions.

Mafalde Wide noodles with wavy edges.

Manicotti rigati Large, ridged tubes for stuffing.

Maruzze "Seashells"; available in many sizes.

Mostaccioli "Moustaches"; medium-sized tubes available ridged and smooth and cut diagonally on ends.

Occhi di lupo "Eyes of the wolf"; tubular form.

Orzo "Barley"; often used in soup.

Pastina General term for tiny *pasta* forms used in soup.

Penne "Quills"; tubular form cut diagonally on ends and available in a variety of sizes.

Rigatoni Large, ridged, tubular form, slightly curved.

Rotelle Tiny rings with points; used in soup.

Ruote "Wheels"; used in soup.

Semi di mela "Apple seeds"; used in soup.

Semi di melone "Melon seeds"; used in soup.

Spaghetti Long thin rods; *spaghettini* is a thinner version. The term is also used in a generic sense for all long, rod *pasta*.

Stelline "Stars"; used in soup.

Tubetti "Tiny tubes"; used in soup.

Tufoli Large tubes for stuffing.

Varnishkes Bow ties with notched edges; Russian.

Vermicelli "Little worms"; long, thin rods bought straight or in "nests." *Vermicellini* is a thinner version. *Vermicelli* is also a common term for noodles in the Middle East.

Ziti Long hollow form, slightly larger than *spaghetti; zitoni* are almost twice the size.

Oriental Noodles

I have included only the most commonly used noodles in this section, and for the most part they are eaten all over the Orient. When you purchase these noodles dried, they may be a product of any of a number of countries—Singapore, Thailand, China, Hong Kong, Malaysia, etc. This leads to a great confusion of names. I have given the common English translations, along with some of the most frequently encountered foreign names to help lessen some of the confusion. Cooking directions will also vary from package to package, so I have attempted to simplify these. But as with all noodles, testing for doneness by tasting is the best way. Because many of the Japanese noodles are unique to the cuisine, I have grouped them together at the end.

Egg Noodles *(mein, min, mee)* These are probably the most popular of the Oriental noodles and can be found fresh or dried in markets. The dried ones are usually sold in one-pound (500 g) packages consisting of several bundles. To use them, untie the bundles and soak them in hot water for 10 minutes, then cook in boiling water until tender. (The soaking will help to separate the strands.) A teaspoon (5 ml) or so of oil added to the cooking water prevents the noodles from boiling over and from sticking together. They are easy to overcook, so test repeatedly for doneness. When they are tender, add a cup of cold water (250 ml) to stop the cooking. Drain thoroughly and toss with a little oil if not using immediately. The very thin variety is used in soups; the wider ones (about an eighth of an inch or 3 mm) are pan fried, tossed with stir fries or used in braised dishes. Though one most readily thinks of Chinese *mein,* similar noodles of varying widths and a variety of names are found in all countries of the Orient. If you cannot find *mein* in your area, *linguine* makes a good substitute in pan-fried or stir-fried dishes. (To make these noodles at home, see page 46.)

Rice Noodles *(fun, kway teow)* There are several widths available of these rice flour noodles. The dried ones have to be soaked in cold water until softened, anywhere from 15 minutes to an hour, depending upon the size. They can then be cooked briefly in boiling water until tender, drained and rinsed to remove excess starch. If cooking ahead of time, drizzle with a little oil to prevent them from sticking together. They may then be stir fried or added to soup. Fresh rice noodles may be stir fried without precooking (see page 47).

Rice *Vermicelli (mi fun, py mei fun, beehoon, meehoon, sen mee)* Also called rice stick noodles, these very fine, transparent, dried rice noodles are found all over the Orient and cook very quickly. You may prepare them in two ways: Simply drop into boiling water and cook, stirring constantly, for only two to three minutes, then drain well and serve mixed with dishes that have a good amount of sauce or in soup. Or soak in hot water for 10 minutes or until softened, drain and add to soups or dishes with sauce and cook for a few minutes until tender. If the noodles are to be used as a crisp base or topping for a dish, drop by handfuls straight from the package into hot oil for just a few seconds; they will inflate to many times their original size and become starch white. Lift out with a slotted spoon or skimmer and drain on paper toweling. When cooking in this manner, be sure the oil is very hot by first testing a few noodles to see if they puff immediately.

Bean Thread Noodles *(fun see, sohoon, bi fun, harusame, fenzu, saifun, woon sen)* Also commonly known as cellophane noodles, shining noodles, pea starch noodles and silver threads, these fine, transparent noodles are made from the starch of the mung bean. To use in braised dishes and soups, soak in hot water until softened, then cook briefly in boiling water until tender. For a crisp garnish, deep fry in the manner of rice *vermicelli*, above.

Japanese Noodles *Udon* (page 48) are thick, whole wheat noodles usually served in broth. *Somen* are much like *udon* but thinner, and are generally used in soups and cold noodle dishes. *Soba* (page 49), one of the most popular Japanese noodles, are made from buckwheat flour and are often served cold. *Shirataki*, made from the starch of a tuberous root, are the noodles traditionally used in *sukiyaki*. They can be purchased dried, in which case they must first be soaked for 20 to 30 minutes in hot water and then cooked for 4 to 5 minutes in boiling water, or presoaked (in cans or plastic containers) and ready to use.

EQUIPMENT

The following recommendations are not meant in a general sense for all kitchens, but rather precisely for the *pasta*-making function in the kitchen. Certainly, many of the items may well be found in any well-appointed kitchen.

As with making bread, so does the *pasta* maker have to give thought to the place where *pasta* will be made. It should be warm and dry, but free of draughts and not so hot as to dry the *pasta* too quickly. And it should be out of the way of general movement (of family and friends), so a careless gesture will not upset the board and send the *pasta* flying. If necessary, use the dining room table with a folded sheet or tablecloth over it.

The Board and Rolling Pin

The *pasta* board should be of hard wood, unvarnished and unwaxed, or of formica, plastic or even of marble. I consider the latter a poor choice, however, for the material should be "friendly to your hands," as my mother used to say, unlike the pastry making surface where coolness is welcome. The surface should be steady, level and easy to clean and about a yard (1 m) by two feet (60 cm) wide, though a bit more or less makes little difference. It is advisable, however, to have one raised edge to prevent flour and dough from spilling over. A good kitchenware shop should carry the boards.

The rolling pin I learned to use in Rome was a new broomstick! Here, I go to the lumberyard for a thick dowel stick one and a half to two inches (4 to 5 cm) in diameter and as long or longer than the width of the working board. While in the lumberyard, buy some medium and some fine sandpaper, and when you get home, sand down the surface and round off the ends to prevent splinters or cuts. First use the medium sandpaper, then finish off with the fine. Now wash the pin very well, rub it with a dry towel and leave it in a warm corner of the kitchen to dry thoroughly. Then lightly grease your hands with cooking oil and rub the surface of the pin with them. When the pin has absorbed the oil, rub flour into it. Repeat this procedure fairly often, so the pin is always smooth and clean. This same procedure will work wonders on your wooden *pasta* board.

Although there is nothing wrong with a thick, heavy rolling pin (the thicker and heavier the bet-

ter for pastry making), I find it somehow makes the *pasta* too satiny smooth to suit me. I think I can promise that, with some practice, the dowel-stick rolling pin will prove much easier to manipulate in rolling out thin *pasta* quickly.

The Pasta *Machines*

It is well established that *pasta* is an international passion for many, everywhere, and making *pasta* at home should become the ambition of most cooks. It does not take half a day to make unless one is making hundreds of little dumplings like *pelmeni, ravioli* or *won ton.* With a *pasta* machine, a pound (500 g) of noodles can take little more than a half hour to make.

There is the manual *pasta* machine with steel rollers used by millions of Italian and American cooks. Then there is the electric *pasta* machine, about twice the price of the manual, but capable of producing *pasta* that is closer to the handmade (pin

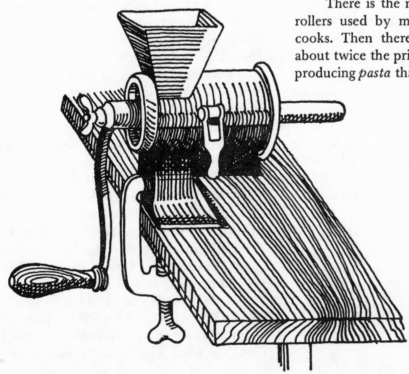

rolled) product, for the plastic covering on the rollers has a slightly textured surface more like the wooden rolling pin.

Both machines will knead, roll out and then cut the noodles for you, and those are the most time-consuming activities of *pasta* making. Both produce a *pasta* comparable to the delicate handmade product. Once eaten, no *gourmand* will be satisfied with the dried commercial product again. If you prefer electrically run machines (as opposed to the elbow grease that runs the manual machines) and can justify the extra expense, do consider the electric machine.

To describe the *pasta* machines more precisely, they have two plain rollers to knead and roll out the dough through progressively narrower spaces to the thinness desired. Most also come equipped with two cutters, one for narrow noodles, the other for slightly wider or medium noodles. If other widths or shapes are desired, they can be cut from the large sheet formed on the rollers.

One *pasta* machine called the Egg Noodle and Macaroni Machine is like the old-fashioned meat grinder, a clamp-on metal affair that forms the *pasta* by forcing it through a plate. A smaller, completely plastic machine operates in somewhat the same fashion and will form *spaghetti,* hollow tubes of macaroni and extra-wide noodles, but is so lightweight that I feel disinclined to use it.

A more specialized machine that looks antique and is quite deliciously attractive is the Teck noodle cutter. Made in West Germany, it sells here around $60 and is imported exclusively by Paprikás Weiss (1546 Second Avenue, New York, New York 10028). It is used by soup lovers for cutting fine noodles.

For *ravioli* lovers, there is the metal "stamp" that will make quick work of forming *ravioli* by "stamping" out the small mounds of filling between two sheets of dough. The Raviolatore comes in two sections, making *ravioli* in several sizes from one to two and three-quarters inches (3 to 8 cm) square; a small rolling pin is included for the cutting and sealing of the *ravioli.* It costs anywhere from $7 to $15, depending on size and style.

The Ravioli Chef is a metal frame with small cavities or indentations. The sheet of dough is laid down and the filling is put on it wherever the dents are. That is covered with another sheet and toothed dividers cut and seal the dumplings when a small rolling pin is pressed over them. This is now available in most kitchenware shops and shops in Italian neighborhoods.

Spaetzle machines are readily available and vary from a colander-like affair with large holes to one that resembles a food mill and another that resembles a ricer. The one I find works most efficiently is an oblong perforated metal plate with a dough hopper that slides back and forth on runners and cuts off pieces of dough as it slides. The simplest is a panlike container with a perforated bottom through which soft dough is pushed with the edge of a spatula. Finally, one that seems to be the most popular, is called the Noodlette or the Babsi Spätzle Machine (about $10 to $12), which sits in an opening in a strip of Masonite board placed on top of a pot.

Cooking Vessels
There are several cooking vessels that will make your *pasta* cookery easier. First, you will need a large kettle of at least five- to six-quart (5 to 6 L)

capacity for boiling the *pasta*. Many recommend—even insist—that the *pasta* kettle be tall, high and narrow, like the classic stock pot. They say with this shape the water does not cool when the *pasta* is added. Others recommend the squat, wide-topped, narrower-bottomed shallow kettle with sides about three and a half to four inches (8 to 10 cm) high. Both work well; the choice is yours.

Further necessities are saucepans of varying capacities: a one-quart (1 L), a one-and-a-half-quart (1.5 L) and a two-quart (2 L) pan for making sauces. For cooking larger amounts of sauce and for braising meats, vegetables and even cooking some fish stews, I use a four-quart (4 L) *sautoir* (or Dutch oven or "chicken fryer").

For Oriental cooking, a large heavy iron wok will prove a good investment. When buying your wok, be sure to tell the salesclerk whether your stove is gas or electric. The classic round-bottomed wok can be used only on gas stoves; there are specially designed flat-bottomed woks for use on electric stoves. Also ask about the supplementary implements for using with the wok—the scoop, the spoon, the wire skimmers, the bamboo whisk, the long cooking chopsticks—that are offered for sale where woks are sold. A further note: The only wok worth having is a carbon steel or iron one, since it is the only material that absorbs and retains high enough heat to cook in the rapid *chow* or stir-fry method.

Before using your steel or iron wok, be sure to "cure" or "season" it as you would any iron or steel frying pan. First scrub the new wok with steel wool and detergent or soap and rinse thoroughly. Dry it completely over moderate heat. Put about a tablespoon (15 ml) of a neutral-flavored oil, such as peanut oil, in the bottom and rub it all over the inside surface with a piece of paper toweling. Put the wok back over moderately high heat for a minute or two. Rub the inside again with oil and repeat the process several times in order to build up a protective covering of oil and to fill the pores. Then feel the inside of the wok with your hand; it should be very smooth and only slightly oily.

After each use of your wok, rub the inside surface with a coarse cloth or paper toweling before storing and never wrap it when storing. If, by some remote chance, food sticks to the wok, rub it first with a paper towel, and only if it cannot be smoothed that way, try very fine dry steel wool. Then again use the oil-and-rub procedure before storing.

If you decide to serve *couscous,* you may want to purchase a *couscoussière,* the traditional pot for cooking this North Africa *pasta.* The pot is generally made of earthenware, stainless steel, copper or aluminum and has two parts. The bottom pan is deep and round sided and is where the stew is cooked or other steaming liquid is simmered. The top pan is smaller, with rather large holes in the bottom, and it fits snugly into the lower pan. There is a tight-fitting lid for the top pan that also often fits on the bottom pan securely.

You can, however, fashion a *couscoussière* from equipment you probably already have in your kitchen. For the bottom pan, use a large stock pot or kettle, and for the top section, a colander or strainer.

Finally, you will need shallow rectangular baking dishes for all the variety of baked *pasta,* such as *lasagne, pasta al forno* and casseroles.

Additional Equipment
- Several well-balanced knives, including a Chinese cleaver, a few paring knives and a honing stone.
- The *mezzaluna* (half-moon blade with handle) for chopping vegetables.
- A sharp vegetable peeler; the rotary type is fine as long as it remains sharp and efficient.
- A food mill with replaceable disks of varying coarseness for puréeing fruits and vegetables.
- A four-sided grater with various cutters and graters for soft cheeses, spices such as nutmeg, some vegetables, etc.
- A fine, efficient cheese grater, either the Mouli rotary type or a flat grater fitted over a box into which the grated cheese drops.
- For lifting out *pasta* (as some authorities believe draining it in a colander is a no-no), there are at least three possibilities: a wooden "hairbrush-type" implement, the same type of implement but with a wooden handle and stainless steel head and spikes or the huge teardrop-shaped skimmer/scoop in stainless steel, which also comes in a wire version.
- A large colander with strong handles and firm feet, so it may be set into the sink for draining *pasta*.
- A sturdy salt mill and peppermill or a "salt box" for coarse salt hung near the stove or cooking work area.
- Several long-handled wooden spoons and forks of varying lengths and capacities.
- A large ladle and a large spoon.
- A slotted spoon and a long-handled skimmer for removing food from deep fat or boiling water.
- A rack on which a steamer may be put in your large pot, or a collapsible steamer (many practical ones are to be found in Chinese stores). With this rack you may also convert your large kettle into a *bain-marie* or double boiler.
- Pastry cutters for cutting wide noodles, *ravioli* disks or squares and other filled shapes. It is best to have a fluted one and a straight one. (They are available singly or together with a single handle.)
- Several asbestos pads or similar devices for setting under pans to rectify uneven heating units or pans that heat unevenly.
- Large and small whisks in a variety of materials.
- Small and large mortars and pestles, of stone, of unglazed ceramic, and as many bronze ones as you like.
- Chinese bamboo baskets for steaming *dim sum* delicacies.

Beyond this list of necessities for the *pasta* maker there are the modern "servants" of hard-working cooks: the electric blender, the electric mixer and the electric food processor. Although chefs and household cooks can, and have for centuries, managed very nicely without these "servants," they do simplify and shorten the cooking periods with almost magical rapidity and ease. Though not inexpensive, they are well worth their price if you value your own time and energy.

It is difficult to advise others on kitchen equipment, so the foregoing suggestions are to be accepted as just that—suggestions that I believe to be helpful to a beginner *mangia-maccherone* or *pasta* lover.

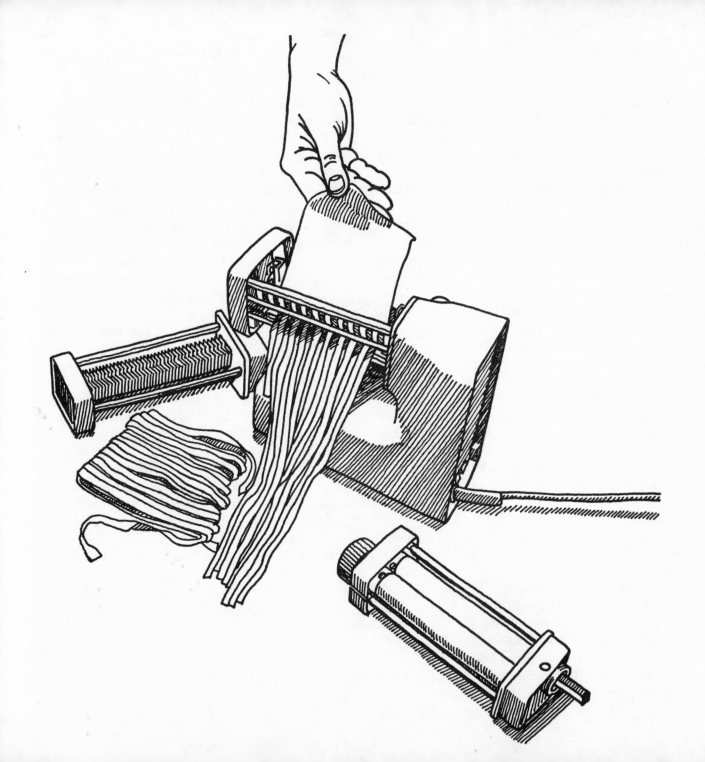

HOMEMADE PASTA

NOODLES MADE AT HOME

Homemade noodles are most commonly made of semolina or unbleached all-purpose flour mixed with eggs *or* water or eggs *and* a bit of water. Semolina, the purest, hardest wheat flour (durum wheat), is, however, extremely difficult to mix with liquid, so making the dough requires an expenditure of great energy and strength.

A few warnings are in order before you begin making noodles at home. Experienced cooks do not always measure ingredients very carefully: a handful of this and a pinch of that and the result, somehow, is always right—and so will yours be after some practice. But to begin with, measure very carefully. All quantities of eggs, flour, etc. given in this book must, however, be considered approximate, although I have worked as "close to the margin" as possible. Eggs vary in size. Flour may be drier or damper, older or fresher and absorb more or less liquid. The weather will also influence the finished product: A damp, sticky day may make the dough stickier; a dry, cool day may cause the flour to absorb more liquid. And then, a box of eggs may be made up of some that weigh a fraction more or less than their neighbors.

If in working with the dough you wish to make the exercise less strenuous, do add a half eggshell of water or milk or that amount of oil. But to get the correct "feel" of the paste, at first use nothing but flour and egg. And remember that dough for stuffed or filled forms sometimes requires a little milk or water so it can be rolled out thinner than for noodles.

It is vital to work as quickly as possible to prevent the dough from becoming dry and brittle. You must also not overwork the dough. As soon as it loses its stickiness and seems silky, alive and vibrant with unseen bubbles, stop kneading! When it is overworked, it becomes too smooth and takes on a sort of cardboard quality. It should have some fine texture to which the sauce—simple or complex—may adhere, and it should be firm without being hard.

Although it may be considered a "rule of thumb" to use one egg to each cup (250 ml) of flour, it is best to begin with one egg to three-quarters cup (175 ml) of flour and add up to one-quarter cup (50 to 75 ml) more for sprinkling the board and to add to the dough during kneading, or sprinkling over the noodles when cut, to prevent them from sticking together. But try to use no more than one cup (250 ml) of flour to each egg. In testing the recipes for this book, I have used unbleached all-purpose flour on the whole and large grade AA eggs.

MASTER RECIPE FOR HANDMADE NOODLES

There are five stages in the making of most noodle doughs: combining the basic ingredients, kneading to the proper consistency, starting to "open" or roll out the dough, stretching the dough as far and as thinly as possible (or as you prefer) and cutting it into varying widths or desired shapes.

For up to 4 servings, use 2 eggs and 1-3/4 cups (425 ml) flour (yield: approximately 1 pound or 500 g)

For 5 to 6 servings, use 3 eggs and 2-3/4 cups (675 ml) flour (yield: approximately 1-1/2 pounds or 750 g)

For 7 to 8 servings, use 4 eggs and 3-3/4 cups (925 ml) flour (yield: approximately 2 pounds or 1 kg)

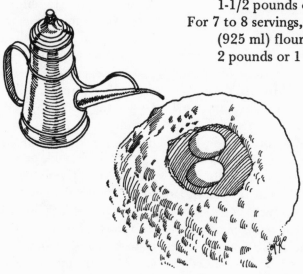

On a firm working surface pour out the flour in a mound, and with your finger, form a deep well in the center (or arrange the flour in a circle). Break the eggs into the well. With a fork or your fingers, beat the eggs lightly, then begin to draw in the flour, bit by bit, mixing the flour and the eggs. To be sure the "wall" of flour does not collapse and the eggs run out over the surface, keep one hand cupped around the outside of the wall, pulling in the flour if it threatens to fall. When you have mixed enough to make a thick mixture, push in the wall, mixing steadily. Now using both hands, push and pull and squeeze the eggs and flour into a solid mass. It will feel sticky and moist, so sprinkle on a

little more flour and continue to "knead" until the mass is no longer sticky and comes cleanly off the surface; it must feel as though the eggs have absorbed as much flour as they can. Set the ball of dough aside, covering it with a bowl or cloth.

While the dough "rests," clean the working surface by scraping off every bit of stuck-on dough until the surface feels smooth and dry again. Then wash your hands to remove caked-on dough and dry them thoroughly. Now lightly flour the surface and your hands, put the ball of dough back on the floured surface and start to knead. Using the heels, palms and fingers of both hands, flatten the dough and push it outward; then with the fingers, lift the far edge of dough and pull it toward you, folding the dough flat. Press down and outward with heels of hands, then again fold the outer surface on the nearer, with the fingers of both hands. Again press down with the heels of both hands. Repeat this motion over and over again, turning the ball of dough as you work, so every side is manipulated. It may take anywhere from 8 to 12 minutes until it feels compact, is silky smooth and seems to contain bubbles within the mass.

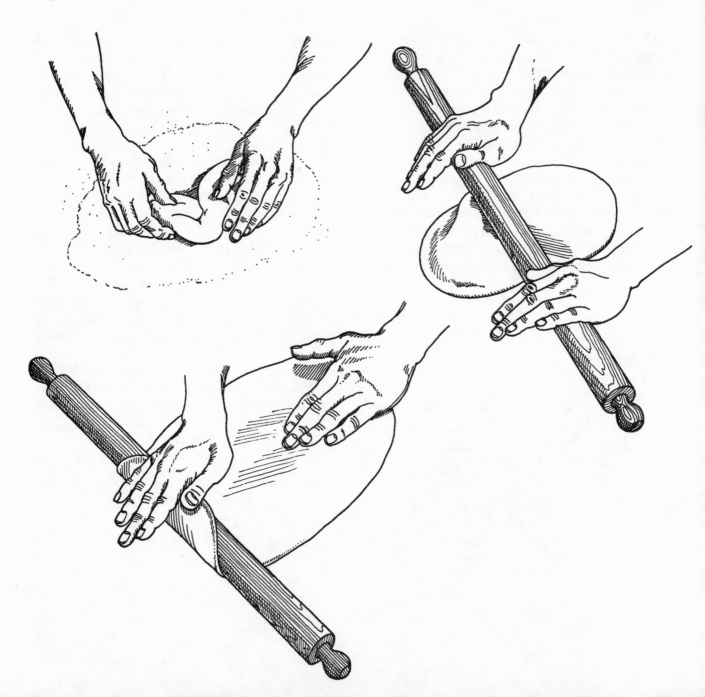

Divide the kneaded ball of dough into quarters or halves (thus broken up into pieces, it will be much easier to roll out). Cover all but one piece and set aside. Sprinkle flour over the work surface, set ball of dough in the center and sprinkle it *lightly* with flour. Flour the rolling pin and set it down on the middle of the dough. Roll it away from you, then forward again, toward you. Turn the dough about a quarter turn and repeat the motions so the finished sheet will be evenly round. The motion is not so much a "pushing down" as a "pressing away" from yourself. When the circle is even, nicely round and less than 1/4 inch thick, or

as thin as you can make it, stop to catch your breath; you'll need full power to push and press the rolling pin, for you must now proceed to stretch the thin dough rather than the comparatively easy "rolling out" you have been doing.

Start the stretching by curling the side of the dough farthest from you around the rolling pin and rolling it toward you, keeping your fingers spread out around the center of the pin. As you move back and forth, however, your hands should move outward from the center, stretching the dough with the fingers and palms of your hands, and rolling and unrolling it as you do. The pin must not

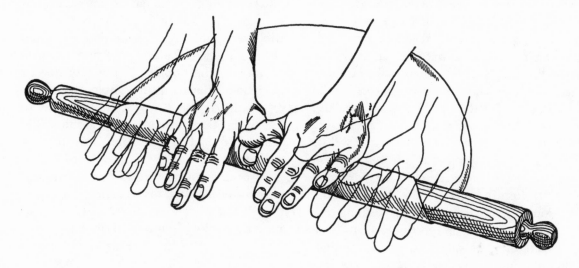

stop; your fingers must not stop, but rather move back and forth, rolling and unrolling the dough. In order to stretch it uniformly, you must, from time to time, turn the entire sheet of dough and replace the pin almost in the center. As you roll and stretch the dough, you will be rolling more and more of it onto the pin. In other words, without stopping the action, you must *not* keep working with the same part of the dough, but change sections with each outward pull and with each turn. Should the dough stick to the board or to the rolling pin, *lightly* sprinkle more flour on the under surface of the dough, on the rolling pin, as well as on the upper surface of the dough. Sprinkle *very, very lightly,* as too much flour can coarsen and toughen the tender dough. As the sheet gets thinner and thinner, you must watch your clock, for this part of the entire process should take no more than 7 to 8 minutes (and the less the better) or the dough will become brittle, overly dry and crackly.

Now, again let the dough "rest." Lay it on a lightly floured surface and cover with a towel or cloth. The easiest way to move it is to roll it up on the rolling pin, move it to a floured warm, dry area and unroll it. Return to work on the remaining pieces of dough. It is wise to keep turning the already rolled out dough and, if possible, to let a third of it hang over the side of the table, though this is not absolutely necessary. It is necessary, however, to flip the sheet over every 10 minutes or so. When after about 15 to 25 minutes the dough has lost its sheen and has a dull, leathery look, loosely roll up the sheet, jelly-roll fashion onto itself, flatten gently and cut out the noodles to the desired width. It is wise to use a heavy well-balanced knife (or cleaver) for this and the safest

method is to make a loose fist of your left hand (if you are right-handed) and place fist with first two sections of your fingers turned under and flat on the roll. Hold the knife in your right hand and cut the noodles, moving your left hand (fist) away and back from the cutting edge, so the knife side is always flat against your knuckles. Lay out a dry cloth, sprinkle it with flour and when noodles are cut completely, move them to the cloth.

To separate the noodles, sprinkle flour or semolina on them lightly, then lift as many noodles as you can grasp *(lightly, lightly)* with the *tips* of your fingers, raising them high, spreading them out and dropping them, again and again, for a few seconds. Sprinkle on more flour or semolina. (The trick of sprinkling on semolina was given me by Ilio Canù, the idea being to add flavor and some texture to the noodles at this late stage, semolina being more flavorful than unbleached flour.)

Now, repeat the procedure until all the dough has been transformed into noodles. Be sure to work as quickly as possible. Once the noodles are cut, drying is naturally accelerated. If where you are working is very hot and dry, cover the noodles with a towel as you make them.

When the noodles are cut and ready, they may be cooked immediately or left to dry a *little* longer for use in the evening or the following day. They must not be left long enough to become brittle; the perfect stage is *leather dry,* when they can still be bent without breaking. At this point they can be put into an airtight plastic bag and refrigerated for up to 1 week, or frozen indefinitely. Of course, if you prefer you may dry the noodles completely (like factory-made noodles) and store indefinitely (see Keeping *Pasta,* page 39).

EXTRA-RICH NOODLE DOUGH
IN THE FOOD PROCESSOR

If you have a food processor, mixing the dough becomes a snap. Mine is a rather early Cuisinart and less powerful than the later ones, but it is a dream to work with, nonetheless. By using the food processor, I am able to treat myself to a richer dough than described above and to use the semolina flour that is otherwise too difficult for me to work with. If you are very strong, you may well be able to make this dough by hand, and, of course, you may make any recipe for noodle dough in the processor.

4 eggs, lightly beaten
1/4 cup (50 ml) water
2 cups (500 ml) fine semolina
Generous pinch of salt
1 tablespoon (15 ml) olive oil

Beat eggs and water together in a small bowl. Pour semolina and salt into the bowl of the processor. Turn the motor on and off several times to mix the flour and salt. Now turn the motor on, and as it processes, add the egg mixture through the feed tube and process until the egg mixture is absorbed by the flour. Pour in the oil and keep processing until the dough forms a compact ball. Turn off promptly and remove dough to a floured working surface. Lightly flour your hands and knead the dough, adding fine semolina as needed to counteract stickiness, until smooth and elastic. Put the ball of dough into a bowl and cover with a towel. Roll out the dough and cut into noodles as described in the Master Recipe, preceding.

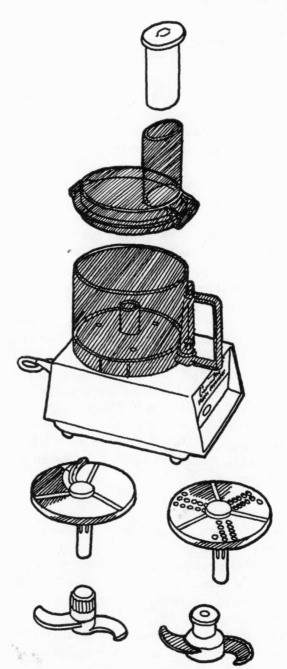

NOODLES MADE WITH
AN ELECTRIC *PASTA* MACHINE

You have simply to form the dough into a ball and the electric *pasta* machine will knead it, thin it to a sheet and cut it into noodles.

Be sure the machine is standing on a firm dry surface. The small suction cups on the bottom of the machine will prevent movement. Cut the dough into four parts or more and cover the ones you are not working with to prevent them from drying out. Set the machine to the widest opening between rollers, #6. With the ball of your hand flatten the dough slightly, particularly at one end. Force the flattest end through the rollers. When it has run through, fold it into four parts upon itself and again pass it through the rollers. Turn the dough each time it is fed into the rollers so different parts of it are pressed together. Each time also feel the dough and stretch it; if it "breaks," keep feeding it through the rollers. It may take as many as fifteen run-throughs or as few as five, depending on how supple the dough is and how well kneaded it is before putting it through the machine. It is important to work quickly to prevent the dough from drying out.

When the dough feels elastic and silky (stretch it between your fingers to ascertain this), stop folding the dough. Move the rollers down to #5 and put the dough through, then to #4, #3 and finally #2. I often stop at #2, since it seems sufficiently thin to me. I prefer a little more "resistance to the teeth" than others, however, so if you like it thinner, do go on to #1. If you are making filled forms rather than noodles, it will be necessary to go on to #1, as they require a thinner sheet.

When the sheet is ready, transfer it to a lightly floured surface, such as a tablecloth or sheet. It may be wise to cut the dough sheet into smaller pieces for easier handling before you move it. Once moved, sprinkle on a little flour or semolina and leave to dry lightly for about 15 minutes before cutting into noodles. Return to the machine and repeat the kneading and rolling out procedure with the remaining dough.

When all the dough is rolled out, remove the roller attachment and attach the cutters, either the very narrow or the quarter-inch (6 mm), the latter usually for more general use. Put the sheets of dough through the cutters, sprinkling flour on the cutters often to keep them clean and to prevent the dough from sticking to them.

When the noodles are cut, follow the directions in the Master Recipe, page 28, for separating them and storing them.

Encouraging Note When familiar with the procedure, it should take no more than 30 minutes or less to make noodles, if you mix the dough in a food processor and roll and cut it in an electric *pasta* machine.

NOODLES MADE
WITH A MANUAL *PASTA* MACHINE

The manual *pasta* machine works on essentially the same principles as the electric. It will knead and roll out the dough for you, then cut it into ribbons; you have only to turn the handle. I do, however, prefer the electric machine for several reasons. The machine "drives itself," which is much easier on arm power, and the machine has greater power. The kneading can be done in 15 run-throughs at the most, while the manual requires many more turns, usually as many as 20 to 25. After having used both the electric machine and the manual, I have discovered that the textures of the rollers differ substantially. The steel rollers on the manual machine create very smooth noodles. The plastic rollers of the electric machine create noodles with a slight texture. My advice to the users of the manual machine is to limit the number of turns through the machine as much as possible, so more of the dough's natural texture remains. Now, mind you, it takes a good deal of searching to see that texture and even more to feel it, but since I did see and feel it, I pass the information on to you.

I like to knead the dough for about five minutes before exposing it to the machine. You may then proceed in the same way as with the electric machine. Please note the numbers carefully, as machines vary; move from wide openings to narrow and narrower.

A Warning on Pasta *Machines* Dust the rollers and cutters of the machine with flour *as often as you can.* It keeps the dough surface dry and prevents sticking or lumping of dough in the machine. Secondly, do not wash the machine. Use a firm brush to whisk off bits of dried dough and excess flour when you have finished making the noodles.

COOKING *PASTA*

"How do you cook *pasta?*" I am often asked.
"In boiling water. How else?"

Since there are so many warnings, so many dos and don'ts, by "experts" in the field, I would first like to reassure my readers that though fresh *pasta* is one thing and dried or manufactured *pasta* is another thing, neither are newborn infants to be handled with infinite care. Secondly, only experimentation will tell you, without argument, just how *you* would like your *pasta* cooked. For instance, most Italians, particularly in the south of Italy, like their *pasta* hard, and at one time *spaghetti* was thrown at a wall to test if it was cooked properly. If it was pasty and overcooked by their standards, it stuck. It it hit with a nice sound and then fell, it was just right. But how do *you* like it? Only by cooking it can you be certain.

Watching the clock will tell you nothing about *pasta* cooking. Instead, the cooking time will be dictated by a variety of things: a little more or a little less flour in the dough; the size and freshness of the eggs or how much of the white you fingered out of the shells; and the degree of dryness of the dough when it is dropped into the boiling water. Naturally, fresh *pasta* requires less cooking time than dried *pasta,* which is concentrated. You must be ready to test fresh *pasta* for doneness the moment the water returns to the boil, whereas you need not start testing dried *pasta* for about five or eight minutes.

In essence, a properly cooked noodle should have a rather firm but not raw core and slight resistance to the teeth when chewed. This is how the Italians consider *pasta* cooked *al dente,* or "to the teeth." If you prefer it less firm, cook it a bit longer, but do not, I implore you, do as the inimitable Mrs. Beaton suggested, "cook it for 2-1/2 hours or until the water is absorbed," for then you may call it paste pudding and a less appetizing prospect I cannot imagine. If the cooked *pasta* is to be recooked in the oven or on the stove top after being mixed with a sauce or other ingredients, it should be cooked only until *almost* tender, or the final result will be much too soft and mushy.

The following cooking directions are applicable to egg noodles eaten just about everywhere. You will find in this book specific directions for cooking noodles (such as the *soba* of Japan, the *mein* of China, the rice *vermicelli* of the Far East, etc.) that do not use this particular cooking method. That is to say, whenever you see the phrase "cook in boiling salted water," the following details are recommended.

It is, in general, best to allow four quarts (4 L) of water for each pound (500 g) of *pasta.* Bring the water to a rolling boil, stir in one tablespoon (15 ml) of salt, and a moment later drop *all* of the *pasta* required for the recipe into the water. If the *pasta* is dried and very long, hold it in your hand at one end and push down the other end. Press a long wooden fork against the middle of the *pasta* and fold over and down. Once it is in the water, the *pasta* bends accommodatingly, but the water will stop boiling. Slap a lid on the pot and listen closely. When it bubbles and sounds as if it has returned to the boiling point, remove the cover promptly and stir the *pasta* with a large wooden fork. If the *pasta* is fresh, draw out a strand with your long fork and taste it. If it is too "firm," wait

a moment and try again. If you are cooking dried *pasta,* permit it to cook about five minutes before tasting. (If you peer into the pot as I do, you may see the *pasta* "curling" in the hot water bath. Sometimes you may be able to judge from the look of it when it is ready, but tasting is really the best way.) When the *pasta* is just as you wish it, pour in a cup (250 ml) of cold water. It will stop the boiling action promptly.

Now lift pot, water and *pasta* and remove to the sink, in which you have set a large footed colander. Drop *pasta* and water into the colander. Lift colander and shake well to remove as much water as possible, and dump *pasta* back into the large kettle you cooked it in. You may, at this point, drizzle on a tablespoon (15 ml) or so of oil or butter and stir with the wooden fork to coat every strand and to prevent the strands from sticking to each other. Now, either serve immediately from a warmed serving bowl or plate with prepared sauce poured over or cover the kettle and let the *pasta* sit for the brief time you require to complete the preparation. It is vital, however, that the *pasta* be served as soon as possible after cooking.

Now, to discuss in greater detail various steps in the above preparation. As much as one and a half pounds (750 g) of *pasta* can, with care, be cooked in the four quarts (4 L) of water. The boiling must be brisk and the stirring vigorous. The *pasta* must not be allowed to settle upon itself or it will stick together. The amount of salt added to the water sometimes depends on the sauce that will be served on the *pasta.* If it will be a butter and cream sauce, by all means add a bit more salt, even as much as two tablespoons (30 ml). But if the sauce is savory with anchovies, capers or other salty ingredients, reduce the amount of salt added to the water.

As I mentioned earlier, even the rather simple process of cooking *pasta* is controversial. Some experts maintain that the *pasta* should not be drained in a colander, but rather lifted out of the water with a large wooden fork or a large skimmer, held over the water for a second to drain, then dropped into a warmed serving bowl or plate. Their reasoning is that the water in which the *pasta* cooked should remain, in small measure, to dilute the sauce, because it retains some of the delicious flavor of the noodle. I, however, have been served *pasta* drained that way and did not appreciate the pool of liquid remaining in my dish after the *pasta* and sauce were eaten.

Another school insists that a tablespoon (15 ml) of olive oil be dropped into the cooking water after the *pasta* has been in it for a second or two. They hold that the *pasta* then does not stick to its neighbors and that the oil brings out the sweetness of *pasta*. I, however, still believe in my rough-and-ready method, but gladly permit you your idiosyncracies, should they develop.

Now to the mysterious numbers on the packets of manufactured *pasta:* "cook for 20 minutes," or for 26 minutes or whatever. How does the manufacturer know how high your heat is, how many quarts of water you are using and how much of it has evaporated from the time it was put on to boil? They don't know, nor do you. So taste, taste and taste again.

A final note on a curious cooking tip that I learned at the home of a friend, Luciano Moroni, in Italy. His gem of a cook, with the delightful name of Leonilda, had prepared a delectable lunch.

Her *pasta* was superb, but above all it was light in texture and flavor. The meal, in my opinion, was gargantuan. Not only was there *pasta* with sauce, but a "stew" of fava beans and prosciutto, veal sautéed with herbs, a huge salad and dessert. I expected to have to be helped from the table, but nothing of the sort. At the end of the meal, I felt quite comfortable. I questioned Luciano on this and he told me the secret. "Both the pasta and beans were cooked in *acqua minerale.*" For a second I thought him mad, and then it hit me. "Bicarbonate of soda!" I said. He nodded happily.

When I started the research for this book, I took the question of using baking soda or bicarbonate of soda in the cooking of *pasta* to Dr. George K. York, the eminent food scientist at the University of California in Davis, who is currently involved in experimenting with flour-and-egg and flour-and-water mixtures *(pasta)*. Not only that, but he is a *gourmand,* an excellent cook and a perfectly charming companion. When I put the question to him he thought a moment and then replied. "Why not? Of course, it would certainly have the effect of 'lightening' the doughy food." I then asked if it would in any way effect the nutritive properties of *pasta* or *pasta* and beans, which prepared together form a complete protein. He assured me it would not in any way alter that aspect of it.

Only afterward did I note that one of the most important Italian food writers, Anna Gosetti della Salda, in her definitive work, *Le Ricette Regionali Italiane,* suggests the use of a *pinch* (no more, mind you) of bicarbonate of soda in her directions for recipes of any mixture of *pasta* and legumes.

PASTA: HOW MUCH TO SERVE AND HOW

It is generally thought by Europeans that we in the United States use far too much sauce on our *pasta,* and while we often eat *pasta* as a main course, they usually serve it as a first course with meat or fish to follow. Europeans value *pasta* for itself and the sauce is merely meant to enhance the delicate flavor and to keep it from being dry. They are shocked to find that Americans may sometimes use as much as a pound (500 g) of meat in a sauce for two persons, and compare that with the usual two to three ounces (56 to 84 g) used for the same number of persons served in Europe.

As a general rule, it is conceded that one pound (500 g) of uncooked fresh *pasta,* or three-quarters pound (375 g) dried will serve four persons or even six as a main course. As a meat accompaniment or side dish this same amount should easily satisfy eight to ten persons; for a first course, it can serve about eight persons.

Of course, there are other considerations. Young adults, 16 to 25 years old, can easily eat twice the above amount in the same situations, especially if they are athletic or otherwise active, and an athletic 12-year-old can alone do credit to the above amounts. The leanness or richness of the sauce will affect the amount of the dish consumed. With a sauce like that of *Spaghetti alla Carbonara* (butter, bacon and eggs) in generous amounts, much less *pasta* will be consumed even as a main course, particularly if diners have gorged themselves on tidbits and drinks before dinner. It must be remembered, too, that many Americans refuse to eat bread with *pasta,* as almost all Europeans do—for eating, pushing and sopping up sauce and because they love bread. The amount of bread consumed will make a difference in the amount of *pasta* to serve. For instance, if I am planning to serve *pasta* as a first course to be followed by a fish or meat course and am not serving bread, I figure about one and a half pounds (750 g) fresh *pasta* and one and a quarter pounds dried for eight persons. This amount works out well for me, though I find many cookbooks figure more or less than that.

I think the advice offered by Dr. Ancel Keys in his book, *How to Eat Well and Stay Well, the Mediterranean Way,* most apt. He advises the cook to take careful note of the type of work done by one's guests in order to judge their caloric needs. He feels that four to five ounces (112 to 140 g) of uncooked fresh *pasta* or three to four ounces (84 to 112 g) dried is sufficient for most adult Americans. For active teenagers and athletes, allow six to seven ounces (168 to 196 g) uncooked fresh and four to six ounces (112 to 168 g) dried; for their sisters, three to four ounces (84 to 112 g) uncooked fresh and two to three ounces (56 to 84 g) dried—and even less for their grandparents.

Finally, I would like to comment on the common notion that *pasta* is fattening. An ounce (28 g) of uncooked *pasta* has 100 calories, the same amount as in a banana, apple or orange. A moderate amount of fresh plain tomato sauce and a little cheese will add perhaps 125 calories to an average three-ounce (84 g) serving. Certainly, a 425-calorie portion at a meal cannot be considered exorbitant.

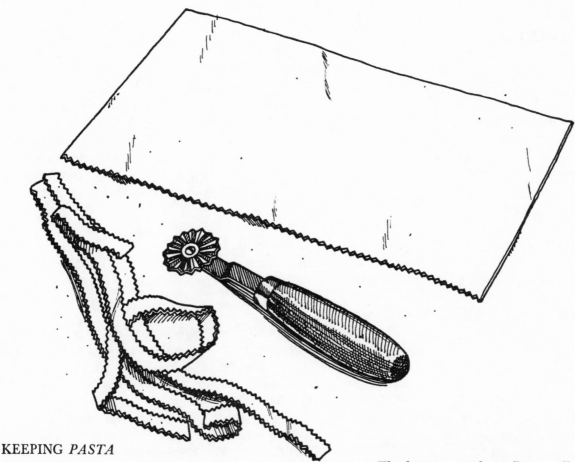

KEEPING *PASTA*

The flat noodle type of *pasta* may be wrapped securely in an airtight plastic bag and refrigerated for up to five to seven days or frozen *almost* indefinitely. The filled forms—*pelmeni, ravioli, tortellini,* etc.—are best if used immediately upon making. They may be refrigerated for a few days or frozen for about a week, but be warned that the flavors of the filling begin to evaporate very quickly and the dumplings dry out.

The best way to keep flat noodle forms over a long period is to dry them completely. Spread them on a floured surface or hang them from poles or sticks until they are quite dry and brittle, like factory-made noodles. Handling them carefully, put the noodles into a large receptacle, leave it uncovered and store in a cool, dry place. They will then keep almost indefinitely. They will take longer to cook that fresh noodles, but not nearly as long as the commercial dried product.

EGGLESS NOODLES
(International)

A most unusual, ultra-rich *pasta*.

4 tablespoons (60 ml) butter or margarine
2 cups (500 ml) unbleached all-purpose flour or
    fine semolina
1/8 teaspoon (scant 1 ml) salt
Approximately 3/4 cup (200 ml) water, boiling

In a large mixing bowl mix the butter and flour together with your hands. Mix in the salt and just enough boiling water to make a stiff dough. Knead the dough on a lightly floured board until smooth and elastic. Cover and let rest for 30 minutes.

Roll out the dough and cut into noodles as described in the Master Recipe, page 28. The dough may feel rather sticky, so dust with flour as you work.

This dough will lend itself to the same uses as the regular egg-and-flour dough, and I think you will find it easier to manipulate. But be warned that it does dry out quickly, and must be kept under a cloth when it is not being worked.
Makes approximately 1 pound (500 g); 4 servings

GREEN NOODLES
Pasta Verde (Italy)

When spinach is added to *pasta* dough, it colors it a lovely soft green, but it also makes it a little creamier, and a bit sweeter, it seems to me. It is used in much the same way as ivory *pasta*—as noodles, *lasagne, tagliatelle,* or the stuffed forms. It is very pretty when served with a fresh tomato sauce or a *béchamel,* or very simply with butter and cheese.

1/2 pound (225 g) spinach
Pinch of salt
1-3/4 cups (425 ml) unbleached all-purpose flour
2 eggs

Remove all stems and discard any imperfect spinach leaves. Wash well and cook with a pinch of salt in the water clinging to the leaves, until just wilted. Drain well, squeeze out all excess moisture and chop finely.

To make the dough, mound the flour on a working surface and make a well in the center with your finger. Break the eggs into the well and add the spinach; beat them together with a fork or your fingers. Now proceed to make the dough and cut the noodles as described in the Master Recipe, page 28. Be prepared to find this *pasta* dough much softer and more malleable than the basic egg-and-flour *pasta.* Cook in the standard manner.
Makes approximately 1 pound (500 g); 4 servings

Note Swiss chard leaves may also be used. I find it produces an even more delicately flavored *pasta.*

RAINBOW *PASTA*
(International)

I have seen these lovely colored noodles made up by wonderful delicatessens in Milan, in Nice, in Aix-en-Provence and in New York. They are easy to make and very appealing for a child's birthday party, no matter what age the "child" may be.

Yellow Noodles
2 cups (500 ml) unbleached all-purpose flour
2 whole eggs
1 egg yolk
Half eggshell water

Green Noodles
1-1/2 cups (375 ml) unbleached all-purpose flour
3 tablespoons (45 ml) finely minced cooked
    spinach (squeezed completely dry)
2 eggs

Brown Noodles
1-1/2 cups (375 ml) unbleached all-purpose flour
1/4 cup (75 ml) whole wheat flour
1-1/2 tablespoons (22 ml) unsweetened cocoa
    powder
2 eggs

Red Noodles
1-1/2 cups (375 ml) unbleached all-purpose flour
1 small beet, boiled, peeled and mashed
2 eggs

The main difference between making colored *pasta* and the usual ivory one is that the eggs must be mixed with the coloring agent before adding to the flour. It is easiest to mix each of them in a blender or in a small bowl with a fork before pouring into the flour well. They can, of course, be mixed in the well with a fork or your fingers, but this is more difficult.

Make each dough separately, proceeding as described in the Master Recipe, page 28, and cutting into noodles approximately 1/4 inch (6 mm) wide. Keep the colors in separate mounds, covered with a towel, until you are ready to cook them. They are then cooked in the standard manner.

Serve these "rainbow" noodles with a simple sauce: cheese and cream, cheese and butter, or minced prosciutto, cream, butter and lightly cooked peas or broccoli flowerets.
Makes approximately 3 pounds (1.5 kg);
10 servings

PARMESAN NOODLES, ROMAN STYLE
Fettuccine Parmigiana Romana (Italy)

A rather unusual type of *pasta*. The cheese becomes an intrinsic part of the noodle and the noodles are often served with only melted butter. I am grateful to Kirk Long for suggesting this delicious *pasta* form.

4 eggs, beaten until light
1/4 cup (50 ml) milk
1 cup (250 ml) freshly grated Parmesan cheese
Approximately 3 cups (750 ml) unbleached
    all-purpose flour

In a large mixing bowl mix together the eggs and milk until well blended. Then mix in the Parmesan cheese. Gradually add the flour, working it in with a fork or your fingers, to form a stiff dough. Knead the dough briefly on a *very* lightly floured surface until it is smooth and elastic. If the dough seems too dry, knead in a little more milk; if too moist, knead in more flour.

    Roll out the dough as described in the Master Recipe, page 28, and cut into noodles approximately 1/4 inch (6 mm) wide. Cook in the standard manner.
Makes approximately 1-1/2 pounds (750 g);
6 servings

HERB NOODLES
Pâtes aux Herbes (France)

This produces a very delicate and unusual noodle, and it is wise to select herbs that blend well together. For example, herbs like rosemary, sage or savory are, for some, a bit overpowering, while parsley, basil, tarragon, sorrel, dandelion (when very young), lemon thyme and marjoram alone or in any combination are very pleasant; try combinations in which each herb is separate yet compatible. But do make your own combinations, for it must, after all, please you.

2-1/4 cups (300 ml) unbleached all-purpose flour
1 teaspoon (5 ml) salt
2 eggs
4 tablespoons (60 ml) chopped fresh herbs,
    pounded in a mortar to a fine paste
Approximately 2 tablespoons (30 ml) lukewarm
    water

Combine the flour and salt and mound on a working surface. Make a well in the center with your finger and break in the eggs. Add the herbs and water to the well and beat them with the eggs using a fork or your fingers. Now proceed to make the dough as described in the Master Recipe, page 28. When a compact mass is formed, move the dough to a floured surface and knead for at least 20 minutes, dusting with flour until the dough becomes firm and smooth. The herbs will absorb much more flour than other *pasta*, so keep dusting as necessary. When it is no longer sticky, form the dough into a ball, cover and let it rest for a good hour or so.

Roll out dough as described in the Master Recipe and cut into 1-1/2-inch (4 cm) squares. Cook the squares in boiling salted water for no more than 4 minutes. Drain promptly as they easily overcook.

These noodles may be served simply with butter and freshly grated cheese. For a more elaborate presentation, put them into a buttered and Parmesan cheese-sprinkled *gratin* dish, pour on 1 cup (250 ml) heavy cream, sprinkle the top with more cheese and bake in a preheated 425°F (220°C) oven for no more than 20 minutes. The cream and cheese are perfect complements to the fresh herbs.

Makes a little over 1 pound (500 g); 4 or 5 servings

HOMEMADE "LITTLE EARS"
Orecchiette Casalinga (Apulia, Italy)

Apulia is the province that is the farthest south on the mainland of Italy—around the heel and part of the instep. The *pasta* in Apulia is as different from northern *pasta* as the sauces are. It is made of semolina and water. The hard durum wheat does not mix easily with water, so making it must be a labor of love (unless you have a food processor). The result is a tougher, chewier dough, but very satisfying, especially after the second or third time you have eaten it. The fourth time, one remembers only that northern *pasta* barely touches one's teeth!

1 cup (250 ml) fine semolina
2 cups (500 ml) unbleached all-purpose flour
1/2 teaspoon (3 ml) salt
Approximately 3/4 cup (175 ml) lukewarm water

Combine the semolina, flour and salt and mound it on a large working surface. Make a well in the center with your finger and pour in 3 to 4 tablespoons (45 to 60 ml) of the water. Begin pulling the flour from the inner wall of the well into the liquid. Add more water and continue forming a paste until the flour has absorbed as much water as possible without becoming hard or dry. The perfect consistency is softer than the basic egg-and-flour *pasta*, but not at all sticky. Knead vigorously on a lightly floured board until the dough is smooth and elastic. This may take 20 minutes or so. Form into a ball and cover.

To make the "little ears," pull off a scant handful of the dough (keep remaining dough covered) and roll into a rope about 3/4 inch (2 cm) in diameter on a lightly floured board. Cut the rope into slices 1/8 inch (3 mm) thick or less to form small circles of dough. Now put one of these circles into the cupped palm of your hand, and with the thumb of the other hand, press and turn the circle at the same time to form a dent in the center that will spread the dough a little on each side. It should look like a small "ear," with slightly thicker "ear lobes." Repeat with all the remaining dough, placing the *orecchiette* on a lightly floured cloth as they are made.

The *orecchiette* are cooked in the same manner as fresh flour-and-egg *pasta*, though they do take somewhat longer to cook. Watch them carefully and taste steadily for doneness. They also dry very well, and can be kept for a month or so in a dry, cool cupboard.

Makes approximately 1-1/2 pounds (750 g); 6 servings

NOODLE "NESTS" MADE ON A "GUITAR"
Tondarelli alla Chitarra (Abruzzi, Italy)

If this ponderous title sounds odd, it's because it is odd. The "guitar" in this context is a homemade frame of wood, rectangular in shape and about eight by twenty inches (20 by 50 cm). On each of the shorter ends, small nails are hammered rather close together and thin but strong wires are strung around the nails, back and forth from side to side. The frame is laid flat (so the top is now the strung wires and the bottom is the table top) and a sheet of *pasta* is laid on the wires. A rolling pin is pressed and rolled over the *pasta*, which is cut by the wires and falls in plump "nests" onto the table. The frame is lifted and the "nests" of tangled *pasta* are removed to a lightly floured cloth. The *pasta* may then be cooked as usual and served with any sauce desired, though the traditional one in Abruzzi is *Ragù di Agnello con Peperoni* (Lamb with Pepper Sauce, page 126).

2-3/4 cups (675 ml) fine semolina
5 eggs
1/2 teaspoon (3 ml) salt

Make the dough according to directions in Master Recipe, page 28, adding the salt to the flour. You will need to knead the dough at least 20 minutes before it is smooth and elastic. Divide the dough into 4 portions and roll out each portion into a rectangle as described in the Master Recipe. If you have a *chitarra*, cut the noodles as described above. If not, roll up the rectangle and cut as finely as possible or cut on the narrowest cutter on your *pasta* machine. Pick up the noodles by the handful and lay them down in small tangled nests on a lightly floured cloth to dry. Or wrap a few noodles around 3 or 4 fingers and drop onto cloth in resulting shape. When they are "leather dry," store them in a cool, dry cupboard.
Makes approximately 1-1/2 pounds (750 g);
6 servings

NOODLE SQUARES
Fleckerl (Austria)

Fleckerl, similar to the *quadrucci* of Italy, are small *pasta* squares generally cooked and served in broth. They may also, however, be cooked in boiling water, drained and served with melted butter or as in *Schinkenfleckerl* (Ham and *Fleckerl* Casserole, page 135).

Noodle dough made with 2-3/4 cups (675 ml)
    flour and 3 eggs, page 28

Make noodle dough according to directions in Master Recipe. Roll out the dough as thinly as possible into a rectangle. Cut into strips 1/2 inch (12 mm) wide. As the strips are cut, stack them on top of one another, dusting them well with flour. Then cut the stack of strips into 1/2 inch (12 mm) squares. Dry lightly for immediate use or dry thoroughly for storing.
Makes approximately 1-1/2 pounds (750 g);
6 servings

"PINCHED" NOODLES
Csipetke (Hungary)

A popular soup noodle in Hungary. It is said that bean soup with *csipetke* is an excellent tonic for a hangover, overeating or a nervous condition.

3/4 cup (175 ml) unbleached all-purpose flour
1/2 teaspoon (3 ml) salt
1 egg

Combine the flour and salt and mound on a working surface or in a mixing bowl. Make a well in the center with your finger and break in the egg. Gradually work the flour into the egg until a distinct mass is formed. Knead on a lightly floured surface for about 5 to 8 minutes, or until dough is smooth and elastic. Form into a ball, cover and let rest for 15 minutes.

Divide the dough into 6 pieces. On a lightly floured board, roll each piece by hand into a rope about the thickness of your index finger and 6 inches (15 cm) long. Dust the ropes lightly with flour.

Bring a large kettle of salted water to a boil. Dust your hands well with flour, "pinch" off little pieces of the ropes and drop the pieces into the boiling water. When they rise to the surface, remove with a slotted spoon, testing first to be sure they are cooked. They can now be dropped into a good goulash or bean soup or eaten with melted butter.
Enough for 8 servings in soup;
4 servings as a side dish

Note Straccia, meaning "torn rags," is a specialty of Sardinia. The dough, very like that used for *csipetke,* is made in the evening, covered and left until morning, when it is rolled out, torn into uneven pieces—as small as an inch (3 cm) across or as large as 3 inches (8 cm) or so—and set on a floured surface. Semolina is sprinkled on and the noodles are left to dry until the evening meal. They are then cooked like any *pasta* and served with a hearty meat-tomato sauce or with the *pesto* sauce on page 52 (Ilio's Sardinian *Pesto*).

SPAETZLE
(Central Europe)

2 cups (500 ml) sifted unbleached all-purpose flour
3 eggs, beaten until light
2/3 cup (150 ml) milk
1 teaspoon (5 ml) salt
Pinch of freshly grated nutmeg
4 tablespoons (60 ml) butter, melted

Put the flour in a large mixing bowl. Add the eggs to the flour, stirring with a large wooden spoon or wire whisk. Very gradually stir in the milk, beating or stirring constantly. Stir in the salt and nutmeg. The dough should be bubbly and elastic.

Bring a large kettle of salted water to a boil. If you do not have a *spaetzle* maker (a colander-like implement), use a colander with large holes. Hold the colander over the boiling water, and with a wooden spoon, press the dough through the holes to make small strands. Boil for about 1 to 2 minutes, or until the noodles rise to the surface. Remove with a slotted spoon to a warmed serving dish. When all of the batter is cooked, toss the noodles with the melted butter.

Serve as a side dish to goulash or stew. You may also sprinkle some grated cheese on top and place in the broiler or oven until cheese melts.
Makes 6 servings

WON TON SKINS OR WHEAT NOODLES
(China)

Won ton dumplings are probably the best known and most popular of Chinese foods. They may be floated in soup, fried for a snack and even served as dessert. This dough may also be cut into strips as noodles called *mein*.

3-1/2 cups (875 ml) unbleached all-purpose flour
1 teaspoon (5 ml) salt
3 eggs
Water
Cornstarch for dusting

Combine the flour and salt and mound it on a large working surface. Make a well in the center with your finger and break in the eggs. With chopsticks or your fingers, work the flour into the liquid, adding water only if needed to form a solid mass. Knead for about 5 minutes, or until the dough is smooth and elastic. Form into a ball, cover and let rest 20 minutes.

Roll out the dough on a lightly floured board into a tissue-thin sheet. Dust with flour and let rest 5 minutes. If to be used for *won ton* skins, cut into 4-inch (10 cm) squares or 3-inch (8 cm) rounds. Sprinkle with cornstarch and stack one on top of another. Cover until ready to use. If to be used for noodles, roll up and cut into desired width as described in the Master Recipe, page 28, then dust with cornstarch.

The noodles may be cooked in boiling water until tender and then served in soup, pan fried or tossed and stirred with vegetables and meat. The *won ton* skins are filled and boiled and served in broth or deep fried, as on page 174.

Makes approximately 55 skins;
1-1/2 pounds (750 g) noodles

Note Won ton skins and fresh wheat noodles may be purchased in Oriental markets and some supermarkets. They both most frequently appear in 1-pound (500 g) packages. Dried wheat noodles are also available.

RICE NOODLES
Fun (China)

I am grateful to Maggie Gin, excellent cook and superb teacher, for permission to reprint this recipe from her book *Regional Cooking of China*. These noodles are not like any made anywhere else, that I know of, and are delicious hot or cold.

2 cups (500 ml) rice flour
1/2 teaspoon (3 ml) powdered alum
1/2 teaspoon (3 ml) salt
2-3/4 cups (675 ml) water
Peanut oil

Using a pastry board, place the rice flour in the center and sprinkle the alum and salt over it. Blend these dry ingredients together and then slowly add some of the water, a little at a time, along with 3 tablespoons (45 ml) of peanut oil. Add only enough water to make a ball of smooth dough and knead 10 minutes to give an elastic texture to the finished noodle. Place kneaded dough into a mixing bowl, break dough up with fingers and slowly add remaining water to make a batter, mixing in well. The batter should be very smooth and completely free of lumps. Let batter rest for about 30 minutes.

Oil a large pie pan and place on a rack over 2 inches (5 cm) of water in a large pot. Ladle enough batter into the pie pan to cover the bottom; the amount of batter used will determine the thickness of the noodles. Cover the pot and bring the water to a boil over high heat. Reduce heat to medium and steam 15 minutes or until batter is set. When the noodle round is cooked, remove pie pan from rack and have another oiled pie pan ready to repeat the process. Let the noodle round cool in the pan until it can be handled, then roll it off onto a plate and set aside until all the noodle rounds are made. To make noodles, cut into 1/2-inch (12 mm) strips, or as desired, and separate.

Makes approximately 2 pounds (1 kg); 6 servings

Note Rice noodle skins or rounds, called *bok fun*, may be purchased in Chinese take-out pastry shops. They can be filled and rolled as they are or cut into noodles. Fresh and dried rice noodles may also be purchased.

WHEAT STARCH DOUGH
Fun Goh (China)

This is the transparent, glistening dough used in making *dim sum* dumplings. The wheat starch can be found in Oriental markets.

2-1/2 cups (625 ml) wheat starch
6 tablespoons (90 ml) cornstarch
1-3/4 cups (425 ml) water
1 tablespoon (15 ml) lard
Oriental sesame oil or peanut oil

Combine the wheat starch and cornstarch in a large mixing bowl. Put the water and lard in a small saucepan and bring to a boil. Gradually add the boiling water to the mixing bowl, stirring vigorously with chopsticks or a fork. When cool, knead the dough in the bowl until smooth and elastic, adding more flour or boiling water, if needed. Form into a ball, rub the surface lightly with oil, cover with a dampened towel and let rest for 30 minutes.

Divide the dough into 4 parts. On an oiled surface form each part into a long rope about 1 inch (3 cm) in diameter. Cut 1/2- to 1-inch (12 mm to 3 cm) pieces from the ropes and press each piece flat with the side of an oiled cleaver or with a rolling pin into a 3-inch (8 cm) circle. Fill and shape dumplings as directed in recipes.
Makes approximately 50 circles

WHOLE WHEAT NOODLES
Udon (Japan)

1 cup (250 ml) whole wheat flour
3 cups (750 ml) unbleached all-purpose flour
1 teaspoon (5 ml) salt
Approximately 2/3 cup (150 ml) water

Combine the flours and salt in a large mixing bowl. Add the water, a little at a time, until a moist dough that you can shape into a ball is formed. Knead the dough on a lightly floured board for about 20 minutes, or until smooth and elastic. Roll out dough and cut into noodles 1/8 to 1/4 inch (3 mm to 6 mm) thick as described in the Master Recipe, page 28.

To cook the *udon,* bring a saucepan of water to a boil and drop them in. When the water returns to the boil, add 1 cup (250 ml) cold water. When it returns to the boil again, cook only until noodles are tender. Drain in a colander placed over a large pan to reserve the cooking water. Rinse the noodles under cold running water to separate the strands. Cool them thoroughly.

The *udon* may be served with a dipping sauce of some of the reserved cooking water and soy sauce or with any preferred dipping sauce. They are also often served in *dashi* (broth), plain or with meats and/or seafood, and vegetables.
Makes approximately 1-1/2 to 2 pounds
(750 g to 1 kg); 6 servings

BUCKWHEAT NOODLES
Soba (Japan)

4 cups (1 L) buckwheat flour
1 teaspoon (5 ml) salt
1 egg, beaten
Approximately 1/2 cup (125 ml) water

Combine the flour and salt in a large mixing bowl. Make a well in the center with your finger and put the egg and a little of the water in the well. Gradually work the flour into the liquid, adding more water, little by little. Add only enough water to form a soft ball. Knead the dough on a lightly floured board for at least 15 minutes, or until the dough is firm and smooth. Work in more flour if dough becomes too sticky. Roll out dough and cut into fine noodles as described in the Master Recipe, page 28.

To cook the *soba*, bring a saucepan of water to a boil and drop them in. When the water returns to the boil, immediately add about 1 cup (250 ml) of cold water. When it again returns to the boil, add another cup (250 ml) of cold water. Repeat this procedure twice more. When the noodles reach the fifth boil, remove from heat and drain in a colander set over a large pan to reserve the cooking water. Rinse the noodles well under cold running water to separate the strands. Cool them completely.

The *soba* may be served with a dipping sauce of some of the reserved cooking water and soy sauce or with any preferred dipping sauce. They are also good tossed with sesame oil and stir fried with vegetable and meat or chilled and served with shrimp *tempura* and a dipping sauce.
Makes approximately 1-1/2 to 2 pounds
(750 g to 1 kg); 6 servings

Note This noodle dough may be used in recipes calling for *bigoli*, the whole wheat noodles of Venice. Roll out the dough 1/8 inch (3 mm) thick and cut into noodles about 3/8 inch (9 mm) wide.

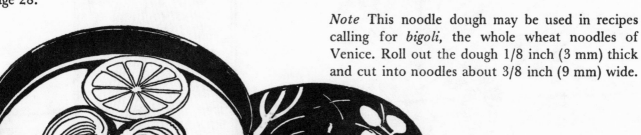

BASIC SAUCES

Though many of the sauces in this chapter are excellent over *pasta* on their own, they have been grouped together because they are called for in several other recipes. Other sauces in this book are grouped according to their most identifiable ingredients, i.e., cheese, beef, seafood, etc.

GENOESE BASIL SAUCE
Pesto alla Genovese (Genoa)

The Genoese assert *pesto* can only be made in a mortar and pestle. And Norman Douglas, that irresistible Italophile, wrote that basil should never be treated more roughly than shredding with the fingers, for otherwise the aromatic oils would be ruined and lost. I have made it in an electric blender, so I do agree with him; the blender batters the fine essences to an offensive mishmash, and not only can one not make out the individual ingredients of the *pesto,* but the sauce becomes slick and unctuous.

I have also made *pesto* in my Cuisinart food processor. I do it with infinite care, turning the motor on and off, so that I do not miss that essential and irretrievable moment when it all may become an eviscerated phantom of a sauce.

The mortar and pestle is, however, the best method of preparation. It gives a rich result in which each ingredient can be tasted and savored, yet blends magically with its neighbor.

Since basil has so relatively brief a season and using frozen or dried basil is hardly comparable to the fresh, make *pesto* when fresh basil is abundant in gardens and markets and freeze it in small batches. It keeps very well this way and you can enjoy it all year. (If you are freezing *pesto,* do not add the cheese until it is thawed and ready to be served, then beat it in thoroughly.)

A warning on the cheese you use: The Genoese use a marvelously piquant Pecorino Sardo cheese, often mixed with Parmesan. The Pecorino available in the United States is a much harsher cheese and is called Pecorino Romano. It should be used with care. Experiment with it, mixing two parts Parmesan and one part Romano, or half and half or however it pleases you, to preserve the balance of flavors of the *pesto*.

Pesto is not only used as a sauce for all kinds of *pasta,* but can also be added to minestrone or other kinds of bean or vegetable soups (just a tablespoon or 15 ml will do it), baked or boiled potatoes and even to rice.

PESTO MADE IN A MORTAR

2 cups (500 ml) gently packed shredded fresh
    basil leaves
2 tablespoons (30 ml) pine nuts
1 to 2 garlic cloves, chopped
Pinch each of salt and freshly ground black pepper
1/2 cup (125 ml) freshly grated Parmesan cheese
2 tablespoons (30 ml) freshly grated Pecorino
    cheese
3/4 cup (175 ml) finest olive oil
Approximately 2 tablespoons (30 ml) water
    from cooking *pasta*

If you are lucky enough to have a large marble mortar and pestle, use it. If not, use whatever you have in the way of a mortar and pestle. Wood is fine and so is unglazed porcelain, with that slight roughness it has.

Put into the mortar the basil, pine nuts, garlic, salt and pepper. Using a circular motion, grind and crush the ingredients against the side of the mortar with the pestle, until you have obtained a very fine paste. Now add both cheeses and blend into basil mixture. When well blended, take a large wooden spoon and start stirring as you add the olive oil, a few drops at a time, and beat it into the mixture. When ready to serve the *pesto,* save out a little *pasta* water and stir it into the sauce.

Makes approximately 6 servings on *pasta;*
8 to 10 servings in soup

PESTO MADE IN A FOOD PROCESSOR

Use the steel blade and turn the machine off and on frequently. The ingredients are the same as used in the preceding recipe. First grind down the pine nuts, then add basil, garlic, salt and pepper. Then add the cheeses, little by little, putting them in through the feed tube. (If your cheeses are very hard, grind them first, then add nuts, basil, garlic, salt and pepper.) After each addition, stop the machine and taste the mixture or touch it with your finger; it should be a creamy, thick paste. Start adding the olive oil, a few drops at a time, with the machine going steadily. The result should be a mixture *almost* as thick as mayonnaise. Stir in *pasta* water when ready to serve.

ILIO'S SARDINIAN *PESTO*
Pesto de Sardegna (Sardinia)

Ilio Canù was born and raised in a mountain town in Sardinia. In his later teens, he came to Rome, where I knew him as a wonderfully inventive cook. Once we contributed together to a friend's *fête* and he brought his *straccia* (page 45), sauced with my *pesto*. He sat beside me at table and, having tasted the dish, whispered: "Not enough lemon." As I have about 14 recipes for *pesto* in my library and not one that includes lemon in any form, I was rather taken aback, but said nothing. Recently, hearing I was working on a *pasta* book, Ilio sent me the following recipe—in Italian, of course, so the translation is mine. I hope he approves of it.

1/4 cup (75 ml) pine nuts
1/4 cup (75 ml) freshly grated Parmesan cheese
1/4 cup (75 ml) freshly grated Pecorino Sardo or
    Pecorino Romano cheese
3/4 cup (175 ml) tightly packed fresh basil leaves
3 garlic cloves, coarsely chopped
2 heaping tablespoons (30 ml) unsalted butter
3/4 cup (175 ml) olive oil
Juice of 1/2 lemon
Salt to taste
Generous pinch of freshly ground white pepper

With a mortar and pestle, grind the pine nuts, cheeses, basil, garlic and butter to a smooth paste. Then add the olive oil, alternately with the lemon juice, very very slowly, drop by drop, grinding steadily and amalgamating the ingredients until the sauce has the consistency of heavy cream and is very smooth. Stir in salt and pepper and serve with *linguine* or other fine noodles.
Makes approximately 1-1/2 cups (375 ml);
4 servings on *pasta*

TOMATO SAUCE
Salsa di Pomodoro (Italy)

1/2 cup (125 ml) olive oil
1 medium onion, finely chopped
1/2 cup (125 ml) sliced fresh mushrooms
1-1/2 pounds (750 g) ripe tomatoes, peeled
3/4 cup (175 ml) dry white or red wine
2 garlic cloves, mashed
1 tablespoon (15 ml) minced fresh oregano
1 tablespoon (15 ml) minced fresh basil
2 teaspoons (10 ml) sugar
2 tablespoons (30 ml) freshly grated Parmesan
    cheese
Salt and freshly ground black pepper to taste

In a small skillet heat 2 tablespoons (30 ml) of the olive oil and sauté the onion until translucent; set aside. In another small skillet heat 2 tablespoons (30 ml) of the olive oil and sauté mushrooms until soft; set aside. Heat remaining olive oil in a heavy medium-sized saucepan and add the tomatoes. Simmer over low heat, breaking up the tomatoes with a wooden spoon, about 10 minutes. Add the onion, mushrooms, wine, garlic, oregano, basil, sugar and cheese, cover and simmer very gently for 2-1/2 to 3 hours. Season with salt and pepper.
    This recipe may be multiplied, poured into glass jars or plastic boxes or bowls, tightly covered and frozen. The containers should hold enough for your usual servings: 4, 6, 8, etc.
Makes approximately 2-1/2 cups;
4 servings on *pasta*

TOMATO SAUCE WITH BASIL
Salsa di Pomodoro e Basilico (Naples)

3 tablespoons (45 ml) olive oil
1 pound (500 g) ripe tomatoes, peeled, seeded
    and chopped
1 garlic clove, minced
Salt and freshly ground black pepper to taste
1/2 cup (125 ml) chopped fresh basil
2 tablespoons (30 ml) chopped fresh Italian
    parsley
1/2 teaspoon (2 ml) sugar

In a large skillet heat olive oil over moderate heat and add the tomatoes. Cook for about 8 to 10 minutes, until soft but not mushy. Stir in garlic, salt, pepper, herbs and sugar. Cook 3 minutes longer and adjust seasonings to taste.
Makes approximately 2 cups (500 ml);
4 servings on *pasta*

TOMATO PURÉE
(International)

2 tablespoons (30 ml) butter
1 pound (500 g) ripe tomatoes, peeled, seeded
    and coarsely chopped
1 teaspoon (5 ml) sugar
1 teaspoon (5 ml) salt
1/2 teaspoon (3 ml) freshly ground black pepper
8 fresh basil leaves, shredded

In a 1-quart (1 L) saucepan melt butter and add all remaining ingredients. Cook, uncovered, over medium heat until thickened, about 30 minutes. Stir mixture from time to time. Remove from heat and put through a food mill.
Makes approximately 1-1/2 cups (375 ml);
4 servings on *pasta*

Variation This purée may be used as a quick fresh tomato sauce by not putting it through the food mill.

BOLOGNESE MEAT SAUCE
Ragù (Northern Italy)

When you see a dish listed on a menu as Bolognese, you know it will have this exciting sauce. It may be with *lasagne,* with *tagliatelle,* with *rigatoni, ziti* or other large tubed forms of *pasta;* this rich sauce will cling to the *pasta* and to folds or holes in it.

Use a large deep kettle of about four-quart (4 L) capacity of enameled ware or even better, flameproof earthenware, set on an asbestos pad, for the long, slow simmering of this fine sauce. The vessel does not require a lid, but long cooking is vital—three to five hours.

4 tablespoons (60 ml) unsalted butter
4 tablespoons (60 ml) olive oil
1 medium onion, chopped
2 celery stalks with leaves, chopped
1 small carrot, scraped and chopped
1 pound (500 g) ground lean beef
1/2 teaspoon (3 ml) salt
1 cup (250 ml) dry white wine
1/2 cup (125 ml) milk
Generous pinch of freshly grated nutmeg
1-1/2 pounds (750 g) ripe tomatoes, peeled and
    chopped

Heat the butter and olive oil over medium heat and sauté the onion for several minutes or until soft. Add the celery and carrot and cook very gently for 2 to 3 minutes. Add the ground meat, breaking it up with a fork, and cook just until all of the raw redness is gone. Stir in salt and wine. Raise heat to moderately high and cook until the wine has completely evaporated, stirring frequently. Reduce heat to medium, add the milk and nutmeg and cook until the milk has evaporated.

Now add the tomatoes and stir for several minutes, so ingredients are thoroughly blended. When the sauce starts to bubble, reduce heat as low as possible, so the sauce barely simmers. Continue cooking, uncovered, for at least 3 to 4 hours or more. It should be watched fairly steadily during this time. Taste and correct seasoning.
Makes approximately 2-1/2 cups (625 ml);
6 servings on *pasta*

Freezing Ragù Ragù freezes very well. It should be given plenty of time to thaw in its freezing container in the refrigerator. Unfortunately, many rush home, try to hurry the thawing process and manage only to cause a loss of precious fresh flavor.

If in a rush, cut a slice of bacon into fine dice and heat it slowly in a heavy saucepan. When it starts to color, add 1 green onion, chopped, and cook until soft. Add a scant handful each of chopped fresh Italian parsley and basil and cook for about 3 to 4 minutes. Then add the thawed or partially thawed *ragù,* and heat through, stirring often. Do not let it boil, but when it is thoroughly heated, serve it immediately. Throughout this process it is vital to keep the heat very low.

BÉCHAMEL SAUCE
Sauce Béchamel (France)

2 cups (500 ml) milk
4 tablespoons (60 ml) unsalted butter
3 tablespoons (45 ml) all-purpose unbleached flour
1/2 teaspoon (1 to 2 ml) salt

Scald the milk in a small saucepan just until it begins to bubble; remove from heat. In a heavy enameled saucepan melt the butter over low heat. Then stir in all of the flour at once, stirring constantly with a wooden spoon until flour is absorbed. Let it bubble for a few minutes—no more than 2 for it must not brown—stirring all the time. Then remove from heat and stir in a little of the hot milk, no more than 1 to 2 tablespoons (15 to 30 ml) to begin with. Only when it has been properly absorbed by the flour and butter paste, add more milk, stirring steadily. When about 1/2 cup (125 ml) of the milk has been added, begin adding about 4 to 5 tablespoons (60 to 75 ml) at a time, stirring constantly, until all the milk is incorporated. Place saucepan over low heat, add the salt and cook, stirring constantly, until the sauce is as thick as heavy cream.

Remember that the sauce thickens as it stands and cools, so it is best to make it just before using. If you must set it aside for some time before using, reheat it over very low heat or in the top of a double boiler over simmering water.
Makes approximately 1-2/3 cups (400 ml)

White Sauce is made much the same way, using cold milk.

Mornay Sauce has small cubes of cheese, usually Gruyère, added after the sauce has begun to thicken. Alternately, see *Mornay* Sauce, page 106, for a particularly rich version.

Cream Sauce is made by adding a few tablespoons of heavy cream to the *béchamel*. Heat it gently, and for a fine, shiny glaze, stir in a tablespoon (15 ml) or so of unsalted butter just before serving.

NEAPOLITAN STYLE BÉCHAMEL SAUCE
Salsa Besciamella alla Napoletana (Naples)

2 cups (500 ml) milk
1 small onion, chopped
1 celery stalk, chopped
6 peppercorns
2 parsley sprigs
2 bay leaves
4 tablespoons (60 ml) unsalted butter
4 tablespoons (60 ml) unbleached all-purpose flour
1 egg yolk

In a small heavy saucepan combine the milk, onion, celery, peppercorns, parsley and bay leaves. Bring just to the boiling point, but do not let it boil. Remove from heat and let stand about 15 minutes. Strain milk and set aside.

In a 1-1/2- to 2-quart (1.5 to 2 L) saucepan melt the butter, then blend in the flour with a wooden spoon. Cook about 2 minutes, stirring constantly; remove from heat. Now add the milk very gradually, stirring constantly, until all of it is incorporated into the flour-butter mixture. Place over moderate heat, still stirring steadily, until it comes to a boil. Cook about 2 to 3 minutes, until thick and creamy. Remove from heat.

In a small bowl beat the egg yolk and quickly stir about half the sauce into it. Return mixture to saucepan and cook over very low heat about 1 minute.

The sauce will thicken as it cools, so it is best to make it just before using. If this is not possible, reheat it very gently over very low heat or in the top of a double boiler over simmering water. Makes approximately 1-2/3 cups (400 ml)

CLARIFIED BUTTER
(International)

This is the pure butterfat, also called *ghee, smen,* etc., that gives the rich and distinctive flavor to many exotic dishes. Moreover, it is used to give silkiness to sauces, and can be heated to higher temperatures and blended more thoroughly over heat than when using ordinary butter, since the milk solids have been eliminated. (It is the milk solids that turn butter rancid and that burn so quickly during cooking.)

It is advisable to make a good amount of clarified butter at a time. It keeps, even without refrigeration, for several weeks. It is used in many parts of the world where refrigeration is a stranger: India, Africa, Mongolia, Tibet, etc. Refrigerated, it will keep for several months.

The best pan for making clarified butter is enameled iron or steel, the heavier, the better. Melt any amount of butter over low heat, and when the foam subsides, remove the pan from the heat and let it stand. The milk solids will drop to the bottom and you will be able to spoon off the clear liquid on top, or you may pour the melted butter through cheesecloth to obtain the clear liquid. Pour the clear liquid into a jar with a tight-fitting lid and store it in a cool, dry place. This clarified butter can be used for all recipes calling for butter.

COMPOUND BUTTERS
(International)

For a simple but elegant *pasta* dish. If you have a food processor, it will make fast and thorough work of these.

Garlic Butter Mash 1 garlic clove and blend it with 1/4 pound (125 g) of unsalted butter, which is at room temperature. Mix in some freshly ground white pepper and any other herbs or seasonings desired.

Whole Shrimp Butter Wash 1/2 pound of whole shrimp—heads, tails and all. Put into a medium-sized saucepan with cold water to cover. Add salt, if desired, a few grinds of pepper, a few drops fresh lemon juice and cook until shrimp are quite red, about 8 to 10 minutes. Remove from heat, drain and set aside to cool. Then put into a mortar with about 1 tablespoon (15 ml) unsalted butter and crush the shrimp with the butter until completely smooth. Add more butter—up to 1 pound (500 g)—as required to make a good butter-shrimp balance. Then force through a fine strainer into a small crock. You will be amazed at how little shell remains in the strainer.

Herb Butter Combine 4 tablespoons (60 ml) unsalted butter, 1 tablespoon (15 ml) minced fresh herbs of choice, 1/4 teaspoon (1 ml) salt, freshly ground white pepper to taste, 1/4 cup (50 ml) heavy cream and 1 teaspoon (5 ml) or more fresh lemon juice in a mortar. Mix with the pestle until smooth and well blended. Let stand several hours before using.

MAYONNAISE
(International)

I cannot imagine a reason for buying this lovely sauce, for with a little practice it takes less time to make than it takes to drive to the nearest grocery store. No, it is not cheaper to make it at home, but no more expensive than buying it either.

Years ago, I was taught by a French friend, Philippe, to make mayonnaise. He used a flat dinner dish and an ordinary kitchen fork. He beat an egg yolk in the dish and added salt, pepper and a little Dijon mustard. Then, with the fork (tines up, back down), he stirred in a wide circle, setting a rhythm and *never, never* changing directions (don't ask me why). The fork in his left hand, the bottle of olive oil in his right, he gradually added the oil, stopping only to put down the oil bottle and pick up the vinegar bottle when the sauce became too thick. At the very end, Philippe squeezed in the juice of half a lemon, and finally, a tablespoon (15 ml) of hot water. It was a beautiful performance.

Now, Philippe used half olive oil (the lovely, pale, light, fruity kind) and half peanut oil, and I decided that his choice was made by what was available. I tried that combination and liked it very much, but the olive oil available in the United States is a little too "heavy" and somewhat bitter, by comparison, so I use all peanut oil except for a tablespoon (15 ml) of olive oil at the very end. It gives me the light, delicate sauce I prefer. You may, of course, substitute olive oil for the peanut oil in the following recipe.

It is very important that all the ingredients and implements be at room temperature, for if cold, the mayonnaise may not blend as well as it should. You may prefer to use a deep bowl and whisk, rather than the plate and fork. Or, of course, you may prefer to use your food processor, which makes very quick work of mayonnaise.

2 egg yolks
Pinch of salt
1 teaspoon (5 ml) Dijon-style mustard or
　　dry mustard
1-1/2 cups (375 ml) peanut oil or vegetable oil
2 tablespoons (30 ml) fresh lemon juice or
　　white wine vinegar, or to taste
1 tablespoon (15 ml) olive oil

Beat the egg yolks very thoroughly until they are light. Add the salt and Dijon mustard and blend in. Now start stirring and adding the oil, drop by drop. Stop adding the oil from time to time, so that the oil already added is properly absorbed by the egg yolks. Then start adding the oil again and continue until the mayonnaise is too thick to absorb more and you can barely stir it. Dribble in a few drops of the lemon juice until the mixture is again thin enough to stir easily. Add the remaining oil, in larger quantities at a time now, until all the oil is used. Taste and add more salt if needed. Stir in the olive oil and the remaining lemon juice.
Makes approximately 1-1/2 cups (375 ml)

Note If you intend to keep the mayonnaise before using, beat in 1 tablespoon (15 ml) hot water once mayonnaise is thickened to your liking. It will keep up to a week in the refrigerator.

DIPPING SAUCE
Tim Sun Jeung (China)

A dipping sauce for deep-fried *wontons, dim sum* dumplings and boiled noodles.

3 tablespoons (45 ml) light soy sauce
3 tablespoons (45 ml) rice vinegar
3 slices ginger root, shredded or minced
1 tablespoon (15 ml) sugar
2 garlic cloves, mashed
2 tablespoons (30 ml) peanut oil
1 tablespoon (15 ml) cornstarch, mixed with
1 tablespoon (15 ml) water
1/2 teaspoon (2 ml) Oriental sesame oil

Combine soy sauce, vinegar, ginger root and sugar in a bowl and stir until sugar dissolves. Sauté garlic in peanut oil for 1 minute. Add the soy sauce mixture and stir until heated. Stir in the cornstarch mixture and cook over low heat until slightly thickened. Stir in sesame oil. Remove from heat and let cool. If the sauce is too thick, add a little hot water until desired consistency is obtained.
Makes approximately 1/2 cup (125 ml)

Variation A little cayenne pepper or Oriental chili oil may be added, if a "hot" sauce is desired.

PASTA WITH EGGS, CREAM AND CHEESE

CUCUMBER AND YOGURT SOUP
(Middle East)

Capelli d'angelo (angel's hair) is a *pasta* that is impossible to make at home, by hand or any machine you might have. The strands are so infinitely fine that the name is quite apt. In Middle Eastern shops, it is called *vermicelli* and is even finer than the Italian variety.

5 cups (1.25 L) plain yogurt
12 ice cubes
2 large cucumbers, peeled and finely grated or
   sliced
1 cup (250 ml) ice water
2 ounces (56 g) *vermicelli* or *capelli d'angelo*
1 teaspoon (5 ml) shredded fresh mint leaves
1 teaspoon (5 ml) minced fresh parsley
Salt and freshly ground white pepper
1/4 cup (75 ml) shredded green onions
1 hard-cooked egg yolk, sieved

Put yogurt into a large bowl and stir in ice cubes. Place bowl in the refrigerator for about 30 minutes, then remove ice cubes. Stir cucumber and ice water into yogurt and return to refrigerator until ready to serve.

Twenty minutes before serving, drop *vermicelli* into boiling salted water and cook just until water returns to the boil. Drain through a fine strainer, rinse under cold running water and drain well again. Chill.

Stir mint and parsley into yogurt mixture, place noodles on top, salt lightly and grind on pepper to taste. Sprinkle on green onions and garnish with egg yolk. Chill well. Serve in shallow soup plates.
Makes 6 servings

FETTUCCINE WITH FOUR CHEESES
(Fettuccine con Quattro Formaggi (Italy)

Noodle dough made with 2-3/4 cups (675 ml)
    flour and 3 eggs, page 28
12 tablespoons (180 ml) unsalted butter, melted
1-1/2 cups (375 ml) half-and-half (light cream),
    warmed
3 tablespoons (45 ml) each freshly grated
    Parmesan, Fontina, mild provolone and
    Gruyère cheese, mixed together

Make noodle dough according to directions in Master Recipe and cut into noodles 1/4 inch (6 mm) wide. Cook the noodles in boiling salted water until tender. Drain and put into a warmed large serving bowl. Pour on the melted butter and toss quickly. Immediately pour on the cream and toss again. Add the cheeses and continue tossing until cheeses begin to melt and get slightly stringy. Serve promptly.
Makes 6 servings

SPAGHETTINI WITH BÉCHAMEL SAUCE
(Central Europe/Italy)

This is one of the most delicate of all noodle dishes and is served in almost all Central European countries and in Italy. Sometimes a little minced parsley or a dash of paprika is sprinkled over the top when serving, but I do not think it necessary.

1 pound (500 g) *spaghettini*
1 recipe *Béchamel* Sauce, page 56
1 tablespoon (15 ml) butter, cut into small pieces
2/3 cup (175 ml) freshly grated Parmesan cheese

Cook the *spaghettini* in boiling salted water until tender. Drain and put into a warmed serving bowl with the butter and half of the cheese. Toss lightly and quickly. Pour on the *Béchamel* Sauce, toss again and serve immediately with remaining cheese on the side.
Makes 4 servings

Note It is rather decorative to toss the *spaghettini* with about three-fourths of the sauce and to pour the remaining sauce in the center on top.

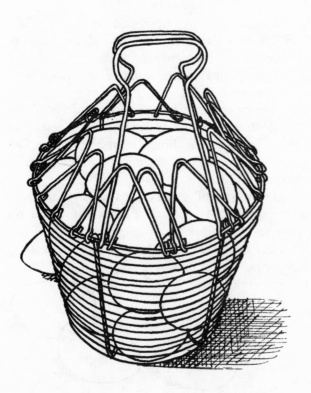

SPAGHETTI FRITTATA
(Italy/Southern France/Northern Spain)

This dish may be served either hot or at room temperature. It is a very popular picnic dish along the Mediterranean. Left in the pan, it is covered, then wrapped in newspaper or whatever is handy. At the picnic grounds it is unwrapped and eaten with crisp, crunchy bread, cheese and fruit, and lots of wine.

3/4 pound (375 g) *spaghetti*
4 tablespoons (60 ml) unsalted butter
1/2 cup (125 ml) freshly grated Gruyère or
    Parmesan cheese
2 eggs, beaten
2 tablespoons (30 ml) minced fresh parsley or
    chives
Salt and freshly ground black pepper to taste
2 tablespoons (30 ml) olive oil

Cook the *spaghetti* in boiling salted water until tender. Drain and transfer to a large mixing bowl. Mix in the butter and half the cheese. Let cool completely, stirring from time to time to prevent noodles from sticking together. Stir in remaining cheese, the eggs, parsley, salt and pepper, mixing thoroughly.

Heat olive oil in a large heavy skillet and pour in the *spaghetti* mixture, spreading it evenly over pan bottom. Cook over low heat for about 10 to 15 minutes or until set; lift edges from time to time to determine if bottom is browning and to loosen it from the pan. Then place pan in a pre-heated broiler for about 1 minute to lightly brown top. Remove from broiler and let stand for 2 minutes, then slide out onto a warmed serving dish. Cut into wedges to serve.
Makes 4 servings

COTTAGE CHEESE WITH NOODLES
(Central Europe)

A delicate, summery dish.

Noodle dough made with 1-3/4 cups (425 ml) flour
    and 2 eggs, page 28
1 pint (500 ml) small curd cottage cheese
1 red or green bell pepper, chopped
1 cucumber, finely diced
1/2 cup (125 ml) or more commercial sour cream
Salt and freshly ground white pepper to taste
1 tablespoon (15 ml) minced fresh parsley

Make noodle dough according to directions in Master Recipe and cut into broad noodles. Cook the noodles in boiling salted water until tender. Drain and put into a warmed large shallow serving bowl. Add cottage cheese, bell pepper, cucumber and half of the sour cream. Toss well and quickly. Add salt and pepper and toss again. Garnish with parsley and serve immediately. Serve remaining sour cream on the side.
Makes 4 servings

BUTTER AND CHEESE SAUCE WITH NOODLES
Salsa al Burro e Formaggio (Italy)

1 pound (500 g) fresh egg noodles
1/4 pound (125 g) unsalted butter
1 cup (250 ml) freshly grated Parmesan cheese
Additional freshly grated Parmesan cheese

Cook the noodles in boiling salted water until tender. While noodles are cooking, cut butter into small bits and put in a warmed serving bowl. Drain noodles and put into bowl with butter bits; toss quickly. Add the cheese and toss so that noodles are well coated with sauce. Serve immediately with additional cheese on the side.
Makes 4 to 6 servings

SPAGHETTI WITH BACON AND EGGS
Spaghetti alla Carbonara (Italy)

The true origin of this now-popular dish is as vague as the mists over the Tiber River. I have always heard it called a *specialitá di Trastevere*, the ancient part of Rome, where it is translated as "coalman's wife's style." It was there I first gorged myself on it many years ago in one of the cavelike restaurants where the *Trasteverini* go to eat and drink and sing and dance. Since those days, however, I have learned that the dish may well have been named for a gang of patriots who called themselves *Carbonari*, or it may have originated during World War II, when American G.I.'s brought their bacon and eggs to the impoverished Neapolitans and ate with them. A third theory calls it an ancient dish of the poor and indeed of the coalmen. And so on and on. Whatever its origin, it is delicious, quick and easy to prepare.

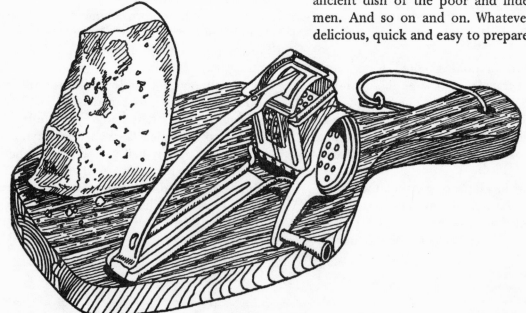

1 pound (500 g) *spaghetti*
6 ounces (170 g) bacon or pancetta, coarsely diced
3 whole eggs
2 egg yolks
1/4 cup (75 ml) freshly grated Parmesan cheese
1/4 cup (75 ml) freshly grated Pecorino cheese
Freshly ground black pepper to taste
Pinch of salt

Cook the *spaghetti* in boiling salted water until tender. Drain and set aside; keep warm.

Fry the bacon over moderate heat until the fat is released and the meat begins to brown. Remove the bacon with a slotted spoon and set aside; keep warm. Drain off about 1 tablespoon (15 ml) of the drippings and reserve; discard remaining drippings. Beat the whole eggs and egg yolks together in a warmed large deep bowl. Add half of each of the cheeses, the pepper and a pinch of salt and beat again. Add the *spaghetti* and quickly toss to distribute the sauce and to "cook" the eggs with the hot *spaghetti*. Add half of the cooked bacon and the drippings and toss again. Add remaining bacon and sprinkle on a little of the remaining cheese. Serve immediately with the remaining cheese on the side. An abundance of pepper is not too much for this rich dish.
Makes 4 to 6 servings

Note Cream is sometimes added to the egg mixture, but I find it an unnecessary refinement. I also prefer to use all Pecorino cheese (a ewe's milk cheese), which is rather piquant and "bitey"; it lends a distinctive flavor and a rich contrast to the silkiness of the eggs and *pasta*.

NOODLE OMELET
Omelette aux Nouilles (France)

Leftover noodles that have been mixed only with butter and cheese may be used in this omelet.

3 tablespoons (45 ml) butter
1/2 cup (125 ml) thinly sliced fresh mushrooms
8 eggs
1 teaspoon (5 ml) salt
Freshly ground black pepper to taste
2 tablespoons (30 ml) finely chopped mixed fresh herbs (chives, parsley, tarragon, chervil, thyme, whatever you prefer)
2 tablespoons (30 ml) water
1-1/2 cups (375 ml) cooked fine egg noodles

Melt 1 tablespoon (15 ml) of the butter in a small skillet and sauté the mushrooms 3 to 4 minutes; set aside. Combine eggs, salt, pepper, herbs and water and beat lightly. Stir in noodles. Heat remaining butter in a large omelet pan or skillet, and when the foam starts to subside, pour in the egg mixture. Over medium heat cook until sides and bottom begin to set. Put cooked mushrooms and their butter in a strip in the center of the omelet. Loosen sides of omelet from pan with spatula and fold one side over the other, covering the mushrooms. Shake pan to loosen bottom of omelet. Cover with a lid for about 3 minutes, then slip out onto a warmed serving dish.
Makes 4 servings

Variations Any sautéed chopped vegetable, such as spinach, broccoli, snow peas, green beans, etc., may be substituted for the mushrooms.

CHEESE PANCAKES WITH FINE NOODLES
Ajja B'Shaariyah (Baghdad)

I am told that when these pancakes are eaten, the diners agree that *"Baghdad set-el-Beled"*—Baghdad is the ancestor of all countries.

1/2 cup (125 ml) very fine egg noodles
2 large eggs
Salt and freshly ground white pepper to taste
1/2 cup (125 ml) crumbled or grated white cheese, such as feta or Syrian halumin
4 tablespoons (60 ml) unsalted butter

Cook the noodles in boiling salted water until tender. Drain and set aside.

Beat the eggs and add the salt, pepper, cheese and noodles; mix thoroughly.

In a large wide frying pan or on a griddle melt the butter. When it begins to foam, pour 2 tablespoons (30 ml) of the egg mixture into the butter for each pancake, making only as many pancakes at a time as the pan will comfortably hold. Turn the pancakes when the undersides are golden and cook second sides until nicely browned. Serve hot with fruit preserves or syrup, if desired.
Makes 4 servings

SPAGHETTI PANCAKES
Froja (Malta)

1/2 pound (250 g) *spaghetti,* cooked and cooled
2 eggs, beaten
1/3 to 1/2 cup (75 to 125 ml) freshly grated
    Parmesan cheese
Salt and freshly ground black pepper to taste
3 tablespoons (45 ml) unsalted butter

In a mixing bowl combine the *spaghetti*, eggs, cheese, salt and pepper. In a 10-inch (25 cm) skillet heat 2 tablespoons (30 ml) of the butter until it starts to foam. Then add the *spaghetti* mixture and press down with a spatula to form a compact cake. Sauté over moderate heat for about 10 minutes or until bottom is nicely browned. Dot top with remaining butter, cut into bits. Cover pan with a serving dish and invert pancake onto dish. Then slide pancake back into pan, browned side up. Cook until underside is brown. Slide out onto the serving dish. Cut into wedges and serve hot with sausages.
Makes 4 servings

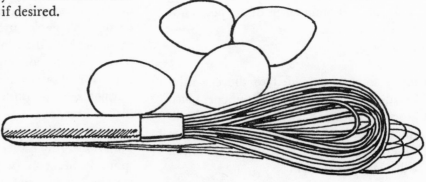

BAKER'S CHEESE NOODLES
Stiriaeh Metelt (Hungary)

This is quite a distinct variation on noodles and a delicious dish for a light supper; the tender noodle and the gentle sugaring are delightful and subtle.

Approximately 2 cups (500 ml) unbleached
    all-purpose flour
1 pound (500 g) baker's cheese
6 eggs
Pinch of salt
1 cup (250 ml) sugar
1 cup (250 ml) commercial sour cream
1 teaspoon (5 ml) freshly grated lemon or
    orange zest
3 tablespoons (45 ml) unsalted butter, softened
1 tablespoon (15 ml) vanilla extract
1/2 cup (125 ml) white or golden seedless raisins

Mix flour and baker's cheese in a bowl and form a well in the center. Drop 2 eggs, salt, 1 tablespoon (15 ml) of the sugar and 1 tablespoon (15 ml) of the sour cream into the well. With a fork or wooden spoon, stir together all ingredients in the well, then gradually add to it, little by little, the flour and cheese mixture, until all are well mixed and form a dough that is soft yet firm. Lightly flour a working surface and knead the dough lightly for about 5 minutes, then divide the dough into 3 or 4 parts and form into balls. Roll each ball out to about 3/4-inch thickness and cut into 1/2-inch-wide (12 mm) noodles. Sprinkle the noodles lightly with flour as you cut them and stack one noodle on top of another. Drop them into boiling salted water and stir with a long-handled wooden fork;

when they rise to the surface they are cooked. Drain and rinse under warm water. Set aside and keep warm.

Separate remaining eggs. Beat yolks with lemon zest, remaining sugar and sour cream, butter, and vanilla extract. Beat egg whites until stiff and fold raisins in, then fold this mixture into the egg yolk mixture. Gently combine noodles and egg mixture and spoon into a buttered baking dish. Bake at 350°F (170°C) for about 30 minutes. Serve warm.
Makes 6 servings as a main dish;
8 to 10 servings as a dessert

NOODLES WITH CHEESE
(Israel)

Noodle dough made with 1-3/4 cups (425 ml)
    flour and 2 eggs, page 28
4 tablespoons (60 ml) unsalted butter
3/4 teaspoon (4 ml) salt
3/4 pound (375 g) baker's cheese, crumbled, or
1-1/2 cups (375 ml) low-fat cottage cheese

Make noodle dough according to directions in Master Recipe and cut into noodles 1/4 inch (6 mm) wide. Cook the noodles in boiling salted water until tender and drain.

In a large flameproof casserole melt the butter and stir in the noodles. Cook over moderate heat until the noodles just start to brown. Be sure to stir lightly but steadily. Remove from heat and stir in salt and baker's cheese, mixing well. Place in a preheated 450°F (230°C) oven for 10 minutes or until heated through.
Makes 4 to 6 servings as a side dish

MACARONI IN CREAM
Macaroni à la Crème (France: The Languedoc)

3 tablespoons (45 ml) unsalted butter
1/2 pound (250 g) elbow macaroni, cooked
3/4 cup (175 ml) ground cooked ham
2 egg yolks, beaten
1 cup (250 ml) heavy cream
3/4 cup (200 g) freshly grated Swiss cheese
Pinch of freshly grated nutmeg
Salt and freshly ground white pepper to taste

Melt the butter in a large saucepan and add the macaroni, ham, egg yolks, cream and cheese, mixing well. Season with nutmeg, salt and pepper. Heat over very low heat, stirring constantly but carefully so as not to mash the macaroni. Serve immediately.
Makes 3 or 4 servings

Macaroni in Cream with Truffles (Macaroni à la Crème avec les Truffes) Omit ham and substitute 2 to 3 small truffles, finely chopped or sliced tissue thin.

MACARONI AND FETA CHEESE
Macaronada (Greece)

This dish can be made with Kefalotyri, Parmesan or any other hard cheese, but I once ate it with feta cheese and it was absolutely unforgettable. Once cooked, the macaroni should be quickly mixed with the butter and feta, which will then melt ever so slightly.

1 pound (500 g) long macaroni, broken into
        1-inch (3 cm) lengths, or elbow macaroni
1 cup (250 ml) crumbled feta cheese
1/4 pound (125 g) unsalted butter

Cook macaroni in boiling salted water until tender. Drain and put into a warmed large serving bowl. Sprinkle the feta cheese over the macaroni and toss until well mixed.

In a large heavy saucepan melt the butter. When it is lightly browned, quickly pour in the macaroni and toss lightly. Serve immediately.

Serve as a side dish to lean meats or as a main dish for a light meal with salad.
Makes 4 servings as a main dish;
6 to 8 servings as a side dish

NOODLE RING WITH CREAM CHEESE
(International)

An attractive way to serve noodles for a light lunch.

2 eggs
1/4 cup (50 ml) sugar
1 teaspoon (5 ml) salt
1/2 pound (250 g) cream cheese, softened
3 cups (750 ml) cooled cooked fine egg noodles
2 tablespoons (30 ml) cracker or bread crumbs
3 tablespoons (45 ml) butter, melted

Beat eggs with sugar and salt. Cream the cheese and blend in the egg mixture. Stir in the noodles.

Generously butter a 9-inch (23 cm) ring mold and spoon in the noodle mixture. Sprinkle with crumbs and melted butter. Bake in a preheated 375°F (190°C) oven for 40 minutes or until nicely browned. Unmold very carefully, first loosening edges with a sharp knife.
Makes 6 servings

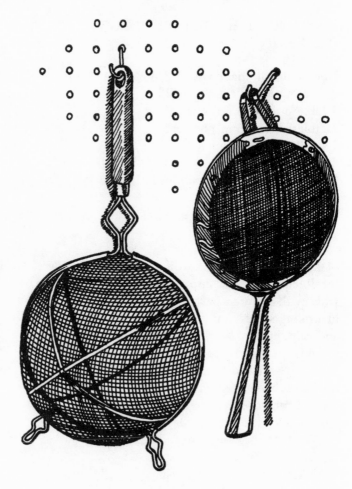

LASAGNE WITH SCRAMBLED EGGS, CHEZ MOI

Noodle dough made with 1-3/4 cups (425 ml)
    flour and 2 eggs, page 28
1 tablespoon (15 ml) olive oil
1 tablespoon (15 ml) butter
1 small onion, chopped
3 eggs
2 tablespoons (30 ml) milk or heavy cream
Generous pinch of salt
1/2 cup (125 ml) freshly grated Gruyère or
    Parmesan cheese

Make noodle dough according to directions in Master Recipe and cut into noodles 2 inches (5 cm) wide with a fluted pastry cutter. Cook the noodles in boiling salted water until tender. Drain noodles and slip into a bowl of warm water to prevent them from sticking together.

Heat oil and butter in a large skillet and sauté the onion over medium heat until soft and translucent. Beat together the eggs, milk and salt until frothy and stir into skillet with onions. Stirring constantly, cook eggs until they are set but still creamy.

Arrange a layer of drained noodles in a buttered rectangular baking dish, spoon on half the egg mixture, cover with remaining noodles and top with remaining egg mixture. Sprinkle on half of the cheese. Place in a preheated 375°F (190°C) oven until top is lightly browned and cheese begins to melt, no more than 15 minutes. (Longer cooking will toughen eggs.) Serve cut into squares with remaining cheese on the side.
Makes 4 servings

SPAGHETTI SOUFFLÉ WITH "NUT BUTTER"
Spaghetti Soufflé avec Buerre Noisette (France)

1-1/2 cups (375 ml) broken spaghettini (1-inch
    or 3 cm lengths)
1 large ripe tomato, peeled, seeded and chopped
5 tablespoons (75 ml) unsalted butter
1 tablespoon (15 ml) dry white wine
1/2 cup (125 ml) milk
1/2 cup (125 ml) heavy cream
4 eggs, separated
1 very small onion, minced
1/2 cup (125 ml) freshly grated Parmesan cheese
1/2 cup (125 ml) freshly grated dry Monterey
    Jack, Cheddar or Gruyère cheese
2 tablespoons (30 ml) fine dry bread crumbs
Freshly ground white pepper to taste

Buerre Noisette
1 pound (500 g) unsalted butter
Juice of 1 lemon

Cook *spaghettini* in boiling salted water until tender. Drain and set aside.

In a small saucepan sauté tomato in 1 tablespoon (15 ml) of the butter until soft. Add wine and cook until tomato is smooth. Let cool. Combine milk and cream in a saucepan. Add remaining butter and heat, stirring lightly, until butter is melted; remove from heat. Beat egg yolks until light. Beat in 1 tablespoon (15 ml) of the milk mixture, then pour egg yolks into milk mixture in saucepan, stirring well. Add the tomato, onion, *spaghettini*, cheeses and bread crumbs; season with a few grinds of pepper. Let cool. Beat egg whites until stiff but not dry and stir one-fourth of egg whites into *spaghettini* mixture to lighten it. Then gently fold in remaining egg whites.

Butter a 1-1/2 quart (1.5 L) *soufflé* dish and spoon in *spaghettini* mixture. Place in a baking pan holding hot water to reach halfway up the sides of the *soufflé* dish. Bake in a preheated 375°F (190°C) oven for 30 minutes; the *soufflé* should be quite high and golden brown on top.

Just before *soufflé* is done, prepare *buerre noisette.* In a small heavy saucepan placed over low heat, melt the butter and cook it until it is "nut brown" (be careful it does not burn). Pour lemon juice into a sauceboat and pour on the browned butter. Stir and pass with the *soufflé.*
Makes 4 to 6 servings

NOODLE *PILAF*
Pilaf de Nouilles (France: Savoie)

This is a dish of that lovely and rather remote region of France that one passes en route from Paris to Geneva. Once I stopped the night in Aix-Les-Bains and could find a room only in a tiny *pension* outside the town. This dish was the first course at dinner that evening and it took me awhile to figure out the recipe. Once I did, I made it often.

2 onions, chopped
1/4 pound (125 g) unsalted butter
1 pound (500 g) fine egg noodles or any small,
    fine *pasta,* such as *orzo,* etc.
2-1/2 cups (625 ml) chicken or beef broth, heated
Salt and freshly ground white pepper
1/4 pound (125 g) or more freshly grated
    Gruyère cheese

In a flameproof casserole sauté the onions in butter. Add the noodles and toss well in the butter until very hot and just barely beginning to color. Add broth and salt and pepper to taste. Bring to a boil, then reduce heat so noodle mixture just simmers. Fold a kitchen towel into several thicknesses and cover top of pot. Place a lid over the towel and cook for about 15 minutes, until liquid is absorbed.

To serve, have ready a warmed casserole; sprinkle some of the cheese over the bottom. Put one-third of the noodle mixture over the cheese, sprinkle on another layer of cheese and top with more noodles. Continue alternating until all ingredients are used, ending with a layer of cheese. Work quickly so food remains quite hot. Set under preheated broiler to melt cheese and brown lightly.
Makes 6 servings as a first course;
3 to 4 as a main dish

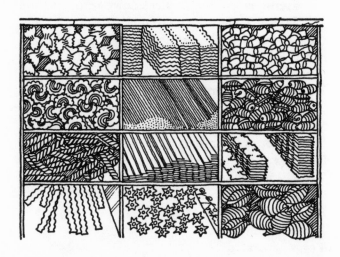

VERMICELLI CAKE
Gâteau de Vermicelles (France)

One of my neighbors in Paris was a woman from the area around Tours. She would not admit to liking Paris and indeed, rarely went farther than the market around the corner. But she loved La Boudrie, the tiny town where she had been born and raised, and if the perfumes that issued forth from her open windows were any indication, it is a town I plan to visit some day for an eating spree.

One day I could not contain myself and had to identify the sweet aroma coming from her flat. "Madame Gregoire, what are you making that smells so wonderful?"

"*Gâteau de vermicelles et merci beaucoup.* You shall have a piece," she added when I looked puzzled by her answer.

And she was as good as her word, for late in the afternoon she sent a piece down with her little girl. It was a marvelous mixture of the crisp and the smooth with the softness of foam, and here is her recipe.

1 cup plus 2 tablespoons (250 ml plus 30 ml)
    hot water
3/4 cup (200 ml) sugar
6 tablespoons (90 ml) unsalted butter
6 ounces (170 g) very fine *vermicellini*
1 cup (250 ml) heavy cream, scalded
Generous pinch of salt
Finely grated zest of 1 lemon
12 whole cloves
4 eggs, separated
Whipped cream

In a heavy-bottomed but small saucepan mix 2 tablespoons (30 ml) of the hot water with 1/4 cup (75 ml) of the sugar. Cook over a low flame until a moderately dark-brown caramel, being careful it does not burn. As it cooks, heat a 1- to 1-1/2-quart (1 to 1.5 L) *soufflé* dish with very hot tap water, then empty it and wipe it dry. Pour in the caramel immediately and tip the dish so that the caramel covers the bottom quite evenly. Set aside to cool and harden. Use 1 to 2 tablespoons (15 to 30 ml) of the butter to grease the sides of the *soufflé* dish above the caramel. Set aside.

In a medium-sized skillet heat the remaining butter. Crush the *vermicellini* into small pieces and toss them in the melted butter until they are moderately browned and crisp. Add the hot water and toss lightly until *vermicellini* begins to soften. Then add the cream, 1/2 cup (125 ml) of the sugar, salt, and lemon zest and mix well; remove from heat. Quickly crush the cloves and pass through a strainer so only crushed parts are added to *vermicellini* mixture; stir well. Beat the egg yolks thoroughly until very light and stir into the *vermicellini* mixture. Now whip the egg whites vigorously and long so they are thick enough to be almost dry, and fold them gently into the *vermicellini* mixture. Pour the batter into the prepared *soufflé* dish. Bake in a preheated 325°F (160°C) oven for 35 to 40 minutes.

Butter a serving platter lightly, and as soon as the cake is taken from the oven, unmold it onto the plate. Serve with whipped cream.
Makes 6 to 8 servings

SWEET NOODLE PUDDING
Lukshen Kugel (Jewish Russian)

Noodle dough made with 1-3/4 cups (425 ml)
    flour and 2 eggs, page 28
1/4 pound (125 g) unsalted butter
1 cup (250 ml) sugar
4 eggs
1 teaspoon (5 ml) vanilla extract
1 teaspoon (5 ml) fresh lemon juice
1-1/2 cups (375 ml) creamed cottage cheese
1 cup (250 ml) seedless golden raisins
1 cup (250 ml) milk
Ground cinnamon and sugar for topping
Heavy cream

Make noodle dough as directed in Master Recipe
and cut into noodles approximately 1/4 inch
(6 mm) wide. Cook the noodles in boiling salted
water until tender. Drain and set aside.

Cream together butter and sugar and beat in
eggs, one at a time, adding each one only after
previous one is thoroughly mixed in. Add vanilla
extract, lemon juice, cottage cheese, raisins and
milk in order given, mixing in each one thoroughly
before adding the next. Finally, fold noodles into
cottage cheese mixture and pour into a large buttered casserole. Sprinkle top with cinnamon and
sugar. Place in a preheated 375°F (190°C) oven.
The "dough" will be very liquid at this point. As a
crust forms, cut into it with a knife and press the
crust inwards; do this every 15 or 20 minutes.
After an hour in the oven, the pudding should
appear quite solid and ready to take out. Serve at
room temperature or chilled, with heavy cream on
the side.
Makes 6 servings

NOODLES WITH POPPY SEEDS
Makos Metelt (Hungary)

Noodle dough made with 1-3/4 cups (425 ml)
    flour and 2 eggs, page 28
1/2 cup (125 ml) milk
1/2 cup (125 ml) honey
1/2 cup (125 ml) heavy cream
1/4 cup (75 ml) ground poppy seeds
Whipped cream

Make noodle dough according to directions in Master Recipe and cut into noodles approximately 1/4
inch (6 mm) wide; set aside.

Combine the milk, honey, cream and poppy
seeds in a small heavy saucepan. Cook over moderate-low heat for 5 to 8 minutes. Meanwhile, cook
the noodles in boiling salted water until tender.
Drain and put into a warmed buttered serving dish.
Pour on the sauce, toss well and serve immediately,
accompanied with whipped cream.
Makes 6 to 8 servings

PASTA WITH VEGETABLES AND HERBS

VEGETABLE SOUP WITH BASIL
Soupe au Pistou (Provence)

1 tablespoon (15 ml) olive oil
5 medium onions, chopped
3 small slices lean salt pork, diced
5 medium carrots, scraped and diced
6 celery stalks, sliced
1 large leek, sliced
1 small head white cabbage, chopped
1/2 pound (250 g) green beans, cut into
    1-inch (3 cm) pieces
6 medium potatoes, peeled and diced
1 turnip, peeled and diced
5 zucchini, diced
1/2 pound (250 g) fresh lima beans, shelled
2 quarts (2 L) water, boiling
2 cups (500 ml) small dried white beans, soaked
    overnight in water to cover and drained

Bouquet garni of 2 parsley sprigs, 2 bay leaves,
    small handful celery leaves
Salt and freshly ground black pepper to taste
1/4 cup (75 ml) Genoese Basil Sauce, omitting
    nuts, page 51, or to taste
Freshly grated Parmesan cheese

In a very large soup kettle or heavy-bottomed saucepan heat the olive oil and sauté the onions until translucent. Add the salt pork and sauté 5 minutes. Add the carrots, celery, leek, cabbage, green beans, potatoes, turnip, zucchini and lima beans and sauté for 6 to 8 minutes. Add the water, white beans and *bouquet garni* and bring to a boil. Reduce heat, cover and simmer very gently for about 45 minutes. Remove *bouquet garni* and continue simmering for 1 hour longer. Season with salt and pepper and stir in basil sauce. Serve with Parmesan cheese on the side.
Makes 8 servings

BLACK BEANS AND MACARONI
Frijoles Negros y Macarrones (Latin America)

This is a modern version of the old *moros y cristianos,* black beans and rice.

2 cups (500 ml) dried black beans, soaked over-
    night in water to cover and drained
1 entire head garlic, separated into cloves,
    peeled and chopped
1/2 pound (250 g) salt pork, finely minced
1 pound (500 g) small elbow macaroni or shells
1 tablespoon (15 ml) ground cumin
1 teaspoon (5 ml) ground turmeric
Dash of cayenne pepper
1 tablespoon (15 ml) salt
Freshly ground black pepper to taste
Finely minced fresh coriander leaves
Finely minced fresh parsley leaves

Put the beans into a large heavy kettle and pour on water to cover. Add 2 of the garlic cloves and bring to a boil. Reduce heat and simmer, covered, until beans are tender, about 1-1/2 hours. Drain off liquid and reserve. Pour beans into a large casserole and set aside.

In a heavy skillet sauté the salt pork over low heat until crisp and browned. Remove with a slotted spoon and drain on paper toweling. Add remaining garlic to the drippings in the skillet and cook over low heat until garlic is soft; set aside.

Cook the macaroni in boiling salted water until tender. Drain and pour over the beans in the casserole; toss beans and macaroni together; add salt pork bits, reserved garlic, cumin, turmeric, cayenne pepper, salt and black pepper and toss again. Pour on about 1 cup (250 ml) of the bean cooking liquid, cover and bake in a preheated 325°F (160°C) oven for about 1 hour. Taste and correct seasoning if necessary. Sprinkle on the coriander and parsley and serve.
Makes 8 servings

"STRAW AND HAY" *ALLA* CARLO
Paglia e Fieno alla Carlo (Italy)

Noodle dough made with 1-3/4 cups (425 ml)
    flour and 2 eggs, page 28
1 recipe Green Noodle dough, page 40
1 small onion, finely minced
6 tablespoons (90 ml) unsalted butter
1 pound (500 g) fresh white mushrooms,
    coarsely chopped
Salt and freshly ground black pepper to taste
1/2 pound (250 g) boiled ham, shredded
1 cup (250 ml) heavy cream
Olive oil
1/2 cup (125 ml) freshly grated Parmesan cheese
Additional freshly grated Parmesan cheese

Make the noodle dough according to directions in Master Recipe and cut into noodles approximately 1/4 inch (6 mm) wide; set aside. Make Green Noodle dough and cut into noodles approximately 1/4 inch (6 mm) wide; set aside.

In a large skillet placed over moderate heat sauté onion in half the butter until soft and lightly colored. Add the mushrooms, raise heat and cook quickly for 2 minutes or until mushrooms have absorbed the butter. Sprinkle on salt and pepper and reduce heat; cook, shaking pan from time to time, until mushrooms release their liquid. Then raise heat again and cook rapidly to reduce liquid, about 3 to 4 minutes. Reduce heat to moderate, stir and add the ham and stir again. Now add half of the cream and cook until mixture thickens. Taste and correct seasoning, if necessary. Remove from heat and set aside.

In a large flameproof casserole combine remaining butter and cream and set over very low heat. Stir, remove from heat and set aside.

Cook the noodles separately in boiling salted water until just tender; drain and toss with a little olive oil. Reheat mushroom sauce gently. Add all the noodles to the casserole holding the cream and butter mixture. Put over low heat and gently toss the noodles to be sure they are well coated with the mixture. Add half the mushroom sauce and toss again, then the grated cheese and toss once more, working very quickly. Remove from heat and add remaining mushroom sauce. Serve immediately with additional Parmesan cheese on the side.

This is a delicately flavored dish and should be served with a light fresh white wine, like an Alsatian wine or a Traminer or similar American wine. If served as a first course, follow with a delicately flavored veal, chicken or fish dish.
Makes 8 to 10 servings as a first course

"THUNDER AND LIGHTNING"
Tuoni e Lampo (Naples)

"Thunder and lightning" is a delightful dish, especially appealing to children (of any age). The *pasta* traditionally used is a mixture of broken ends of *pasta* found in the bottoms of almost empty sacks (and usually very inexpensive, thus very popular with parents).

I encountered this dish, most appropriately, one very stormy night in 1952, en route by car to Sicily. A companion and I had come all the long way down the boot from the usually cheery Côte d'Azur, where we had spent a dour Christmas holiday, and were now reaching desperately for the sun. It had eluded us fiercely the farther south we came in our tiny unheated car. A snow storm had begun suddenly and furiously about two in the afternoon and night had settled soon after, as it has a way of doing in the mountains. "We'll stop at the very next town," we muttered again and again, but no town had appeared. Now, after a particularly sharp turn, there was a real town (of sorts) and even a hotel sign, lit by a five-watt bulb. We skidded to a halt and flew inside. The patron greeted us with a mixture of amazement and gallant pleasure.

Yes, he had a room and could even supply a meal, though we would be sharing the family meal of *tuoni e lampo*. As my Italian was then rather basic at best, and my friend's even shallower, I was accused of overconfidence when I translated it for her. We giggled, certain we had misunderstood.

The dining room was just barely lit, but we could make out the dripping stone walls; the touch of damp napery did not improve our humor. The plates arrived—the rims icy cold—bearing a huge mound of steaming "food." The mixture of very firm *pasta* and chewy smooth beans, lightly colored with a delicate and direct tomato sauce and sharpened with abundant freshly ground black pepper and grated cheese, was not only delectable, but warming and very satisfying. Later I asked our patron for the recipe, which the eldest boy laboriously wrote out for me. I slipped it into my Baedecker (of 1924) and it was years before it again turned up. When I translated it, lo and behold! it was indeed "thunder and lightning."

1/2 pound (250 g) dried chickpeas, soaked
    overnight in water to cover
1/2 pound (250 g) mixed *pasta* (see note)
1/2 cup (125 ml) freshly grated Parmesan cheese
1 teaspoon (5 ml) salt
1 tablespoon (15 ml) olive oil or butter
2 tablespoons (30 ml) Tomato Sauce, page 53,
    or leftover *ragù*
1/2 teaspoon (3 ml) freshly ground black pepper

Bring the chickpeas and their soaking water to a boil in a heavy kettle over moderately low heat. Reduce heat and simmer until beans are just tender and *still chewy,* about 45 minutes to 1 hour. (See following note.)

Cook *pasta* in boiling salted water until tender. Because you will be working with different sizes and thicknesses, it will be difficult to judge when it is cooked. Work it out, it's worth it. But be certain not to overcook the *pasta!*

When both the beans and *pasta* are cooked, drain them and mix them together in a warmed large serving bowl. Toss them with 2 large wooden forks to prevent mashing. Stir in cheese, salt and olive oil until blended. Pour on the Tomato Sauce and grind on the pepper. Serve *immediately.*

This dish is enhanced by a good Zinfandel or Chianti, and a salad of mixed greens (be sure to include a little sorrel, *arugula* or other sharp-flavored green) with a simple oil and vinegar dressing. Makes 6 servings

Note The *pasta* is probably only obtainable in Italian grocery shops, where it is sold from great sacks by weight. Ask for leftovers, mixed together.

A further hint: A pinch (no more!) of baking soda in the chickpeas cooking water may prevent after dinner embarrassment and discomfort. The Italians warn gleefully that the name of this dish is inspired by the physical (abdominal) aftereffects of eating it, rather than any tribute to the weather.

FIDELLO
(Middle Eastern or Sephardic Jewish)

Sephardic Jews are those who have lived in Eastern countries since their exile from Spain during the Inquisition, while the Ashkenazic Jews are from Russia and the European world. Their foods are as dissimilar as their speech. They celebrate the same religious holidays, but in different ways.

Fidello is a fine *pasta* form wound into "nests" and dried in thick coils. It is available in all Middle Eastern shops.

1 pound (500 g) *fidello* coils
1/2 cup (125 ml) olive oil
1 tablespoon (15 ml) tomato paste
Salt to taste
5 cups (1.25 L) water or chicken broth

Separate coils of *fidello* as much as possible without breaking them up too much. Heat oil in a large skillet and cook noodles in it until golden brown, turning and tossing from time to time. Remove the noodles with a slotted spoon, draining off as much oil as possible. Add the tomato paste, salt and water to the oil in the pan. Cover and simmer gently until sauce begins to bubble. Add the *fidello,* stir quickly and cover pan. Simmer, stirring frequently to keep noodles from sticking to the pan and to separate the coils. Cook until noodles are tender and all the liquid is absorbed, about 20 minutes.
Makes 6 servings

STUFFED NASTURTIUMS AND CAPELLI D'ANGELO
(International)

12 large, well-formed nasturtium flowers
1/2 pound (250 g) cream cheese, softened
1 tablespoon (15 ml) unsalted butter, softened
4 tablespoons (60 ml) commercial sour cream
8 fresh basil leaves, finely shredded
1/2 teaspoon (2 ml) ground cinnamon
3/4 pound (375 g) *capelli d'angelo* or
    finest *pasta* available
2 tablespoons (30 ml) mayonnaise (preferably
    homemade, page 58)

Wash the nasturtiums very lightly and carefully, being careful not to bruise them; shake off excess water and set aside. Blend together the cream cheese, butter, 2 tablespoons (30 ml) of the sour cream, the basil and cinnamon and let stand for 2 hours to blend flavors.

Drop the *capelli d'angelo* into boiling salted water. As soon as the water returns to the boil, drain noodles through a fine strainer. Remove to a bowl and toss with the mayonnaise blended with the remaining sour cream. Chill.

Just before serving, make a bed of one-fourth of the noodles on each of 4 serving plates. Stuff each nasturtium flower with some of the cream cheese mixture and arrange three of the stuffed flowers on top of each bed of noodles.

This is an attractive dish and delicious to boot. By all means, serve champagne with it.
Makes 4 servings

NOODLES WITH TOMATO SAUCE
(Tibet)

The following sauce may be served over tiny meat-filled dumplings, called *momos*, or thin egg noodles, as below. Years ago, a little restaurant in New York City, near the port end of the island (to be available to sailors coming off their ships), served this dish. Apparently, it is a very common dish in Tibet.

Noodle dough made with 1-3/4 cups (425 ml)
    flour and 2 eggs, page 28
2 tablespoons (30 ml) peanut oil
1 small onion, finely chopped
1 teaspoon (5 ml) fenugreek seeds
4 large ripe tomatoes, peeled, seeded and
    coarsely chopped
3 tablespoons (45 ml) chopped fresh coriander
    leaves
Pinch of cayenne pepper
Pinch of salt

Make noodle dough according to directions in Master Recipe and cut into very fine noodles; set aside.

In a large heavy saucepan or skillet heat the peanut oil and sauté the onion until lightly colored. Stir in the fenugreek seeds and cook a few minutes longer. Stir in the tomatoes, coriander, cayenne pepper and salt and simmer, uncovered, for 30 minutes. It may require the addition of a little water if it begins to dry out.

Cook noodles in boiling salted water until tender. Drain and put into a warmed serving bowl. Pour sauce over and serve immediately.

Makes 4 to 6 servings

SPAGHETTI WITH OIL AND GARLIC
Spaghetti con Olio e Aglio (Italy)

A garlic press is the perfect gadget for this dish. It mashes garlic so finely you will not find yourself chomping on pieces of it. But remember, mashed garlic is much stronger in flavor than chopped garlic.

1 pound (500 g) *spaghetti*
6 to 8 tablespoons (90 to 120 ml) olive oil
3 garlic cloves, mashed
1 tablespoon (15 ml) chopped fresh basil
Freshly ground black pepper
Freshly grated Parmesan cheese

Cook the *spaghetti* in boiling salted water until tender. Drain and put into a warmed serving bowl; keep warm.

In a small heavy skillet heat the oil with the garlic for several minutes; do not let the garlic brown. Remove from heat and mix in basil. Pour sauce over the *spaghetti*, sprinkle on pepper and toss quickly. Serve immediately with Parmesan cheese on the side.

Makes 4 servings

Note Grated cheese is not traditionally served with this dish, but I like a little, anyway.

SPAGHETTI WITH BASIL AND TOMATOES
Spaghetti con Basilico e Pomodori (Italy)

4 large ripe tomatoes, peeled and chopped
1 pound (500 g) mozzarella cheese, shredded
1/2 cup (125 ml) chopped fresh basil
2 garlic cloves, minced
1 cup (250 ml) olive oil
Salt and freshly ground black pepper
1 pound (500 g) *spaghetti*
Freshly grated Parmesan cheese

Combine all ingredients except *spaghetti* and Parmesan cheese and mix thoroughly. Set aside for at least 1 hour for flavors to blend.

Cook *spaghetti* in boiling salted water until tender. Drain and put into a warmed serving bowl. Pour over sauce, toss lightly and serve with Parmesan cheese on the side.

Makes 4 to 6 servings

TRENETTE WITH PESTO SAUCE AND POTATOES
Trenette con Pesto e Patate (Italy)

Trenette is the Genoese word for what is called *fettuccine* in other parts of Italy. This dish is the traditional one for *pesto,* and if *pasta* and potatoes seems too starchy a combination for you, leave out the potatoes. But do try it once; it is surprisingly delicious.

Noodle dough made with 1-3/4 cups (425 ml)
    flour and 2 eggs, page 28
3 medium potatoes, peeled and thinly sliced
1 recipe Genoese Basil Sauce, page 51

Make the noodle dough according to directions in Master Recipe and cut into noodles approximately 1/4 inch (6 mm) wide; set aside.

Cook the potatoes in boiling salted water until barely tender. Add the noodles to the pot and cook until tender. Drain and put noodles and potatoes on a warmed serving platter. Pour on the sauce and toss thoroughly but rapidly to prevent cooling. Serve immediately.

Makes 4 to 6 servings

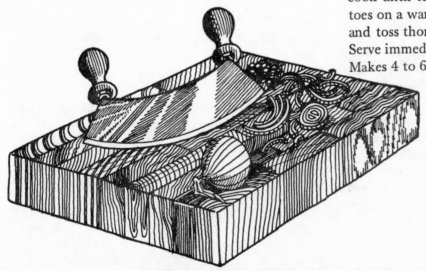

SPAGHETTI WITH MUSHROOM-CAPER SAUCE
(Mediterranean Area)

1 tablespoon (15 ml) butter or olive oil
1/2 pound (250 g) fresh mushrooms, sliced
1 garlic clove, mashed
1/2 cup (125 ml) dry white wine
Juice of 1 lemon
4 teaspoons (20 ml) salt-cured capers, soaked in
    several changes of water to remove excess
    salt and drained well
1 pound (500 g) *spaghetti*
Minced fresh parsley
Lemon wedges

In a medium-sized heavy skillet melt the butter and sauté the mushrooms and garlic over moderately high heat until mushroom liquid has evaporated but the mushrooms are still firm. Add wine and lemon juice and simmer over low heat, stirring often, until liquid has reduced by one-half, about 5 to 10 minutes. Stir capers into sauce and cook no more than 5 to 8 minutes, then remove from heat and keep warm until *spaghetti* is cooked.

Cook *spaghetti* in boiling salted water until tender. Drain and put into a warmed serving bowl. Pour on the sauce, toss quickly, sprinkle with parsley and serve immediately with lemon wedges on the side.
Makes 4 to 6 servings

Note A simpler caper sauce is obtained by combining butter, fresh lemon juice and capers in quantities to suit your taste in a small saucepan. Heat just to boiling point and pour over hot *spaghetti*.

EGG BARLEY CASSEROLE
(Jewish American)

1/2 pound (250 g) egg barley *pasta*
1/4 pound (125 g) butter
1 small onion, chopped
1/2 celery stalk with leaves, chopped
1/2 pound (250 g) fresh mushrooms, sliced
1 cup (250 ml) beef stock
Salt and freshly ground black pepper to taste
1 small ripe tomato, peeled and chopped (optional)
Minced fresh parsley for garnish

Drop egg barley into boiling salted water and cook about 6 to 7 minutes. Drain and put in a warmed casserole. Toss with 1 tablespoon (15 ml) of the butter; set aside.

In a medium-sized skillet melt remaining butter and sauté onion and celery until soft. Add mushrooms, raise heat and cook, stirring from time to time, for 4 to 5 minutes, or until liquid from mushrooms has evaporated. Pour on the stock and add the salt and pepper; cook, stirring frequently, for about 5 minutes. If using tomato, add now and cook 5 minutes longer. Pour mushroom mixture over egg barley in casserole. Sprinkle on the parsley and bake in a preheated 375°F (190°C) oven for about 25 minutes.

Serve this as a side dish to a meat roast or as a main dish for a light meal. A mixed greens salad with avocado slices is delightful with this dish, and cheese and fruit for dessert.
Makes 4 servings as a main dish;
6 servings as a side dish

VEGETABLES AND MACARONI
Alecha (Ethiopia)

1-1/4 pounds (625 g) elbow macaroni or other
    thick *pasta* form
1/3 cup (75 ml) peanut oil
3 medium onions, chopped
3/4 pound (375 g) green beans, broken into
    1-inch (3 cm) lengths
1-1/2 teaspoons (8 ml) ground turmeric
3 medium ripe tomatoes, peeled and
    finely chopped
1/2 teaspoon (3 ml) sugar
1/2 cup (125 ml) water
2 garlic cloves, mashed
Salt and freshly ground black pepper to taste

Cook macaroni in boiling salted water until tender. Drain and put in a bowl with 1 tablespoon (15 ml) of the peanut oil; toss and set aside.

In a large heavy skillet heat remaining oil and sauté onions until golden. Add green beans and turmeric and sauté for 10 minutes. Then add tomatoes, sugar and water. Cook over high heat, stirring constantly, for 2 to 3 minutes. Add macaroni to vegetable mixture with the garlic. Cook gently for 15 to 20 minutes, stirring often. Season with salt and pepper and serve immediately.
Makes 6 servings

NOODLES WITH ZUCCHINI AND MUSHROOMS
Nouilles aux Courgettes et Champignons (France)

Noodle dough made with 1-3/4 cups (425 ml) flour
    and 2 eggs, page 28
12 tablespoons (180 ml) unsalted butter
1/2 pound (250 g) fresh mushrooms, thinly sliced
1-1/2 pounds (750 g) zucchini, cut into julienne
1 cup (250 ml) heavy cream
1 cup (250 ml) freshly grated Parmesan cheese
1/2 cup (125 ml) chopped fresh Italian parsley
Additional freshly grated Parmesan cheese

Make noodle dough according to directions in Master Recipe and cut into noodles approximately 1/4 inch (6 mm) wide. Cook the noodles in boiling salted water until tender. Drain and set aside; cover and keep warm.

In a large skillet heat 4 tablespoons (60 ml) of the butter over moderately high heat and sauté the mushrooms for 2 to 3 minutes. Add the zucchini, cream and remaining butter, cut into small bits. Bring to a boil (liquid will have formed from the vegetables), reduce heat and simmer for 3 minutes. Add the noodles to the skillet, sprinkle in the Parmesan and parsley and toss, using 2 wooden forks, until well blended. Remove to a warmed serving platter and serve with Parmesan cheese on the side.
Makes 6 servings

EGGPLANT WITH MACARONI
Melanzane alla Parmigiana con Maccheroni (Italy)

2 tablespoons (30 ml) salt
2 large unpeeled eggplants, sliced
1/2 cup (125 ml) olive oil (or half olive oil and
　　half corn oil)
2 garlic cloves, bruised
4 large ripe tomatoes, peeled, seeded and chopped
1 tablespoon (15 ml) chopped fresh basil, or
1 teaspoon (5 ml) crumbled dried basil
Freshly ground black pepper to taste
1-1/2 pounds (750 g) medium macaroni, cooked
1/2 pound (250 g) mozzarella cheese, thinly
　　sliced or shredded
1/2 cup (125 ml) freshly grated Parmesan cheese

Salt the eggplant slices and put into a colander to drain for about 30 minutes; pat dry. Heat 6 tablespoons (100 ml) of the oil in a large skillet and cook the eggplant, a few slices at a time, until nicely browned, adding oil if needed. Remove slices to a dish; set aside.

Add remaining oil to the skillet and sauté garlic until browned; remove cloves and discard. Add tomatoes, basil and pepper to the skillet and simmer gently for about 15 minutes, or until thickened to a fine sauce.

In a large buttered casserole, layer the ingredients: first some of the macaroni, then some of the eggplant and tomatoes. Repeat until all ingredients are used. Top with the mozzarella, then the Parmesan. Bake in a preheated 350°F (170°C) oven for 30 to 40 minutes, or until cheeses melt and are lightly browned. Serve immediately.
Makes 6 to 8 servings

"BASILIZZA"

This wonderfully quick and easy (to say nothing of economical) dish with its obviously invented title has been served by my good friends, Betty Clark and Virginia Dantanville, for impromptu dinners for years. Origin? Who knows?

1 pound (500 g) *spaghettini* or *linguine*
1/4 pound (125 g) butter
14 to 16 green onions and tops, chopped
2 handfuls fresh parsley leaves
1 heaping teaspoon (7 ml) crumbled dried basil
1/2 cup (125 ml) freshly grated Parmesan cheese

Cook the *spaghettini* in boiling salted water until tender. Drain and put into a warmed shallow serving bowl or platter; keep warm.

In a large skillet melt the butter and add the green onions, parsley and basil. Sauté until limp and very lightly browned. Pour over the noodles and sprinkle on half of the cheese. Toss lightly and quickly and serve immediately. Pass remaining cheese.

Serve with a green salad and warmed crispy rolls. A fairly rough red wine, like a Zinfandel, complements this rather direct dish.
Makes 4 to 6 servings

CHILLED "ANGEL'S HAIR" WITH TOMATO SAUCE
Capelli d'Angelo Freddo (Jewish Italian)

1 pound (500 g) *capelli d'angelo* or very fine
    spaghettini
3 tablespoons (45 ml) olive oil
3 garlic cloves, finely minced
2 tablespoons (30 ml) finely chopped fresh
    Italian parsley
6 tablespoons (90 ml) Tomato Sauce with Basil,
    page 54
1/2 teaspoon (3 ml) sugar
1 teaspoon (5 ml) salt
Freshly ground black pepper to taste

Cook the *capelli d'angelo* in boiling salted water until tender. Drain and rinse with cold water, stirring to separate the strands. Drizzle on 1 tablespoon (15 ml) of the olive oil and toss; set aside.

In a small saucepan heat the remaining oil and add the garlic. Cook over very low heat until garlic is lightly golden. Stir in the parsley, tomato sauce, sugar, salt and pepper. Cook for no longer than 5 minutes, stirring occasionally.

Put noodles into a deep bowl and pour on the sauce. Toss until the noodles have absorbed the sauce, then cover the bowl and refrigerate for several hours until chilled.

This dish may be served as a first course or as a side dish to a meat roast or steamed, cold fish dish. On a hot day, it will be very satisfying as an entrée with a salad of mixed greens.

Makes 6 to 8 servings as a first course or side dish;
4 servings as a main dish

FETA AND SPINACH SALAD WITH *FARFALLETTE*
(Greek adaptation)

2 pounds (1 kg) spinach
1/2 cup (125 ml) olive oil
2 tablespoons (30 ml) fresh lemon juice
2 tablespoons (30 ml) white wine vinegar
1/2 teaspoon (3 ml) salt
1/4 teaspoon (1 to 2 ml) ground cinnamon
1/4 teaspoon (1 to 2 ml) dry mustard
1/8 teaspoon (1 ml) freshly ground black pepper
2 tablespoons (30 ml) toasted pine nuts
1 pound (500 g) *farfallette*, cooked and chilled
2 cucumbers, peeled and sliced
5 hard-cooked eggs, sliced or cut into wedges
1/4 pound (125 g) feta cheese, diced or crumbled
4 green onions, finely chopped

Wash the spinach very carefully. Put it into a bowl of water and pick out good leaves. Change the water and rinse leaves again. Discard any imperfect leaves and all stems. Drain well, pat dry with paper toweling and tear leaves into approximately 1-inch (3 cm) pieces. Put spinach in a very large bowl.

In a jar with a tight-fitting lid combine the oil, lemon juice, vinegar, salt, cinnamon, mustard and pepper. Shake well, pour half of the dressing over the spinach leaves and toss well. Sprinkle on the nuts and *farfallette*. Arrange on top in concentric circles or layers the cucumber slices, egg slices and feta cheese. Sprinkle on the onions and pour on remaining dressing.

Makes 8 to 10 servings

VEGETABLE SALAD
WITH PEANUT DRESSING
Gado-Gado (Indonesia)

This colorful and delicious salad may be arranged in small heaps of ingredients or in layers, each ingredient separated from the others. Arrange with a sense of the different colors of the vegetables for best effect. The following amount will serve two generously, but the ingredients may be multiplied to eternity!

1/2 cup (125 ml) finely shredded cabbage
1/2 cup (125 ml) diagonally cut green beans
1/2 cup (125 ml) shredded carrots
1 cup (250 ml) bean sprouts
1/2 pound (250 g) thin Oriental egg noodles
1 tablespoon (15 ml) peanut oil
1 large tomato, cut into wedges
1 cucumber, peeled and thinly sliced

Peanut Dressing
2 tablespoons (30 ml) minced onion
1/2 teaspoon (3 ml) peanut oil
6 tablespoons (90 ml) peanut butter
3 tablespoons (45 ml) sugar
1 teaspoon (5 ml) salt
1 teaspoon (5 ml) Tabasco sauce
2 tablespoons (30 ml) fresh lemon juice
1-1/2 cups (375 ml) water
1 bay leaf
1/2 teaspoon (3 ml) shredded ginger root
1 garlic clove, finely minced

Cook cabbage, green beans and carrots separately until just barely tender; they should be quite firm. Chill each thoroughly. Pour boiling water over bean sprouts and drain immediately; chill. Cook the noodles in boiling water only until barely tender; drain well, toss with the oil and chill. Chill tomato and cucumber.

To make the dressing, fry onion in oil until browned. Combine with all remaining ingredients and cook over low heat, stirring constantly, until thickened. Remove from heat and let cool to room temperature.

Arrange vegetables and noodles on a serving platter as described in introduction. Serve dressing separately.
Makes 2 servings

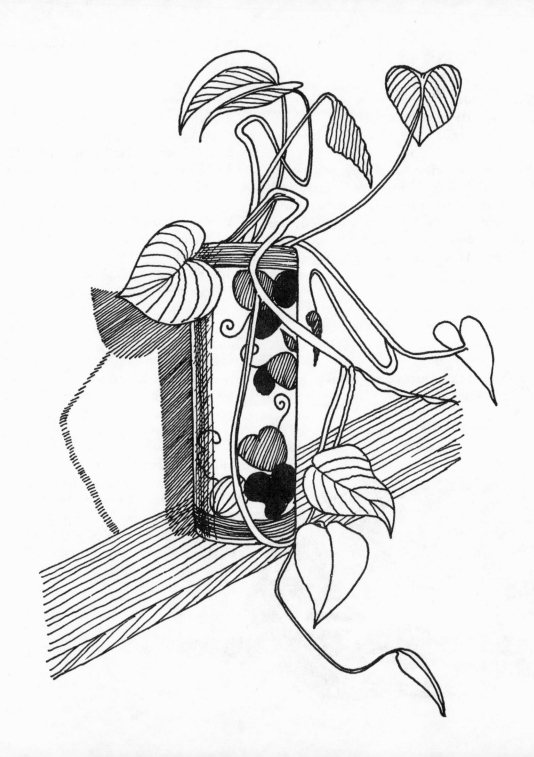

PASTA WITH FRUIT AND NUTS

NOODLES WITH NUT SAUCE
Fideos con Salsa de Nuez (Argentina)

A delightful surprise for those not familiar with this dish.

Noodle dough made with 3-3/4 cups (925 ml)
    flour and 4 eggs, page 28
1/4 cup (75 ml) heavy cream
1/4 cup (75 ml) commercial sour cream
Salt and freshly ground black pepper to taste
4 tablespoons (60 ml) unsalted butter
2 garlic cloves, mashed
1 cup (250 ml) finely chopped walnuts
1 cup (250 ml) freshly grated Parmesan cheese
1/2 cup (125 ml) chicken broth

Make noodle dough according to directions in Master Recipe and cut into noodles approximately 1/4 inch (6 mm) wide. Cook noodles in boiling salted water until tender. Drain and put into a warmed large serving bowl. Mix together the heavy cream and sour cream and add to the noodles with the salt, pepper and half the butter. Toss well, cover and keep warm.

In a small heavy saucepan heat the remaining butter and sauté the garlic. Cook for about 3 minutes, but do not let it brown. Remove saucepan from heat and stir in walnuts, cheese and chicken broth. Pour over the noodle mixture and toss well. Serve immediately.

This may be served as a first course to be followed by a roast and vegetables, or as a main course for a light meal with salad. Crisp rolls may be served with it to sop up the delicious sauce remaining in the dish when the noodles have been eaten.

Makes 6 to 8 servings as a main dish;
10 to 12 as a first course

NOODLES WITH ALMONDS
Nouilles Amandine (France)

Noodle dough made with 1-3/4 cups (425 ml)
    flour and 2 eggs, page 28
1/2 cup (125 ml) slivered blanched almonds
4 tablespoons (60 ml) unsalted butter
1/2 pound (250 g) fresh mushrooms, thinly sliced
2 tablespoons (30 ml) grated onion
1 recipe *Béchamel* Sauce, page 56
3/4 cup (175 ml) freshly grated Gruyère cheese

Make noodle dough according to directions in Master Recipe and cut into noodles approximately 1/4 inch (6 mm) wide. Cook the noodles in boiling salted water until tender, drain and set aside.

In a small skillet sauté almonds in 1 tablespoon (15 ml) of the butter until crisp and golden; set aside. In a large saucepan sauté mushrooms in remaining butter over low heat, stirring, for about 5 minutes. Add the onion and cook until translucent. Mix in the almonds and very gradually add the *Béchamel* Sauce; heat thoroughly but do not boil. Toss the drained noodles in the sauce. Pour the noodles into a warmed serving bowl and sprinkle with the Gruyère. Serve immediately.
Makes 4 to 6 servings

SPAGHETTI WITH FRIED BREAD AND RAISINS
Spaghetti con la Mollica Fritta e L'Uva Passa (Sicily)

Using sweet dried fruits with *pasta* is neither unusual nor modern to the Mediterraneans; honey or other sweet flavorings were often added to anchovy sauce during ancient times and even during the Renaissance.

1/2 cup (125 ml) seedless raisins (golden or dark)
1 pound (500 g) *spaghetti*
4 tablespoons (60 ml) olive oil
1 garlic clove, minced
2 slices dry white bread, crusts removed and
    bread finely grated
2 tablespoons (30 ml) chopped fresh parsley
Salt and freshly ground black pepper to taste

Soak the raisins in warm water to cover for 30 minutes or longer. Cook *spaghetti* in boiling salted water until tender, drain well and toss with 1 tablespoon (15 ml) of the olive oil. Cover and keep warm.

In a large saucepan brown the garlic in remaining oil. Discard garlic and toss in bread crumbs; cook, stirring constantly, until nicely browned. Add *spaghetti* to saucepan and toss lightly. Drain the raisins and add with parsley, salt and pepper to noodles. Mix well and serve immediately.
Makes 4 to 6 servings

SWEET *VERMICELLI*
Seviyan (India)

This is made with the very finest, thinnest *vermicelli,* broken into small pieces to facilitate stirring.

1/4 pound (125 g) very fine *vermicelli*
2 tablespoons (30 ml) *ghee* (clarified butter, page 57)
1/4 teaspoon saffron threads, soaked in
1-1/2 cups (375 ml) hot water
1/2 cup (125 ml) sugar
3 tablespoons (45 ml) seedless golden raisins
3 tablespoons (45 ml) slivered blanched almonds
1/8 teaspoon (scant 1 ml) ground cardamom
Coarsely chopped pistachio nuts for garnish (optional)
Heavy cream

Break the *vermicelli* into small pieces, no longer than 1 inch (3 cm). Put the *ghee* in a heavy saucepan over moderate heat. Add the *vermicelli* and fry until golden, stirring constantly but gently. Add the saffron and water and bring to a boil. Reduce heat to very low, cover and simmer very gently until the *vermicelli* is cooked. This should take only a few minutes. Add the sugar and raisins and cook, uncovered, until the liquid is absorbed. Add the almonds and cardamom and stir them in well. Garnish with pistachio nuts, if desired, and serve warm with cream on the side.
Makes 6 servings

LENTEN *SPAGHETTI* WITH WALNUTS AND SUGAR
Spaghetti di Quaresima (Italy)

This is an ancient dish, still popular all over Italy. It has a quaint and unusual flavor and is much more delicious than you might at first think.

1 pound (500 g) *spaghetti,* cooked
1/2 cup (125 ml) finely chopped walnuts
1 cup (250 ml) dry bread crumbs
2 tablespoons (30 ml) sugar
Freshly grated nutmeg to taste
Salt and freshly ground black pepper to taste
4 tablespoons (60 ml) olive oil

Cook the *spaghetti* in boiling salted water until tender. Drain and put into a warmed deep serving bowl. Combine the walnuts, bread crumbs, sugar, nutmeg and salt and pepper. Add the walnut mixture and olive oil to the *spaghetti.* Toss well and serve promptly.

This is, in Italy, a main dish or first course. You may, however, prefer to eat it as a dessert. Do, by all means.
Makes 4 servings

ARABIAN NIGHTS SALAD
(England/Arabia)

With thanks to Elizabeth David, who inspired me to concoct this salad. She found it in Mrs. Leyel's *The Gentle Art of Cookery* in the chapter "Dishes from the Arabian Nights." It was allegedly brought from the East by Anatole France. The recipe has long intrigued me and I have served it with and without *pasta* and love it both ways.

4 large oranges
2 grapefruits
2 medium white onions, finely chopped
Ice water
1 cup (250 ml) Mediterranean-type black olives, pitted
Several coriander sprigs
Several parsley sprigs
1 recipe *Orecchiette,* page 43, cooked and chilled
Hungarian paprika
Salt
Approximately 3 tablespoons (45 ml) olive oil

Peel the oranges and grapefruits and carefully divide into sections. Remove all the white, bitter pith and chill sections well. Cover the onions with ice water and set aside. Taste the olives, and if very salty, soak in warm water for 30 minutes or so. Drain thoroughly, pat dry and chop coarsely.

Remove stems of herbs and discard. Chop leaves finely. In a large, shallow serving bowl arrange a bed of the *orecchiette.* Mound the orange and grapefruit sections in the center. Drain the onions and arrange on top with the olives. Sprinkle on herbs, then paprika and salt. Drizzle on the olive oil and serve very cold.

Crispy rolls with unsalted butter and a light, dry white wine are fine complements to this salad. A piquant fresh cheese or fresh creamy Roquefort will help make this a memorable luncheon.
Makes 6 servings

RICE WITH *ORZO* AND PINE NUTS
(Lebanon)

Orzo is a small rice-shaped *pasta* form very popular in the Near East. In this dish it is hard to tell the rice from the *orzo*. Care must be taken in stirring not to mash the *orzo*.

1/2 cup (125 ml) *orzo*
1/4 pound (125 g) unsalted butter
2 cups (500 ml) long-grain rice, well washed
2-1/2 cups (625 ml) water, boiling
1 teaspoon (5 ml) salt
1/4 cup (75 ml) pine nuts

In a large saucepan lightly brown the *orzo* in butter. When browned, remove pan from heat and stir in the rice. Return pan to the stove and cook over moderate heat for about 2 minutes, stirring steadily. Add the water and salt. Reduce heat to lowest point, cover tightly and cook until all water is absorbed. Turn mixture frequently so it does not stick to the pan. Just before serving, stir in the pine nuts.
Makes 6 servings

APPLE AND NOODLE PUDDING OR CAKE
Lukshen Cholent (Eastern Europe)

A traditional Jewish pudding, well known from Germany through Russia.

Noodle dough made with 1-3/4 cups (425 ml) flour and 2 eggs, page 28
6 tablespoons (90 ml) butter
1/2 cup (125 ml) milk
6 tablespoons (90 ml) unbleached all-purpose flour, sifted
1 cup (250 ml) sugar
1/4 teaspoon (1 to 2 ml) ground cinnamon
1/2 cup (125 ml) seedless golden raisins
3 eggs, separated
3 small eating apples, peeled, cored and horizontally sliced
Heavy cream

Make noodle dough according to directions in Master Recipe, but roll out slightly thicker than directed. Cut into noodles approximately 1/4 inch (6 mm) wide. Drop the noodles in boiling salted water. One minute after water has returned to the boil, drain noodles, reserving 1/2 cup (125 ml) of the cooking water. In a large bowl combine noodles, reserved cooking water, half the butter and the milk. Mix in the flour, sugar and cinnamon and stir well. Then add the raisins and stir again.

Beat the egg yolks until light and add to the noodles. Beat the egg whites until stiff but not dry and gently fold into noodle mixture. Butter a deep baking dish and pour in half of the noodle mixture.

Lay the apple slices on top and cover with remaining noodles. Dot with remaining butter, cover and bake in a preheated 375°F (190°C) oven for about 45 minutes. Pass the cream for individual servings.
Makes 6 servings

Note I have had this dish with both sweet and sour cream; delicious either way.

NOODLES WITH RAISINS AND ALMONDS
Cataif (Near East/Romania)

This recipe is quite old and is, with variations, eaten in many of the Middle Eastern and North African countries as well as, surprisingly, in Romania.

Noodle dough made with 2-3/4 cups (675 ml) flour, 3 eggs and 2 tablespoons (30 ml) water, page 28
1/4 pound (125 g) unsalted butter
2 teaspoons (10 ml) ground cinnamon
1 teaspoon (5 ml) freshly grated nutmeg
1/2 cup (125 ml) seedless golden raisins
1 cup (250 ml) blanched almonds, chopped and toasted
1/4 cup (50 ml) chopped mixed candied citrus peel
Grated zest of 1 lemon
3 tablespoons (45 ml) sugar
Heavy cream

Caramel Sauce
1/2 cup (125 ml) sugar
1/4 cup (75 ml) water
Juice of 1 lemon

Make noodle dough according to direction in Master Recipe, working the water into the dough. Cut into noodles approximately 1/8 inch (3 mm) wide. Drop noodles into boiling salted water. One minute after water has returned to the boil, drain and put into a large bowl. Toss with half the butter and sprinkle with cinnamon and nutmeg.

Butter a shallow baking dish and pour in one-third of the noodles. Cover with half each of the raisins, almonds, candied peel, lemon zest and sugar. Repeat layers and finish with noodles. Dot top with remaining butter. Bake in a preheated 325°F (160°C) oven for 15 minutes.

While noodles are baking, make the caramel sauce. Put sugar into a small dry saucepan and stir over very low heat until it melts and turns golden brown. Remove from heat and pour in the water. Do it carefully for the mixture will spurt furiously. Return to heat and stir until the mixture becomes a syrup. Slowly add the lemon juice, stir well to blend and then pour over the noodles. Return to the oven for 5 more minutes. Serve with cream on the side.
Makes 6 to 8 servings

NOODLES WITH WALNUTS
Nuss Nudeln (Austria)

Noodle dough made with 1-3/4 cups (425 ml)
    flour and 2 eggs, page 28
2 tablespoons (30 ml) finely ground walnuts
3 tablespoons (45 ml) sugar
4 tablespoons (60 ml) unsalted butter

Make noodle dough according to directions in Master Recipe and cut into noodles approximately 1/4

inch (6 mm) wide. Cook noodles in boiling salted water until barely tender. Drain, rinse under tepid water and drain again. Mix together walnuts and sugar and set aside.

Melt butter in a large saucepan and toss noodles in it. It is best not to cook the noodles further, but simply reheat them and coat them well with the butter. Put noodles in a warmed serving bowl and sprinkle with 2 tablespoons (30 ml) of the nut-sugar mixture. Serve immediately with remaining nut-sugar mixture on the side.
Makes 6 servings

BROAD NOODLES IN MILK
Siroki Resanci u Mljeku (Yugoslavia)

Noodle dough made with 1-3/4 cups (425 ml)
    flour and 2 eggs, page 28
1 quart (1 L) milk
2 tablespoons (30 ml) sugar
2 tablespoons (30 ml) unsalted butter
1/2 cup (125 ml) grated or coarsely chopped
    walnuts
2 tablespoons (30 ml) seedless golden raisins

Make the noodle dough according to directions in Master Recipe and cut into noodles approximately 1/4 inch (6 mm) wide. In a large saucepan combine milk, sugar and butter and heat until scalded. Stir in the noodles and cover with a tight lid. Simmer over low heat until noodles are tender and have absorbed the milk, about 20 to 25 minutes. Sprinkle with nuts and raisins and serve immediately.
Makes 4 to 6 servings

PASTA WITH SEAFOOD

A SOUP OF TOULON
La Soupe à la Toulonnaise (France)

"Do not, *ma chère*," counseled Madame Bouquet, my landlady in Paris, "throw away the court bouillon in which you have cooked a salt-water fish. It is a fine base for an excellent soup." This is how I made it under her supervision.

Strain fish broth through cheesecloth or a fine strainer; add water to make it a full quart (1 L), if it is lacking. In a large soup kettle heat 2 tablespoons (30 ml) olive oil. Add 1 tablespoon (15 ml) flour and cook, stirring often, until it thickens and comes away from the sides of the pan. Then add, little by little, the cold fish broth, stirring constantly. Bring to a boil, reduce heat to medium and cook very gently for 10 minutes.

Stir in a pinch of saffron powder and a few grinds of black pepper. Bring back to a boil and add 1/4 pound (125 g) *spaghettini*, broken into small pieces, and cook until *pasta* is tender, or as Madame Bouquet said, *"jusqu'à gentille ou tendre."* Serve immediately.
Makes 4 servings

SPAGHETTI À LA GRETA GARBO
(United States)

I would like to thank the proper person for this recipe, but I've had it so long I cannot remember where it came from. It has stood me in great stead as a quick and delicious dish.

"Cook *spaghetti al dente* and toss with a sauce of cream, butter and minced smoked salmon."

NOODLES ROMANOFF WITH RED CAVIAR
(Russian American)

Noodle dough made with 1-3/4 cups (425 ml)
    flour and 2 eggs, page 28
1 pound (500 g) natural cream cheese, softened
1 pint (500 ml) commercial sour cream
4 green onions, finely minced
Dash of Tabasco sauce or cayenne pepper
1/2 teaspoon (3 ml) salt
1/2 cup (125 ml) dry bread crumbs
2 tablespoons (30 ml) unsalted butter, thoroughly
    chilled
1 jar (2 ounces or 56 g) red caviar

Make noodle dough according to directions in Master Recipe and cut into noodles approximately 1/8 inch (3 mm) wide. Cook the noodles in boiling salted water until tender. Drain and set aside.

In a medium-sized bowl mix together the cream cheese, sour cream, green onions, Tabasco sauce and salt. Stir very well to blend, then stir into the noodles. Pour into a buttered 2-quart (2 L) casserole and sprinkle bread crumbs over the top. Dot with cold butter and arrange the red caviar in center on top (or any preferred design). Bake in a preheated 350°F (170°C) oven for about 30 minutes or until heated through.

This makes a lovely buffet dish, served with a crisp green salad and fresh hot French bread.
Makes 6 servings

Note Black caviar may be used in place of the red caviar, but only if it is of fine quality. Otherwise it may well be too salty.

SNAIL BUTTER WITH NOODLES
Buerre d'Escargot aux Nouilles (France)

Although I first made this with snails from my garden in Paris and later in California with my garden snails (after a two-week feeding of moist cornmeal, followed by several boilings), there is no reason that canned snails wouldn't do as well—and save all the preliminary labor.

Noodle dough made with 1-3/4 cups (425 ml)
    flour and 2 eggs, page 28
12 tablespoons (180 ml) unsalted butter
4 green onions, finely minced
4 garlic cloves, finely minced
Salt and freshly ground black pepper to taste
2 cans (4-1/2 ounces or 130 g each, drained weight)
    snails, drained and coarsely chopped
1 cup (250 ml) finely chopped fresh Italian
    parsley

Make noodle dough according to directions in Master Recipe and cut into noodles approximately 1/8 inch (3 mm) wide; set aside.

In a small saucepan melt the butter and add the green onions, garlic, salt and pepper. Sauté over low heat until onions and garlic are soft; they must not brown. Add the snails and heat thoroughly, shaking the pan from time to time. Add parsley and let stand over very lowest heat until needed.

Cook the noodles in boiling salted water until tender. Drain and put into a warmed serving dish. Pour on the snail sauce and toss quickly. Serve immediately with plenty of crusty bread to sop up the sauce, and a light red wine, like a fine claret.
Makes 6 servings as a first course

NOODLES AND OYSTERS
(New England)

Noodle dough made with 1-3/4 cups (425 ml) flour
    and 2 eggs, page 28
24 small oysters in the shell, shucked and liquor
    reserved
1 quart (1 L) oyster water (oyster liquor plus
    water to make measure)
1/4 pound (125 g) butter
1/4 cup (50 ml) unbleached all-purpose flour
1/2 cup (125 ml) minced fresh parsley
4 green onions, finely chopped
Pinch of cayenne pepper
Salt and freshly ground black pepper to taste

Make noodle dough according to directions in Master Recipe and cut into noodles approximately 1/4 inch (6 mm) wide; set aside.

Simmer the oysters in the oyster water until their edges curl. Remove oysters with a slotted spoon and reserve. Melt the butter in a saucepan and blend in flour. Cook, stirring, 2 to 3 minutes; do not brown. Gradually add half the oyster water and cook over moderate-low heat, stirring constantly, until sauce is smooth and thick, about 10 minutes. Raise heat slightly and add parsley, onions, cayenne pepper, salt and black pepper. Cook, stirring frequently, for about 8 minutes.

While the sauce is cooking, cook the noodles in boiling salted water until tender. Drain and put into a warmed large serving bowl; keep warm.

Add oysters to sauce and heat through, only a few minutes. Pour sauce over noodles, toss quickly and serve immediately.
Makes 4 servings

CRAB IN NOODLE RING
(California)

Noodle Ring with Cream Cheese, page 69
1 pound (500 g) crab meat
6 tablespoons (90 ml) butter
2 tablespoons (30 ml) flour
2 cups (500 ml) heavy cream
Milk, if needed
2 tablespoons (30 ml) chopped fresh parsley
1 teaspoon (5 ml) curry powder
1 tablespoon (15 ml) cognac or brandy
Salt and freshly ground white pepper to taste
Minced fresh parsley for garnish

Prepare noodle ring and place in oven to bake as directed. While ring is cooking, prepare the crab mixture. Pick over the crab meat and discard any cartilege or shell fragments. Shred crab meat finely, or leave in lumps, as preferred; set aside.

In a heavy saucepan melt the butter and stir in flour. Cook, stirring, 3 minutes; do not let it brown. Gradually stir in cream, adding a little milk if mixture seems too thick. Add parsley, curry powder, cognac, salt and pepper. Stir in crab meat and cook, stirring constantly, for 10 minutes. Taste and adjust seasonings.

Unmold noodle ring onto a warmed platter. Spoon crab mixture into center and garnish with parsley.
Makes 4 servings

MUSSELS WITH *SPAGHETTI*
(Mediterranean Area)

3 pounds (1.5 kg) mussels in the shell
1 small onion, chopped
1 garlic clove, chopped
1 cup (250 ml) water
3/4 cup (175 ml) dry white wine
2 tablespoons (30 ml) olive oil or unsalted butter
1/2 celery stalk with leaves, chopped
1 bay leaf
1 parsley sprig
1 thyme sprig
Freshly ground black pepper to taste
1 pound (500 g) *spaghetti,* cooked and kept warm

Scrub mussels, remove beards and soak in water to cover a few minutes to remove as much sand as possible; drain.

In a very large kettle combine the onion, garlic, water, wine, oil, celery, bay leaf, parsley, thyme and pepper. Bring to a boil and drop in mussels. Cook until shells open.

Put hot, drained *spaghetti* in a warmed serving bowl. Remove mussels from kettle with a large slotted spoon and place on top of *spaghetti*. Quickly strain the hot mussel broth and put into a warmed tureen with a ladle. Pour 2 tablespoons (30 ml) of the broth on the mussels and *spaghetti* and toss well. Serve promptly.

Fill a cup with the mussel broth for each guest to drink or to pour on the *spaghetti*. Grated cheese is usually not served with this dish, but a little would not hurt, if preferred.
Makes 6 servings

SPAGHETTI WITH RED CLAM SAUCE
Spaghetti con le Vongole e Salsa Rossa
(Italo-American)

2 tablespoons (30 ml) olive oil
2 medium onions, chopped
1 garlic clove, minced
1 bay leaf, crumbled
6 fresh basil leaves, shredded, or
1/4 teaspoon (1 ml) crumbled dried basil
1 teaspoon (5 ml) salt
Several grinds black pepper
2 teaspoons (10 ml) sugar
4 large ripe tomatoes, peeled, seeded and chopped
1/4 cup (75 ml) dry white wine
1/4 cup (75 ml) minced fresh parsley
1 can (7 ounces or 200 g) minced clams, drained
    and liquid reserved
1 pound (500 g) *spaghetti*
Freshly grated Parmesan cheese

Heat olive oil in a large heavy skillet over moderate heat. Sauté onions and garlic, stirring occasionally, until soft and just starting to color. Add the bay leaf, basil, salt, pepper, sugar, tomatoes, wine, parsley and clam liquid. Simmer, uncovered, stirring often, until sauce thickens slightly and has the consistency of good light gravy. Stir in the clams and heat 4 to 6 minutes longer.

While the sauce is cooking, cook the *spaghetti* in boiling salted water until tender. Drain, arrange in a mound on a warmed platter and pour clam sauce over the top. Sprinkle with Parmesan cheese and pass extra cheese for individual servings.
Makes 6 servings

LINGUINE WITH WHITE CLAM SAUCE
Linguine con le Vongole "In Bianco"
(Italo-American)

Not too long ago I was asked by that San Francisco "Underground Gourmet," Bob Read, to a banquet at the nonpareil Mandarin Restaurant to celebrate the Chinese New Year. Mayor George Moscone and his wife, Gina, were also there, and we were seated around the same table. Of course, the subject of food filled the evening and I found the opportunity to ask the Mayor which *pasta* he preferred. He answered with spirit: "The simplest is the best! *Linguine* with cheese, *linguine* with clams and white sauce; those are my favorites." I hope he finds this recipe to his taste.

Noodle dough made with 1-3/4 cups (425 ml)
    flour and 2 eggs, page 28
1/2 cup (125 ml) olive oil
1 tablespoon (15 ml) unsalted butter
1 garlic clove
1 can (7 ounces or 200 g) minced clams, drained
    and liquid reserved
Pinch of salt
Freshly ground black pepper to taste
1/2 teaspoon (3 ml) crumbled dried marjoram
3 tablespoons (45 ml) chopped fresh Italian
    parsley
Freshly grated Parmesan cheese

Make noodle dough according to directions in Master Recipe, roll out slightly thicker than usual and cut into noodles approximately 1/8 inch (3 mm) wide; set aside.

Heat olive oil and butter in a heavy skillet and add the garlic clove. Cook over low heat until garlic browns. Mash clove into the oil with a fork to release garlic essence, then remove and discard clove. Add the clam liquid, salt, pepper and marjoram and simmer for 5 minutes. Add the clams, stir in well and cook, covered or partially covered, for just over 5 minutes. Stir in half the parsley.

While the sauce is cooking, cook the noodles in boiling salted water until tender. Drain and put into a warmed deep serving bowl. Add half the sauce and toss well. Pour remaining sauce over the top, sprinkle on parsley and pass the Parmesan cheese.

Bon appetito, caro Mayor Moscone.
Makes 4 to 6 servings

CLAMS AND *VERMICELLI*
Palourdes et Vermicelle (Basque/French)

In early spring of 1953, I arrived in a deserted Biarritz and went on to the lovely fishing village of St.-Jean-de-Luz, close to the Spanish border. The extraordinary cool, clear light reminded me of my home in Monterey, California, so I settled down for several days stay. My hotel boasted a simple but exquisite cuisine and the following is one of the dishes I enjoyed for three days running at lunch—and often since then.

20 small clams, steamed to open shells
2 garlic cloves
4 tablespoons (60 ml) olive oil
2 large tomatoes, peeled, seeded and chopped
1 small fresh hot chili pepper, finely chopped
2 tablespoons (30 ml) chopped fresh Italian parsley
1/2 teaspoon (3 ml) crumbled dried oregano or basil
1 teaspoon (5 ml) sugar
Salt and freshly ground black pepper to taste
1 pound (500 g) *spaghettini*

Drain clams and remove from shells, reserving liquor. Strain liquor and set clams and liquor aside. In a skillet sauté the garlic cloves in 3 tablespoons (45 ml) of the olive oil until browned; remove and discard cloves. Add clams and their liquor, tomatoes, chili pepper, parsley, oregano, sugar, salt and black pepper to the skillet. Bring to a boil, reduce heat and simmer until sauce is slightly thickened, about 15 minutes.

While the sauce is cooking, cook the *spaghettini* in boiling salted water until tender. Drain and put into a warmed serving bowl with the remaining olive oil. Toss well, pour on the sauce and toss again. Serve immediately.
Makes 4 to 6 servings

"QUILLS" WITH ANCHOVY SAUCE
Penne à la Montégale (Provence)

12 salt-cured anchovies, soaked in several changes of water, boned and mashed
1 garlic clove, minced
1 shallot, minced
3/4 cup (175 ml) minced fresh parsley
1-1/4 cups (325 ml) olive oil
1 tablespoon (15 ml) red wine vinegar
1 tablespoon (15 ml) minced fresh thyme
1 pound (500 g) *penne*
1/3 cup (75 ml) freshly grated Parmesan cheese

Combine all ingredients except *penne* and cheese and let stand 1 hour to blend flavors. Cook the *penne* in boiling salted water until tender. Drain and put into a warmed serving bowl. Pour on sauce, toss quickly and sprinkle with cheese. Serve immediately.
Makes 4 to 6 servings

"LITTLE EARS" IN THE MANNER OF PALM SUNDAY
Orecchiette alla Domenicana (Apulia, Italy)

3 tablespoons (45 ml) olive oil
2 tablespoons (30 ml) water
4 ounces (125 g) dried Italian mushrooms, soaked
    in warm water 20 minutes and well drained
2 garlic cloves
12 anchovy fillets canned in oil, rinsed and
    mashed, or
10 salt-cured anchovies, soaked in several changes
    of water, boned and mashed
1 recipe *Orecchiette*, page 43
1 tablespoon (15 ml) minced fresh Italian parsley
Dry bread crumbs
Unsalted butter

In a medium-sized skillet heat 1 tablespoon (15 ml) of the olive oil and add the water and mushrooms. Cook over low heat for about 15 minutes. Chop mushrooms finely or put through a sieve with half the cooking liquid; set aside.

In a small heavy saucepan of enamelware, glass or earthenware, sauté the garlic in 1 tablespoon (15 ml) olive oil until browned; discard the garlic. Add the mushrooms with their liquid to the garlic-flavored oil along with the anchovies. Cook over low heat for about 5 minutes, then remove from heat.

Cook the *orecchiette* in boiling salted water until tender. Drain and put into a warmed earthenware casserole. Pour on the mushroom-anchovy sauce and sprinkle with parsley. Top with a light coating of bread crumbs, drizzle on remaining olive oil and dot with bits of butter. Bake in a preheated 400°F (210°C) oven for 10 minutes.
Makes 4 servings

Variations Add 1 or 2 hot mashed potatoes to the sauce with a bit more olive oil and perhaps more butter and some freshly grated Romano cheese. *Bucatini,* elbow macaroni, thick *spaghetti* and other large thick forms of *pasta* are also good with this sauce.

SPAGHETTI, PROSTITUTE'S STYLE
Spaghetti alla Puttanesca (Rome)

Whether this dish took its name because of the hot and salty sauce, very quickly made, or from some more honorable method, no one seems to know—or care! In any case, it is said to be an ancient dish and to have its origin in the poor district of Trastevere in Rome, where prostitutes have lived since time immemorial.

On a gray, cold, rainy day in Trastevere, this dish is heaven sent, eaten with crusty bread and a salad of mixed greens, and lots of red wine.

4 tablespoons (60 ml) butter
3 tablespoons (45 ml) olive oil
8 anchovy fillets canned in oil, chopped
3 garlic cloves, minced
1 small dried hot red chili pepper, minced
3 large ripe tomatoes, peeled and thinly sliced
1/4 pound (125 g) Mediterranean-type black olives, pitted and sliced
1 tablespoon (15 ml) salt-cured capers, soaked in several changes of water and drained
1 pound (500 g) *spaghetti*
1 tablespoon (15 ml) chopped fresh parsley

In a large skillet heat the butter and olive oil. When the butter has melted, add the anchovies, garlic and chili pepper and cook for a few minutes, stirring frequently. Add the tomatoes, olives and capers and cook for 3 minutes. Taste and correct seasoning, if necessary.

Cook the *spaghetti* in boiling salted water until tender. Drain and add to the sauce in the skillet and mix well. Add the parsley and cook 30 seconds, stirring constantly. Serve immediately.
Makes 4 servings

"MOUSTACHES" WITH SQUID SAUCE
Mostaccioli con Calamari (Italy)

1 pound (500 g) fresh squid
4 tablespoons (60 ml) olive oil
2 garlic cloves, minced
1 green or red bell pepper, coarsely chopped
3 fresh hot green chili peppers, seeded and
    finely chopped
5 or 6 large ripe tomatoes, peeled, seeded and
    chopped
2 tablespoons (30 ml) tomato paste
Salt to taste
1 pound (500 g) *mostaccioli* or any large *pasta* of
    intricate shape, such as *penne* or *rigatoni*

To clean the squid, cut off the tentacles above the eyes and reserve. Pull the head off, and with it, pull out the innards; discard. Feel around inside the body and pull out and discard the cartilege. Then, with a coarse towel or cloth, rub off the thin purplish skin on the body. Hold the squid bodies under cold running water to rinse them well. Slit bodies open and lay them flat. Cut the bodies into large squares, then "score" the surface of the squares in a crisscross pattern; this will prevent them from curling during cooking.

Heat the olive oil in a large heavy skillet and sauté the squid (including tentacles) over moderate heat until it is no longer translucent, about 2 to 3 minutes. Reduce heat and add the garlic, bell pep-per, chili peppers, tomatoes, tomato paste and salt. Simmer for about 15 minutes, stirring frequently. If sauce is too thin, simmer longer; if too thick, add a little water.

While sauce is cooking, cook the *mostaccioli* in boiling salted water until tender. Drain and put into a warmed large serving bowl. Pour on sauce, toss and serve immediately.
Makes 4 to 6 servings

SPAGHETTI WITH TUNA FISH
Spaghetti con Tonno (Italy)

1 pound (500 g) ripe tomatoes, peeled, seeded and
    chopped
2 garlic cloves, mashed
1 cup (250 ml) minced fresh Italian parsley
2 tablespoons (30 ml) olive oil
1 teaspoon (5 ml) salt
1/2 teaspoon (3 ml) freshly ground black pepper
1 can (6-1/2 ounces or 184 g) tuna fish, drained
3/4 pound (375 g) *spaghetti*

In a heavy saucepan combine the tomatoes, garlic, parsley, olive oil, salt and pepper and cook 20 minutes. Add tuna and simmer 15 minutes longer.

While sauce is simmering, cook the *spaghetti* in boiling salted water until tender. Drain and put into a warmed serving bowl. Pour on sauce, toss quickly and serve immediately.
Makes 3 or 4 servings

COD WITH *MORNAY* SAUCE AND NOODLES
Gratin de Morue aux Nouilles (France)

1-1/2 pounds (750 g) cod fillets
1/2 cup (125 ml) milk
1 bay leaf
1 small onion, stuck with 2 whole cloves
Pinch of cayenne pepper
Salt
10 whole peppercorns
2 parsley sprigs
1/4 pound (125 g) fine egg noodles
2 tablespoons (30 ml) butter
Salt and freshly ground black pepper to taste
1/2 cup (125 ml) freshly grated Gruyère cheese

Mornay Sauce
2 tablespoons (30 ml) butter
3 tablespoons (45 ml) unbleached all-purpose flour
1/2 cup (125 ml) heavy cream
1-1/2 cups (375 ml) milk
Salt and freshly ground black pepper
1 cup (250 ml) freshly grated Gruyère cheese
1 egg yolk
Pinch of freshly grated nutmeg

Put the cod fillets in a saucepan with the milk, bay leaf, onion, cayenne pepper, salt, peppercorns, parsley and water to just cover. Slowly bring to a boil, reduce heat and simmer gently for 1 minute. Remove from heat and lift out fillets with a large slotted spoon; discard liquid and set fillets aside.

Cook the noodles in boiling salted water until tender. Drain, toss with butter and sprinkle with salt and pepper. Pour the noodles into a buttered gratin dish or other baking dish and arrange cod fillets on top; set aside.

To make the sauce, melt the butter in a small heavy saucepan over medium heat and stir in the flour. Cook, stirring, about 3 minutes. Gradually add the cream and milk, stirring constantly. Season with salt and pepper. Add the cheese, and when it melts, bring mixture slowly to a boil. Beat the egg yolk with a little of the hot milk mixture and return to saucepan. Stir rapidly and when it again reaches the boiling point, remove promptly from the heat. Stir in nutmeg.

Spoon the sauce over the fish and sprinkle on the grated cheese. Bake in a preheated 475°F (240°C) oven for 10 to 15 minutes, or until heated through.
Makes 4 servings

STUFFED SHRIMP WITH NOODLE DARIOLES
(Great Britain)

A delicious and attractive dish, the origin of which I cannot now recall I've had it so long.

18 jumbo shrimp, shelled and deveined
Approximately 1/2 cup (125 ml) Whole Shrimp
    Butter, page 58, thoroughly chilled
1/2 cup (125 ml) unbleached all-purpose flour
1 teaspoon (5 ml) salt
1/4 teaspoon (1 ml) freshly ground white pepper
4 eggs, beaten
1 cup (250 ml) fine dry bread crumbs
Peanut oil for deep frying
Noodle Darioles, following

Split the inside curve of each shrimp about three-fourths of the way through to the back. Place, split side down, between sheets of dampened waxed paper and gently pound shrimp until flattened, taking care not to tear them.

Put a rounded 1/2 teaspoon (3 ml) of shellfish butter on the split surface of each shrimp and fold sides together to re-form shrimp. Mix together flour, salt and pepper and dip each shrimp into mixture. Then dip each shrimp into beaten eggs and finally into bread crumbs. Chill shrimp for at least 1 hour.

Pour peanut oil into a pan to a depth of about 3 inches (8 cm). Heat oil to about 375°F (190°C) and fry shrimp until golden brown; remove with a slotted spoon. Drain well on paper toweling and serve immediately with Noodle Darioles.
Makes 6 servings

Noodle Darioles
Darioles are a rather charming and elegant Victorian way of serving side dishes. They are molds shaped much like custard cups or *baba au rhum* molds, with slightly flaring straight sides and flat bottoms. They are available at well-stocked gourmet kitchenware shops.

Noodle dough made with 1-3/4 cups (425 ml)
    flour and 2 eggs, page 28
1/2 cup (125 ml) clarified butter, page 57, melted
2 cups (500 ml) dry bread crumbs
2 tablespoons (30 ml) butter, melted

Make noodle dough according to directions in Master Recipe and cut into noodles as fine as possible. Cook the noodles in boiling salted water until tender. Drain and toss with clarified butter.

Butter the insides of 6 dariole molds and fill with buttered noodles. (If you have too many noodles, reserve some for another use, such as an omelet or casserole.) Set molds in a baking pan with hot water about two-thirds up sides of molds. Bake in a preheated 400°F (210°C) oven for 25 minutes.

While noodle darioles are cooking, toss bread crumbs with melted butter and spread on a baking sheet. Put into the oven with the dariole molds and toast until golden, stirring frequently. Remove from oven and set aside.

When noodle darioles are ready, unmold noodles and sprinkle with toasted bread crumbs. Serve one to each diner with 3 of the stuffed shrimp.
Makes 6 noodle darioles

DEEP-FRIED SHRIMP WITH BUCKWHEAT NOODLES
Soba Tempura (Japan)

A very popular Japanese lunch, snack or light evening meal. The *tempura* can be shrimp or shrimp and a mixture of vegetables, dipped in batter and fried. Eat the *tempura* as soon as possible for the best flavor.

Peanut oil for deep frying
1 pound (500 g) medium shrimp, shelled and deveined with tail intact
1/2 pound (250 g) large fresh mushrooms, thinly sliced
2 green bell peppers, cut into strips
1 recipe *Soba*, page 49
1 large *daikon* (large white radish), finely grated
1 tablespoon (15 ml) grated ginger root

Batter
1 egg yolk
1 cup (250 ml) ice water
1-1/4 cups (300 ml) unbleached all-purpose flour

Dipping Sauce
1 cup (250 ml) *dashi* (see note)
2 tablespoons (30 ml) *mirin* (sweet rice wine) or dry sherry
3 tablespoons (45 ml) Japanese soy sauce
1 teaspoon (5 ml) sugar

To make the batter, put the egg yolk into a large bowl and beat well, adding the ice water gradually. Then add the flour all at once and beat lightly until the flour is moistened, but still quite lumpy.

Heat the peanut oil in a wok or deep skillet until it just barely smokes. Put a drop of batter into the oil to test its readiness; it should brown lightly in 30 seconds. Dip the shrimp in the batter, a few at a time, and drop into the oil. Cook just until lightly golden. Treat the mushrooms and bell peppers in the same way. Drain on paper toweling.

While *tempura* is cooking, heat all of the sauce ingredients in a small saucepan, stirring until sugar is dissolved; keep hot. Cook the noodles as directed in the recipe; drain.

To serve, put equal portions of the noodles in large individual bowls; add some of the grated radish and a little of the ginger and pour on a little of the warm sauce. Top with several pieces of *tempura.*

Naturally, serve tea, and end the meal with fresh fruit.

Makes 6 servings

Note Dashi, Japanese soup stock, can be purchased in instant form at Japanese markets and some supermarkets, or see recipe, page 114.

FRIED RICE NOODLES WITH SEAFOOD
Char Kway Teow (Malaysia)

4 tablespoons (60 ml) peanut oil
3 garlic cloves, minced
2 medium onions, sliced
4 fresh hot red chili peppers, seeded and chopped
1/4 pound (125 g) barbecued pork, thinly sliced
    on the diagonal
1/2 pound (250 g) shrimp, shelled and deveined
1/2 pound (250 g) squid, cleaned and cut into
    rings (see page 105 for cleaning instructions)
1/4 pound (125 g) bean sprouts
1 cup (250 ml) shelled peas
1 recipe Rice Noodles, page 47, cut approximately
    1/4 inch (6 mm) wide
1 tablespoon (15 ml) dark soy sauce
2 tablespoons (30 ml) light soy sauce
2 tablespoons (30 ml) oyster sauce
3 eggs, beaten
4 green onions, chopped

Heat 2 tablespoons (30 ml) of the peanut oil in a wok or deep skillet and stir fry the garlic, onions and chili peppers over moderate heat until they are soft. Add the pork, shrimp and squid and stir fry for 2 to 3 minutes or until seafood is cooked through. Add the bean sprouts and peas and stir fry for 2 minutes. Remove mixture from wok and set aside.

Heat remaining oil in the wok, and when quite hot, add the rice noodles. Stir fry gently until heated through. Add the dark and light soy sauces and the oyster sauce and toss well to blend. Pour in the eggs and stir constantly until eggs set. Return the seafood mixture to the pan, toss well and serve, garnished with green onions.
Makes 6 servings

SEAFOOD WITH NOODLES AND VEGETABLES
Yosenabe (Japan)

2 quarts (2 L) *dashi* (see note, page 109)
1/4 pound (125 g) bean thread noodles, soaked
    in hot water to cover 10 minutes and drained
1 tablespoon (15 ml) Japanese soy sauce
Small piece *kombu* (dried kelp)
3/4 pound (375 g) fish fillets, such as red snapper,
    sea bass or cod, cut into 1-inch (3 cm) pieces
6 clams in the shell, scrubbed
12 medium shrimp, shelled and deveined
2 squares *tofu* (Japanese fresh bean curd cakes),
    cubed
1/4 pound (125 g) spinach, trimmed
Small wedge Napa cabbage, cut into 1-inch (3 cm)
    pieces
6 fresh mushrooms, sliced
6 green onions, cut into 1-inch (3 cm) lengths
Dipping Sauce, page 109

Combine *dashi* and noodles in a saucepan and bring to a boil. Reduce heat and simmer gently for 3 to 5 minutes. Add the soy sauce and *kombu* and simmer for 3 minutes. Then add the fish, clams, shrimp, *tofu*, spinach, cabbage, mushrooms and green onions and simmer for 5 minutes, or until clams open and other ingredients are cooked.

    Ladle into serving bowls, with each diner receiving a sample of all of the ingredients. Serve the sauce on the side.
Makes 6 servings

PASTA-TUNA MOLD
(United States)

3 cups (375 ml) cold cooked *gemelli, mafalde,*
    lasagnette or any preferred *pasta* form
1 can (6-1/2 ounces or 184 g) tuna fish, drained
    and flaked
2 tablespoons (30 ml) chopped fresh parsley
1/2 teaspoon (2 ml) crumbled dried marjoram or
    thyme
1/2 cup (125 ml) Mayonnaise, page 58
2 tablespoons (30 ml) fresh lemon juice
1/2 cup (125 ml) commercial sour cream
Salt and freshly ground black pepper to taste
1/3 cup (75 ml) diced canned pimiento (optional), or
1 teaspoon (5 ml) red caviar (optional)

Combine *pasta,* tuna fish, parsley and marjoram and toss well. Combine all remaining ingredients, stir to blend well and then combine the two mixtures and mix thoroughly. Pack the mixture into a chilled 1-1/2-quart (1.5 L) mold or round-bottomed bowl. Double a towel and put on a firm surface. Holding mold firmly, carefully bounce down on towel several times to eliminate air holes in the salad. Chill thoroughly and unmold to serve.
Makes 6 servings

Variations Chopped hard-cooked eggs, tomato wedges and black olives are often added as garnish with sprigs of fresh herbs.

PASTA WITH POULTRY

BABA'S CHICKEN NOODLE SOUP
(Jewish Ashkenazic)

An old and famous favorite, sometimes dubbed "Jewish penicillin," and considered a panacea against all ailments. Cure-all or not, it is delicious.

1 whole boiling chicken, with fat intact in cavity
1 medium onion, stuck with 3 cloves
3 celery stalks with leaves
2 small carrots, scraped
4 parsley sprigs
1 small parsley root (optional)
1/8 teaspoon (scant 1 ml) crumbled dried
    thyme (optional)
6 peppercorns
1/8 teaspoon (scant 1 ml) powdered saffron
Salt and freshly ground black pepper to taste
2 tablespoons (30 ml) finely chopped fresh parsley
1/4 pound (125 g) fine egg noodles

Put the chicken in a large, heavy kettle with water to cover. Bring slowly to a boil over moderate heat. Skim off any froth that rises to the surface. Reduce heat until water barely simmers, then add the onion, celery, carrots, parsley sprigs, parsley root, thyme, peppercorns and saffron. Put lid on askew and simmer gently for at least 2-1/2 hours, adding boiling water if needed to keep chicken covered. Remove chicken and set aside to cool. Strain the stock and discard vegetables; return stock to kettle. Bone and skin chicken and dice or shred chicken meat; reserve some of the chicken meat to return to the soup and set remainder aside for another use. Add salt and pepper, parsley, chicken meat and egg noodles to the stock. Simmer until noodles are tender, then serve with freshly baked egg bread *(challah)*.
Makes 6 servings

NOODLE SOUP
WITH CHICKEN AND MUSHROOMS
Nabeyaki Udon (Japan)

Dashi
2 quarts (2 L) water
3-inch (8 cm) piece *kombu* (dried kelp), well rinsed
3 tablespoons (45 ml) *katsuobushi* (dried bonita
     flakes)

1 recipe *Udon*, page 48
1/3 cup (75 ml) Japanese soy sauce
1/3 cup (75 ml) *mirin* (sweet rice wine) or
     dry sherry
9 *shiitake* (dried mushrooms), soaked in warm
     water to cover 30 minutes, drained and
     thinly sliced
1-1/2 chicken breasts, boned and thinly sliced
1/4 pound (125 g) *kamaboko* (fish cakes),
     sliced
4 green onions, thinly sliced on the diagonal
Watercress leaves
Matchstick-cut *daikon* (large white radish)

To prepare the *dashi,* bring the water to a boil in a
large saucepan. Add the *kombu* and boil for 3
minutes. Remove *kombu* and add *katsuobushi.*
Bring back to boil and remove from heat. Let stand
until *katsuobushi* settles to the bottom, then strain
and reserve.

Drop the noodles into boiling water, stirring
to separate. When water returns to the boil, add
about a cupful (250 ml) of cold water. Let water
come to the boil again and cook until noodles are
just tender; drain well and set aside.

Bring the *dashi* to the boil and add the soy
sauce and *mirin.* Cover and simmer 10 minutes.
Taste and adjust with more soy sauce or *mirin.*
Add *shiitake* and chicken and let simmer for 8
minutes. Add noodles and heat through. Place
kamaboko, green onions, watercress leaves and
daikon on top, cover and heat gently for a minute
or 2. Serve immediately.
Makes 6 servings

Note Tempura shrimp are usually set on top of
this soup with the *kamaboko.* The shrimp, though
time-consuming to prepare, make a very good addition. You may also poach an egg in the broth.

CHICKEN AND RICE NOODLE SOUP
Pho Ga (Vietnam)

I ate this soup at the home of friends, and was so
delighted with it, I begged the recipe. The one they
gave me was in that delightful "handfuls-and-
pinches-of" method, so it took a good deal of
experimentation to get the recipe on paper. When I
thought I finally had it, I found a recipe for the
same soup in *Craig Claiborne's Favorites.* The following is a combination of his and my own.

1 large fryer chicken (about 4 pounds or 2 kg)
Large handful fresh mint leaves
Large handful fresh basil leaves
Moderate handful fresh coriander leaves
1/2 pound (250 g) bean sprouts
1 small cucumber, peeled
1 small red onion, thinly sliced
1 tablespoon (15 ml) red wine vinegar
2 limes, each cut into 6 wedges
3 green onions, chopped
2 long fresh hot chili peppers, thinly sliced
1 pound (500 g) dried rice noodles (Malaysian
    or Thai if possible; about 1/4 inch or 6 mm
    wide)
6 eggs

Nuoc Mam Sauce
1 cup (250 ml) Oriental fish sauce
1 tablespoon (15 ml) minced ginger root
3 garlic cloves, finely chopped
1 small fresh hot chili pepper, seeded, if
    desired, and chopped
3 tablespoons (45 ml) fresh lemon juice
2 tablespoons (30 ml) sugar
1 teaspoon (5 ml) finely chopped fresh coriander
1/3 cup (75 ml) water

Put the chicken in a kettle with water to cover. Bring slowly to a boil, lower heat, cover and simmer about 15 minutes. Remove from heat and let chicken stand in broth for 30 minutes.

While the chicken is standing in the broth, rinse the mint, basil and coriander leaves and pat dry. Place each herb in a separate bowl. (You may shred the leaves, if desired.) Pour boiling water over the bean sprouts, drain immediately and rinse under cold water, then drain again; place in a bowl. Cut the cucumber in thin slices and then into thin strips; put into a bowl. Put the red onion in a bowl and pour over the vinegar. Put lime wedges, green onions and chili peppers each in a separate bowl.

To make the *nuoc mam* sauce, combine all ingredients in a bowl and mix together well.

Skin and bone the chicken and shred the meat. Remove any excess fat from the broth and pour about 1 tablespoon (15 ml) of the broth over the chicken meat; reserve the broth.

Put rice noodles in a very large bowl and pour on boiling water to cover. Let stand 5 minutes, drain off water and discard it. Repeat until noodles are tender. (The number of times you will need to do this will depend on the noodles you are using; check for tenderness after every dousing with boiling water.)

Bring the broth to a boil. Arrange all the bowls of ingredients in the center of the table. Heat the chicken meat *very gently* in a medium-size saucepan. Divide the drained noodles equally among 6 large soup bowls. Cover with equal amounts of chicken and ladle on the hot broth. Push the chicken to one side and break an egg into the other side. (The eggs will remain fairly raw; if you prefer, you may pre-poach them.) Serve immediately and invite each diner to help himself to the other ingredients according to his taste.
Makes 6 servings

CHICKEN AND RICE *VERMICELLI* SOUP
Soto Ajam (Indonesia)

This dish is often served as part of the array of dishes for a *rijsstaefel*.

1 large whole boiling chicken (4 to 6 pounds or
　　2 to 3 kg)
1-inch (3 cm) piece ginger root
1 teaspoon (5 ml) ground turmeric
3 garlic cloves
1 medium onion, coarsely chopped
Pinch of salt
2 tablespoons (30 ml) peanut oil
2 ounces (56 g) rice *vermicelli*, soaked to soften
　　in warm water 10 minutes and drained
12 green onions, finely minced

Put chicken in a large kettle and add water to cover. Bring to a slow boil over moderate heat and skim any froth that forms on the surface. Reduce heat so water is barely simmering, cover and cook just until chicken is tender; do not overcook. Remove chicken from kettle, drain well and set aside. Raise heat under cooking liquid and cook until reduced to about half the volume. When chicken is cool enough to handle, bone it completely, dropping the bones back into the stock as they become bare; cut the chicken into good-sized chunks.

In a mortar and pestle (or blender or food processor) pound together the ginger, turmeric, garlic, onion and salt to a paste. Heat the peanut oil in a small skillet and quickly fry the paste, stirring constantly, for 2 to 3 minutes. Remove to a bowl. When cooking liquid is reduced, strain it and put it in a large saucepan. Add the chicken pieces to the saucepan and then stir in the seasoning paste. Bring to a boil, reduce heat and simmer, uncovered, for 10 minutes. Raise the heat, add the *vermicelli* and boil rapidly for 5 minutes. Taste to correct seasoning; it may require more salt. Sprinkle with green onions, cook 5 minutes longer and serve with rice.

Makes 4 servings

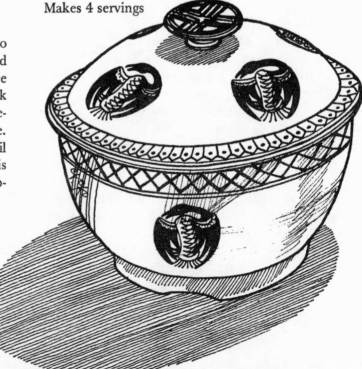

BUCKWHEAT NOODLES WITH CHICKEN GIBLETS
Bigoli con Rovinazzi (Veneto)

Bigoli are specialties of the Veneto area and are rarely seen elsewhere. The dough is made with buckwheat flour and eggs in the proportion of one egg to one cup (250 ml) flour, and is then pressed through a special *bigoli* hand press. If unavailable, use factory-made buckwheat *spaghetti* or noodles, available in health food stores.

1/4 pound (125 g) chicken livers
1/4 pound (125 g) chicken gizzards and hearts
1/4 pound (125 g) unsalted butter
2 to 3 fresh sage leaves
Chicken stock
Salt to taste
1 pound (500 g) *bigoli*
1/2 cup (125 ml) freshly grated Parmesan cheese

Chop the livers and gizzards and hearts very finely, keeping them separate. In a large heavy skillet melt the butter, add the sage leaves and cook gently for a few minutes. Add the gizzards and hearts and cook over very low heat about 30 minutes, adding a little chicken stock if necessary to prevent burning. Add the chicken livers and cook no more than 6 to 8 minutes; season with salt to taste.

While the sauce is cooking, cook the *bigoli* in boiling salted water until tender. Drain and add to the skillet with the sauce. Toss quickly until all the noodles are well coated. Put into a warmed serving bowl, sprinkle with Parmesan cheese and serve immediately.
Makes 4 to 6 servings

FETTUCCINE WITH CHICKEN LIVER SAUCE
Fettuccine con Fegato di Pollo (Italy)

A traditional Italian dish; the sauce is also served with *gnocchi*. If you have avoided eating liver, just try this and you'll be sold.

Noodle dough made with 1-3/4 cups (425 ml)
    flour and 2 eggs, page 28
1 pound (500 g) chicken livers
Salt and freshly ground black pepper to taste
4 tablespoons (60 ml) unsalted butter
1/4 cup (75 ml) Marsala
1 fresh sage leaf, shredded
1/2 cup (125 ml) heavy cream
2 tablespoons (30 ml) minced fresh Italian parsley

Make noodle dough according to directions in Master Recipe and cut into noodles approximately 1/4 inch (6 mm) wide; set aside.

Cut each chicken liver into 4 pieces and sprinkle with salt and pepper. In a large skillet melt the butter, and when the foam subsides, sauté chicken livers just until raw redness disappears. Pour on the Marsala, then raise heat to medium-high and reduce the liquid by cooking 3 to 4 minutes. Lower heat and add sage; keep warm over very low heat.

Cook the noodles in boiling salted water until tender. Drain and put into a warmed serving bowl; keep warm.

Stir the cream into the chicken livers and bring to a boil. Reduce heat immediately and simmer for no more than 1 to 2 minutes. Pour over noodles and garnish with parsley.
Makes 4 to 6 servings

CHICKEN AND VEGETABLES WITH FRIED NOODLES
Kaukswe Kyaw (Burma)

1 pound (500 g) dried Oriental egg noodles
1/2 cup (125 ml) peanut oil
4 medium onions, finely chopped
6 garlic cloves, finely chopped
1 whole chicken breast, boned, skinned and
    thinly sliced
4 or 5 chicken livers, thinly sliced
2 tablespoons (30 ml) soy sauce
1 small head Napa cabbage, shredded
1 celery stalk with leaves, shredded
6 to 8 dried Chinese black mushrooms, soaked in
    warm water to soften, drained and thinly
    sliced
6 to 8 green onions, shredded
3 eggs, beaten
Salt and freshly ground black pepper
Chopped fresh coriander

Put the noodles in warm water to cover about 10 minutes; drain. Cook the noodles in boiling water until tender. Drain and toss gently with about 2 tablespoons (30 ml) of the peanut oil; set aside and keep warm.

Heat 4 tablespoons (60 ml) of the peanut oil in a wok or skillet and stir fry the onions and garlic until translucent. Add chicken and liver and stir fry until no longer pink. Stir in soy sauce, cover and simmer over low heat until meat is tender. Raise heat and add cabbage, celery, mushrooms and green onions. Stir fry until vegetables are just cooked, about 2 minutes. Remove from pan and set aside.

Heat remaining oil in pan and stir fry noodles for a few minutes, turning them carefully so as not to break them. Remove from pan and place on a warmed serving platter. Quickly scramble eggs in oil remaining in pan. Season to taste with salt and pepper.

Cover the noodles with the meat and vegetable mixture and top with the eggs. Garnish with coriander and serve immediately.
Makes 4 to 6 servings

CHICKEN AND VEGETABLE CASSEROLE
Jollof (Liberia)

4 tablespoons (60 ml) peanut oil
3-pound (1.5 kg) fryer chicken, cut into
    serving pieces
1/2 pound (250 g) cooked ham, chopped
2 medium onions, chopped
1/2 teaspoon (3 ml) ground allspice
1/4 teaspoon (1 ml) ground cumin
Salt and freshly ground black pepper to taste
1/2 cup (125 ml) long-grain rice
6 ripe tomatoes, peeled and chopped
1 can (6 ounce or 171 g) tomato paste
3 cups (750 ml) chicken stock
1/2 pound (250 g) green beans, cut into
    1-1/2-inch (4 cm) lengths
2 cups (500 ml) small elbow macaroni, cooked
6 tablespoons (90 ml) minced fresh coriander

In a heavy, 4-quart (4 L) flameproof casserole heat the peanut oil, then add the chicken pieces and brown them on all sides over medium heat. Stir in the ham, onions, allspice, cumin and salt and pepper and cook over moderate heat until onions are translucent, about 5 minutes. Stir in the rice and mix well, then mix in the tomatoes, tomato paste and the chicken stock. Cover and simmer gently for about 15 minutes. Arrange the green beans in a layer on top, cover and cook 15 minutes longer.

Arrange the macaroni on top, like a crust, and check that there is enough liquid on the bottom of the pan to prevent burning by tilting the pan; add additional liquid if necessary. Sprinkle top with coriander, cover and simmer gently until rice is completely cooked and *pasta* is heated through, about 10 minutes. Serve from the casserole.
Makes 4 to 6 servings

TURKEY TETRAZZINI
Tacchina Tetrazzini (Italo-American)

This dish was created at the turn of the century in Chicago by an opera lover/chef to honor the great diva. It has probably been seen on more buffet tables than any other dish—or so it would seem. Oddly enough, I have had a dish much like it in Italy, served by Italians. Turkey was, until fairly recently, a great extravagance and fairly rare in Italy; now it is called "the calf with two legs," and is quite commonplace and a welcome economy.

3/4 pound (375 g) *spaghetti*
1/4 pound (125 g) butter
6 green onions, finely chopped
Salt and freshly ground black pepper to taste
1/2 pound (250 g) fresh mushrooms, sliced
4 cups (1 L) cubed cooked turkey
3 tablespoons (45 ml) unbleached all-purpose flour
2 cups (500 ml) turkey or chicken stock
1/2 cup (125 ml) heavy cream

2 egg yolks, beaten
1/4 cup (75 ml) freshly grated Parmesan cheese
1/4 cup (75 ml) dry bread crumbs
1/2 cup (125 ml) finely minced fresh parsley

Cook the *spaghetti* in boiling salted water until tender. Drain and put into a large bowl. Toss with 2 tablespoons (30 ml) of the butter and set aside.

In a skillet melt 3 tablespoons (45 ml) of the butter and sauté the green onions until soft and translucent. Add salt, pepper and mushrooms and cook over moderately high heat until all the mushroom liquid has evaporated, about 3 to 4 minutes. Remove to a large bowl and stir in the cubed turkey; set aside.

In a saucepan melt remaining butter and stir in the flour all at once. Continue stirring and cooking for about 3 minutes, but do not brown. Gradually add the stock, stirring constantly, and cook until thickened. Simmer very gently for 4 to 5 minutes, then stir in salt and pepper to taste and remove from heat. Beat together the cream and egg yolks and whisk in a little of the hot sauce. Add egg mixture to the sauce, stirring constantly, and place over low heat. Cook for 2 to 3 minutes, or until smooth and hot. Taste to correct seasoning and stir sauce into turkey-mushroom mixture.

Put the *spaghetti* into a large buttered casserole. Make a well in the center and pour in the turkey mixture. Sprinkle Parmesan cheese and bread crumbs on top and then the parsley. Bake in a preheated 350°F (170°C) oven for about 30 minutes, or until bubbly and nicely browned. Serve immediately.
Makes 6 servings

ARISTOCRATS' STUFFED CAPON
Cappone all' Aristocratica (Italy)

6- to 7-pound (3 to 3.5 kg) capon
1 medium onion
1 medium carrot
1 teaspoon (5 ml) salt
1 recipe *Mornay* Sauce, page 56
1/2 pound (250 g) small elbow macaroni
3 tablespoons (45 ml) freshly grated Parmesan
    cheese

Put the capon in a very large kettle with the onion, carrot, salt and water to cover. Bring to a boil, reduce heat to a low simmer, cover and cook 1-1/2 to 2 hours, or until tender. Remove capon from kettle carefully to prevent tearing the skin, and set aside until cool enough to handle.

While the capon is cooking, prepare the *Mornay* Sauce and set aside. Cook the macaroni in boiling salted water until tender, drain and put in a bowl with half the *Mornay* Sauce, mixing thoroughly. Lightly stuff the capon with the macaroni and sew or skewer closed. Butter a baking dish generously and lay the capon in it. Spoon remaining sauce over it and sprinkle with Parmesan cheese. Bake uncovered in a preheated 375°F (190°C) oven until nicely browned and heated through, about 30 minutes.
Makes 6 servings

LIVER AND NOODLE STUFFING FOR TURKEY OR GOOSE
(Hungarian American)

Noodle dough made with 1-3/4 cups (425 ml)
    flour and 2 eggs, page 28
1/4 pound (125 g) unsalted butter
1 medium onion, chopped
Liver from bird to be stuffed, diced
1/2 pound (250 g) *pâté de foie gras* or unsmoked
    fine quality liverwurst, mashed
1 tablespoon (15 ml) minced fresh parsley
Salt and freshly ground black pepper to taste
1 tablespoon (15 ml) Hungarian paprika
1/2 teaspoon (3 ml) minced fresh sage

Make noodle dough according to directions in Master Recipe and cut into noodles approximately 1/4 to 1/2 inch (6 mm to 12 mm) wide. Cook in boiling salted water until tender. Drain and set aside; keep warm.

In a small skillet melt the butter and sauté onion until translucent; do not let it brown. Add liver and *pâté* and sauté for about 5 minutes or until all rawness is gone. Pour over noodles, including any fat remaining in the skillet. Add parsley, salt and pepper, paprika and sage and toss well with 2 forks to distribute evenly.
Makes approximately 8 cups (2 L); enough to
stuff neck and body cavity of a
10- to 12-pound (5 to 6 kg) bird

CHICKEN SALAD WITH COCKSCOMB *PASTA*
Insalata di Pollo con Creste di Gallo (Italy)

Creste di gallo, or cockscomb *pasta,* is a very pretty addition to a salad—and a very substantial addition as well. The curls and crevasses will embrace bits of the salad, so every bite will give a taste of the chicken, dressing and vegetables—a combination of textures: firm and chewy, soft, crisp, oily and altogether delicious.

Dressing
1 teaspoon (5 ml) dry mustard
1/2 teaspoon (3 ml) salt
2 teaspoons (10 ml) red wine vinegar
6 tablespoons (90 ml) olive oil

1 pound (500 g) *creste di gallo,* cooked and chilled
1/4 pound (125 g) Gruyère, Emmental, Monterey Jack or Jarlsberg cheese, finely diced
1/2 cup (125 ml) Mediterranean-type black olives, pitted and diced
2 celery stalks with leaves, diced
1 medium green bell pepper, diced
1 chicken breast, cooked, boned, skinned and diced
Romaine lettuce leaves
2 slices bacon, fried crisp, drained and crumbled

To make the dressing, put the mustard, salt and vinegar in the bottom of a large salad bowl and mix with a wooden fork or spoon. Add the olive oil, stirring vigorously until well blended.

Add the *pasta* to the dressing and toss well. Then add cheese, olives, celery, bell pepper and chicken, mix thoroughly and taste and correct seasoning. Slip the Romaine lettuce leaves down under the edges of the salad so it is surrounded by them. Sprinkle on the bacon and serve.
Makes 4 to 6 main dish servings

PAPRIKA CHICKEN WITH DUMPLINGS
Paprikas Csirke Nockerl (Hungary)

1 tablespoon (15 ml) rendered chicken fat or butter
1 medium onion, chopped
1 garlic clove, minced
3-1/2 pound (1.5 kg) fryer chicken, cut into serving pieces
1 cup (250 ml) water
1 teaspoon (5 ml) salt
1 tablespoon (15 ml) Hungarian paprika
1/2 recipe *Nockerl,* page 153, cooked and drained, omitting butter and cheese topping

In a large heavy skillet heat the chicken fat and sauté the onion and garlic until just beginning to brown. Add the chicken pieces and brown them on all sides over high heat. Reduce heat and cook about 15 minutes. Add the water, salt and paprika and mix in well. Cover pan and simmer very gently for about 45 minutes, adding additional water for gravy, if necessary. Remove chicken and place on a warmed serving platter. Mix *nockerl* with gravy remaining in skillet and put into a warmed serving bowl. Serve immediately.
Makes 4 to 6 servings

PASTA WITH LAMB AND PORK

LAMB, FRUIT AND VEGETABLE SOUP WITH *VERMICELLI*
Cherbah (Tunisia)

1-1/2 pounds (750 g) boneless lean lamb, in 1 piece
2 lamb bones, cracked
2 quarts (2 L) water
2 teaspoons (10 ml) salt
1 teaspoon (5 ml) freshly ground black pepper
Pinch of cayenne pepper
1/4 pound (125 g) dried apricots
4 tablespoons (60 ml) olive oil
4 onions, coarsely chopped
3 green bell peppers, coarsely chopped
2 tablespoons (30 ml) chopped fresh mint leaves
4 ripe tomatoes, peeled and chopped
1/4 pound (125 g) large *vermicelli,* broken into
    short lengths
1 tablespoon (15 ml) fresh lemon juice
Chopped fresh parsley and mint leaves for garnish

In a large heavy soup kettle combine the meat, bones, water, salt, black pepper and cayenne pepper. Bring to a boil and skim off any froth that forms on the surface. Add the apricots, reduce heat, cover and simmer for at least 1-1/2 hours.

In a large skillet heat the olive oil and sauté the onions, bell pepper and mint until onions are translucent. Add to the soup with the tomatoes and continue simmering another hour. Remove meat and bones and discard latter. Cut meat into bite-sized pieces and return to soup. Taste to correct seasoning, if necessary; it should be slightly sweet, slightly peppery and have sufficient salt. Add the *vermicelli* and cook for about 5 minutes or until tender. Pour into a warmed soup tureen, stir in lemon juice and garnish with the parsley and mint.

Makes 4 to 6 servings

LAMB, LEEK AND CHICKPEA SOUP
WITH *ORECCHIETTE*
(Malta)

4 pounds (2 kg) breast of lamb or lamb shoulder,
    cut into serving pieces
4 leeks
1 large onion, chopped
3 celery stalks with leaves, chopped
2 medium carrots, sliced
2 medium ripe tomatoes, peeled and chopped
4 quarts (4 L) water
1 pound (500 g) dried chickpeas, soaked overnight
    in water to cover and drained
Salt and freshly ground black pepper to taste
1/2 cup (125 ml) chopped fresh parsley
2 teaspoons (10 ml) minced fresh oregano
1 small fresh sage leaf, shredded
1 recipe *Orecchiete,* page 43, cooked
Minced fresh parsley for garnish

In an 8-quart (8 L) soup kettle cook the meat over moderate heat, turning often, until nicely browned. (The fat on the meat will be sufficient for browning.) Meanwhile, wash the leeks under cold running water and cut them into 1/2-inch (12 mm) slices, including green tops. Soak in cold water to cover 5 minutes, drain and add to meat in kettle with onion and celery. Cook until vegetables are lightly golden. Stir in the carrots and tomatoes and cook for 5 minutes, stirring lightly, then pour on the water. Raise heat and bring to a boil; skim off any froth that forms on the surface. Add the drained chickpeas, bring back to the boil and skim again until surface is clear. Reduce heat, cover and simmer gently for 1 hour. Add salt, pepper and herbs and continue cooking gently for 2 to 3 hours longer. The cooking time will depend on the age of the lamb; if young, less cooking is needed. The meat should be almost falling off the bones when done. Remove meat from kettle and cut meat off bones. Shred or dice meat and return it to the kettle. Add *orecchiette* and heat through. Garnish with minced parsley and serve with crisp, crusty bread and a mixed greens salad.
Makes 12 servings

LAMB, BEEF AND MACARONI PIE
Pastitsio (Greece)

I was first introduced to a version of this delightful dish by the late artist, Varda.

1 pound (500 g) macaroni
2 tablespoons (30 ml) butter
1/3 cup (75 ml) freshly grated Parmesan cheese
Ground cinnamon

Meat Sauce
2 tablespoons (30 ml) butter
2 tablespoons (30 ml) olive oil
2 large onions, chopped
3 garlic cloves, mashed
1/2 pound (250 g) ground lamb
1/2 pound (250 g) ground beef
3 large ripe tomatoes, peeled, seeded and chopped
Pinch of crumbled dried oregano
1/4 teaspoon (2 ml) ground cinnamon
1/4 teaspoon (2 ml) freshly grated nutmeg
1/4 teaspoon (2 ml) ground cloves
3 eggs, lightly beaten
1/3 cup (75 ml) freshly grated Parmesan cheese

White Cheese Sauce
2 tablespoons (30 ml) butter
2 tablespoons (30 ml) unbleached all-purpose flour
3 cups (750 ml) milk, heated
Salt and freshly ground white pepper
2 eggs, lightly beaten
1 cup (250 ml) crumbled feta cheese

Cook macaroni in boiling salted water until tender. Drain and put into a buttered shallow baking dish; set aside.

To make the meat sauce, heat the butter and oil in a large skillet and sauté the onions, garlic, lamb and beef, breaking up meat with a fork and cooking until browned. Blend in the tomatoes and seasonings. Cook over medium heat for 20 minutes, then remove from heat and let cool slightly. Stir in the eggs and cheese; set aside.

To make the cheese sauce, melt the butter in a heavy saucepan and add the flour. Cook over moderate heat, stirring constantly, until smooth; do not let it brown. Gradually blend in the milk, salt and pepper and cook, stirring constantly, until thickened. Beat a little of the hot sauce into the eggs and return mixture to saucepan, stirring constantly. Blend in the feta cheese.

Cover macaroni with meat sauce and then with cheese sauce. Dot with butter and sprinkle with Parmesan cheese and cinnamon. Bake in a preheated 350°F (170°C) oven until the sauce sets, about 45 minutes. Serve, cut into squares.
Makes 8 servings

Variation Peel and thinly slice a large eggplant. Sprinkle slices with olive oil and broil on both sides until tender. Place the slices on top of the meat sauce layer and cover with the cheese sauce. Bake as directed above.

LAMB WITH PEPPER SAUCE
Ragù di Agnello con Peperoni (Abruzzi, Italy)

This is the traditional sauce used with *tondarelli alla chitarra* in the Abruzzi province of Italy. A curiously subtle sauce, it is also very satisfying with any fine noodle or small smooth *pasta* shape.

4 tablespoons (60 ml) olive oil
2 garlic cloves, chopped
2 bay leaves
3/4 pound (375 g) boneless lamb, cut into small dice
1/2 cup (125 ml) dry white wine
2 large ripe tomatoes, peeled and chopped
2 large green bell peppers, cut into julienne
Salt and freshly ground black pepper to taste
1 recipe *Tondarelli alla Chitarra*, page 44

In a small saucepan heat the olive oil over moderate heat and add the garlic and bay leaves. Sauté for 3 minutes, then add the lamb and brown thoroughly, stirring often. After about 10 minutes, add the wine and raise the heat. Cook until wine is reduced by half and add the tomatoes and bell peppers. Stir well, cook for about 5 minutes, then stir in salt and pepper. Reduce heat to lowest point, cover and simmer for about 2 hours. If the sauce seems dry, add a little water.

Cook the noodles in boiling salted water until tender. Drain and place on a warmed serving platter. Pour sauce over and serve.
Makes 6 servings

MACARONI AND LAMB PIE
Macaron Reyenado (Turkey)

My great friend, Edouard Roditi, prides himself on his Sephardic ancestry and spends much time in Turkey, Greece and the other countries of the Near East. The following dish is one I remember Edouard describing many years ago.

1 pound (500 g) small elbow macaroni
2 tablespoons (30 ml) olive oil
1 pound (500 g) finely ground lean lamb
1 large onion, coarsely chopped
1/2 cup (125 ml) minced fresh parsley
1 hard-cooked egg, sieved
1 teaspoon (5 ml) salt
1/2 teaspoon (3 ml) freshly ground black pepper
1 hard-cooked egg, sieved
5 raw eggs
1/2 teaspoon (3 ml) ground allspice

Cook the macaroni in boiling salted water until tender. Drain and set aside.

In a large skillet heat the olive oil and sauté the lamb, onion and parsley until meat is lightly browned. Add the hard-cooked egg, salt and pepper and stir in well. Beat together 2 of the raw eggs and the allspice and stir into meat mixture. Beat remaining 3 raw eggs and mix with the macaroni. Grease a baking dish and spread half of the macaroni mixture on the bottom. Cover with the meat mixture and top with remaining macaroni. Bake in a preheated 350°F (170°C) oven for 30 minutes or until top is golden. If a crisp top is desired, bake 5 to 10 minutes longer.
Makes 6 servings

LAMB BALLS ON FRESH NOODLES
Ktsitsos (Israel)

Ktsitsos means "chopped" in Hebrew.

Noodle dough made with 1-3/4 cups (425 ml) flour
    and 2 eggs, page 28
2 pounds (1 kg) ground lean lamb or beef
2 medium potatoes, peeled, boiled until tender
    and mashed
1 medium zucchini, grated
2 celery stalks with leaves, finely chopped
2 tablespoons (30 ml) unbleached all-purpose flour
1/2 teaspoon (3 ml) salt
1/4 teaspoon (1 ml) freshly ground black pepper
3 tablespoons (45 ml) olive oil
Dry bread crumbs or matzo meal
3 eggs, lightly beaten
2 cups (500 ml) beef stock, heated

Make noodle dough according to directions in Master Recipe and cut into noodles approximately 1/4 inch (6 mm) wide; set aside.

Mix together lamb, potatoes, zucchini, celery, flour, salt, pepper and 1 tablespoon (15 ml) of the olive oil. Wet your hands and form the mixture into meatballs the size of small eggs. Heat the remaining olive oil in a skillet. Dip the meatballs first in bread crumbs to coat lightly and then in egg. Put in the skillet and fry gently, turning to brown on all sides. When the meatballs are browned, pour on the beef stock, cover and cook over low heat for 15 minutes (less if rare meatballs are preferred).

While the meatballs are cooking, cook the noodles in boiling salted water until tender. Drain and arrange on a warmed large serving platter. Pour on the meatballs and broth and serve immediately. Makes 6 servings

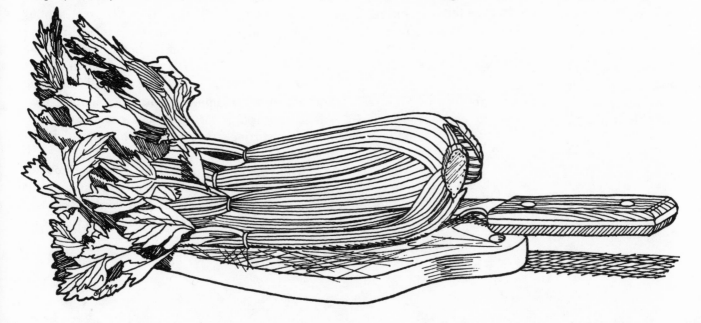

PORK AND BEAN THREAD NOODLE SOUP
Khao Poun (Cambodia)

5 cups (1.25 L) chicken stock
1/2 teaspoon (2 ml) salt
1/4 pound (125 g) bean thread noodles, soaked
    in warm water to soften 10 minutes, then
    cut into 6-inch (15 cm) lengths
1/2 pound (250 g) ground pork butt
2 tablespoons (30 ml) finely minced water
    chestnuts
1/2 teaspoon (3 ml) cornstarch
1 teaspoon (5 ml) light soy sauce
2 teaspoons (10 ml) Oriental fish sauce
1/4 cup (50 ml) finely shredded green onions
Chopped fresh coriander

Bring the chicken stock to a boil and add the salt
and noodles. Boil for 15 minutes.

    While the stock is boiling combine the pork,
water chestnuts, cornstarch, soy sauce and fish
sauce in a bowl and mix together thoroughly.
Shape into small balls, about the size of a hazelnut,
and drop into the boiling soup. Boil for 10 minutes, but do not stir. Ladle into deep bowls and
sprinkle with green onions and coriander. Serve
immediately.
Makes 4 to 6 servings

DRUNKARD'S MACARONI
Maccheroni all' Ubriaca (Milan)

Noodle dough made with 1-3/4 cups (425 ml) flour
    and 2 eggs, page 28
3 tablespoons (45 ml) olive oil
1/2 pound (250 g) mild Italian sausage, skinned
1-1/2 cups (375 ml) half-and-half (light cream)
2 large ripe tomatoes, peeled, seeded and chopped
Pinch of salt
Freshly ground black pepper
6 tablespoons (90 ml) cognac or brandy
2 tablespoons (30 ml) freshly grated Parmesan or
    Romano cheese

Make noodle dough according to directions in Master Recipe and cut into noodles approximately 5/8
inch (12 mm) wide with a fluted pastry cutter; set
noodles aside.

    In a large skillet heat 1-1/2 tablespoons
(22 ml) of the oil and brown the sausage, breaking
it up well with a fork and stirring often. Add the
half-and-half and stir well. Add the tomatoes, salt
and several grinds of pepper and stir well. Continue
cooking about 10 minutes to reduce liquids, then
stir in cognac. Raise heat and cook briskly 10
minutes, stirring frequently, until cognac is reduced by half.

    While the sauce is cooking, cook the noodles
in boiling salted water until tender. Drain and put
into a warmed serving bowl. Pour on the sauce and
toss well. Add the Parmesan cheese, toss well again
and serve immediately.
Makes 6 first-course servings

FRIED *VERMICELLI* WITH MIXED MEATS
Mee Krob (Thailand)

A perfect dish for a buffet. Double the recipe and serve with small bowls of condiments, as you do curry: chopped cucumbers, chopped or shredded radishes, chopped roasted peanuts, chopped chili peppers, curry sauce, chopped preserved ginger, crisply fried onions.

Peanut oil
4 garlic cloves, minced
2 medium onions, finely chopped
1 pound (500 g) pork butt, thinly sliced and
    then shredded
14 to 16 dried Chinese black mushrooms, soaked
    to soften, drained and sliced
2 whole chicken breasts, boned, skinned and
    shredded
1 pound (500 g) medium shrimp, shelled, deveined
    and each cut into 2 or 3 pieces
10 to 12 green onions, cut into 2-inch (5 cm)
    lengths
1/2 pound (250 g) green beans or snow peas,
    sliced on the diagonal
1/4 cup (75 ml) soy sauce
1 tablespoon (15 ml) sugar
1/4 cup (75 ml) white vinegar
2 small dried hot red chili peppers, finely crushed
1/2 pound (250 g) rice *vermicelli*
Chopped fresh coriander

Heat 3 tablespoons (45 ml) peanut oil in a wok or skillet and stir fry the garlic and onion for about 3 minutes, or until they just begin to turn golden. Add the pork and mushrooms and stir fry until pork is no longer pink. Add the chicken and shrimp and stir-fry for about 1 minute. Add the green onions and green beans and stir fry for about 1 minute. Mix together the soy sauce, sugar, vinegar and chili peppers and add to the pan. Stir fry for 2 minutes, turn off heat, cover and let stand while the noodles are cooking.

Heat peanut oil to a depth of about 3 inches (8 cm) in a separate wok or a saucepan. Test to see if the oil is hot enough by dropping in a few strands of the rice *vermicelli*. If the noodles puff up immediately to several times their original size, the oil is ready. Drop the noodles by handfuls into the oil. Turn once to cook evenly. They will cook in about 15 to 20 seconds. Lift out with a slotted spoon and drain on paper toweling. When all of the noodles are cooked, toss all but a few of them into the meat mixture. Mix thoroughly but very quickly so that the noodles do not deflate too much. Place on a warmed serving platter and garnish with coriander and reserved noodles.

Makes 6 to 8 servings

The following two recipes were graciously given to me by Madame Cecilia Chiang, proprietor of the incomparable Mandarin restaurants in San Francisco and Beverly Hills, with permission to use them in this book. I wish to express my gratitude to Madame Chiang for allowing me to use them and for being the first to introduce the dramatic dishes of Szechwan and northern China to the United States.

PORK AND SZECHWAN MUSTARD PICKLE WITH NOODLES
Dan Dan Mein (China)

2 tablespoons (30 ml) peanut oil
1/2 pound (250 g) pork butt, thinly sliced and then chopped
1 tablespoon (15 ml) dry sherry
3/4 cup (175 ml) chicken stock
6 dried Chinese black mushrooms, soaked in water to soften, drained and sliced and then finely chopped
1/2 cup (125 ml) finely chopped bamboo shoots
1/2 cup (125 ml) finely chopped Szechwan mustard pickle (see note)
1-1/2 teaspoons (7 ml) finely chopped fresh hot chili pepper
2 tablespoons (30 ml) soy sauce
1 teaspoon (5 ml) sugar
1/2 teaspoon (3 ml) monosodium glutamate or Accent (optional)
1 teaspoon (5 ml) Oriental sesame oil
1 teaspoon (5 ml) salt
1 teaspoon (5 ml) cornstarch, mixed with
1 tablespoon (15 ml) water
1 pound (500 g) fresh Chinese egg noodles
2 cups (500 ml) cold water
1/2 cup (125 ml) crushed roasted peanuts or cashews (optional)

Heat peanut oil in a wok or skillet over high heat. Add the pork and stir fry for 1 to 2 minutes, adding sherry when it starts to brown. Then add chicken stock and cook until pork is no longer pink. Add mushrooms, bamboo shoots, mustard, pickle and chili peppers and stir fry for 1 minute. Add soy sauce, sugar, monosodium glutamate, sesame oil and salt and stir in well. Add cornstarch mixture and cook until pan liquids have thickened. Set aside and keep warm.

Drop the noodles into boiling water. Bring to a second boil and add the cold water. Bring to a third boil, immediately drain noodles and put into a warmed serving bowl. Pour on the sauce and sprinkle with the peanuts. Toss thoroughly and serve immediately.
Makes 4 servings

Note Szechwan mustard pickle is mustard green preserved in brine and covered with ground chili. It is available in cans in Oriental markets.

PORK AND NOODLES WITH *HOISIN* SAUCE
Cha Chiang Mein (China)

1 pound (500 g) pork shoulder or butt
1 tablespoon (15 ml) peanut oil
2 teaspoons (10 ml) dry sherry
3/4 cup (175 ml) chicken stock
2 tablespoons (30 ml) soy sauce
1/4 teaspoon (2 ml) Oriental sesame oil
1 to 2 tablespoons (15 to 30 ml) *hoisin* sauce
    (sweet, spicy bean sauce)
1/2 tablespoon (8 ml) cornstarch, mixed with
2 tablespoons (30 ml) water
1-1/2 pounds (750 g) fresh Chinese egg noodles
1 cup (250 ml) cold water
1 cup (250 ml) shredded cucumber

Thinly slice the pork, then shred it and finally chop it finely. (Do not use a meat grinder.) Heat peanut oil in a wok or skillet and stir fry pork about 2 minutes. Sprinkle with sherry and add chicken stock, soy sauce, sesame oil and *hoisin* sauce. Mix well and add the cornstarch mixture, stirring until pan liquids have thickened; keep warm.

Drop the noodles into boiling water. Bring to a second boil and add the cold water. Bring to a third boil, immediately drain noodles and put into a warmed serving bowl. Pour on the sauce and sprinkle with cucumber. Toss well and serve.
Makes 6 servings

Note A little Oriental chili oil may be added, if desired.

MIXED MEATS AND MACARONI CASSEROLE
Stuffato (Corsica)

1/2 pound (250 g) boneless pork shoulder
1/2 pound (250 g) boneless veal shoulder
1/2 pound (250 g) boneless beef
1/2 cup (125 ml) olive oil
1/2 pound (250 g) bacon, coarsely diced
2 medium onions, sliced
1 garlic clove, minced
2 ripe tomatoes, peeled and chopped
1 quart (1 L) water
1 cup (250 ml) dry red wine
1 teaspoon (5 ml) salt
1/2 teaspoon (3 ml) freshly ground black pepper
Bouquet garni of 2 oregano sprigs, 1 rosemary
    sprig, 1 bay leaf and 2 parsley sprigs
1/2 pound (250 g) small elbow macaroni
1-1/2 cups (375 ml) freshly grated Gruyère cheese

Cut the meats into serving pieces. In a large heavy skillet heat the olive oil and brown the meats and bacon over moderately high heat, turning often. When nicely browned, remove meats with a slotted spoon and transfer to a large heavy saucepan or kettle. Add the onions, garlic, tomatoes, water, wine, salt, pepper and *bouquet garni* to the kettle. Bring to a boil, then reduce heat, cover and simmer until meats are tender, about 2 to 2-1/2 hours.

Cook the macaroni in boiling salted water until tender. Drain and set aside. When the meats are tender, remove from saucepan with a slotted spoon and keep warm. Raise heat under saucepan and reduce liquid to about 2 cups (500 ml) by boiling briskly. Arrange the meats in a large casserole, then cover with the macaroni and finally the cheese. Pour in the concentrated stock and bake in a preheated 350°F (170°C) oven for 20 minutes.
Makes 6 servings

FETTUCCINE, ROMAN STYLE
Fettuccine alla Romana (Rome)

A classic dish, simple and delicious. It must be put together quickly, so the ingredients must be ready at hand. A perfect chafing dish recipe.

Noodle dough made with 1-3/4 cups (425 ml)
    flour and 2 eggs, page 28
1/4 pound (125 g) unsalted butter, softened
1 cup (250 ml) freshly grated Parmesan cheese
1 cup (250 ml) shelled peas, parboiled 2 minutes
    and kept warm
1/4 pound (125 g) prosciutto, finely chopped
1/2 cup (125 ml) heavy cream, warmed
Salt and freshly ground black pepper to taste

Make noodle dough according to directions in Master Recipe and cut into noodles approximately 1/4 inch (6 mm) wide. Cook the noodles in boiling salted water until tender. Drain and put into a warmed serving bowl that already has the butter in it. Toss lightly, then add the cheese, peas, prosciutto and cream and toss well. Sprinkle with salt and pepper and serve immediately.
Makes 4 servings

NOODLES FOR WEDNESDAY
Nouilles pour le Mercredi (France)

Quick, economical and full of nourishment and good flavor, this dish was introduced to me by a French friend with a good-sized family and a thin pocketbook. She figured that on Monday and Tuesday, she could use the weekend leftovers, but by Wednesday they were quite gone, so she often made this inexpensive dish. It may seem to have expensive ingredients, but so little of each is necessary and goes rather far.

Noodle dough made with 1 scant cup (scant
    250 ml) flour and 1 egg, page 28
3 tablespoons (45 ml) margarine or butter
Salt and freshly ground black pepper to taste
Pinch of freshly grated nutmeg
1/4 pound (125 g) boiled ham, coarsely chopped
1-1/2 cups (375 ml) freshly grated Parmesan cheese
1-1/2 cups (375 ml) freshly grated Gruyère cheese
2 whole eggs
4 eggs yolks
1-1/4 cups (325 ml) milk

Make noodle dough according to directions in Master Recipe and cut into noodles approximately 1/4 inch (6 mm) wide. Cook noodles in boiling salted water until tender. Drain well and return to pot. Add 2 tablespoons (30 ml) of the margarine, the salt, pepper, nutmeg, ham and all but a couple spoonfuls of the cheeses. Toss noodles well, coating them with all of the ingredients. In a small bowl mix together the whole eggs, egg yolks and milk and beat until light and foamy. Grease a large casserole with the remaining margarine and sprinkle it with the reserved cheeses. Pour in the noodle mixture and pour egg mixture over top.

Place the casserole in a baking pan with hot water to about halfway up the side of the casserole. Put in a preheated 350°F (170°C) oven for 30 to 35 minutes, or until top sets and is lightly golden. Let stand 3 to 5 minutes before serving.
Makes 6 servings

Variations This dish may also be made with chicken, turkey or fish, such as tuna fish or other cooked or canned fish, in place of the ham. Use 1/2 pound cooked poultry meat or fish or 1 small can tuna fish. Leftover roast meat may also be substituted, in which case some of the gravy from the roast can be used in place of the margarine.

BAKED *LASAGNETTE*
WITH SAUSAGES AND MEATBALLS
Lasagnette con Salsicce e
Polpettine al Forno (Italo-American)

Noodle dough made with 2-3/4 cups (675 ml) flour
    and 3 eggs, page 28
1/2 pound (250 g) hot Italian sausages, skinned
    and cut into 1-inch (3 cm) pieces
1/2 pound (250 g) sweet Italian sausages, skinned
    and cut into 1-inch (3 cm) pieces
1-1/2 cups (375 ml) freshly grated Parmesan or
    Romano cheese
Additional freshly grated Parmesan or Romano
    cheese

Meatballs
1-1/2 pounds (750 g) ground beef (or half beef
    and half pork)
1 cup (250 ml) fresh bread crumbs
2 tablespoons (30 ml) water
2 eggs
3/4 teaspoon (4 ml) salt

1/2 teaspoon (2 ml) freshly ground black pepper
2 tablespoons (30 ml) chopped fresh Italian parsley
6 fresh basil leaves, shredded
2 tablespoons (30 ml) olive oil
1 tablespoon (15 ml) butter
1 medium onion, finely minced
1 garlic clove, finely minced
Olive oil for browning

Sauce
2 tablespoons (30 ml) olive oil
1 onion, finely chopped
2 garlic cloves, finely minced
6 large tomatoes, peeled, seeded and chopped
1/2 teaspoon (2 ml) salt
1/4 teaspoon (1 ml) freshly ground black pepper
1 tablespoon (15 ml) shredded fresh basil
1 tablespoon (15 ml) finely chopped fresh Italian
    parsley

Make noodle dough according to directions in Master Recipe and cut into noodles approximately 1-1/4 inches (3 cm) wide with a fluted pastry cutter; set aside.

To make the meatballs, mix together the ground beef, bread crumbs, water, eggs, salt, pepper, parsley and basil. Heat the olive oil and butter in a small skillet and sauté the onion and garlic until soft; do not brown. Remove from heat, let cool and add to the meat mixture. With your hands, work the mixture until well blended. Form into small meatballs about the size of walnuts and chill until ready to cook.

To make the sauce, heat the olive oil in a large skillet and sauté the onion and garlic until translucent. Add all the remaining sauce ingredients and cook over low heat for about 30 minutes, or until sauce is slightly thickened.

In another skillet heat a little olive oil and brown the meatballs on all sides, adding more oil if necessary. When nicely browned and firm, remove with a slotted spoon and slip into the sauce.

Pour off any fat remaining in the skillet from cooking the meatballs and add the sausages. Cook until nicely browned.

While the sauce and meats are cooking, cook the noodles in boiling salted water until tender. Drain and slip them into a large bowl of warm water to prevent them from sticking together.

In a large shallow greased baking dish make a layer of one-third of the noodles. Cover with half of the sauce and then half of the sausage. Repeat layers, reserving a little of the sauce, and end with a layer of noodles. Drizzle on remaining sauce and sprinkle with Parmesan cheese. Bake in a preheated 375°F (190°C) oven for 45 minutes. Cut into squares and serve with additional grated cheese on the side.
Makes 6 to 8 servings

HAM AND *FLECKERL* CASSEROLE
Schinkenfleckerl (Austria)

Any tiny *pasta* form may be used, but *fleckerl* are traditional.

1 recipe *Fleckerl,* page 45
2-1/2 tablespoons (35 ml) butter, softened
3 eggs, separated
1 pint (500 ml) commercial sour cream
1/4 pound (125 g) boiled ham, chopped

Cook the *fleckerl* in boiling salted water until tender. Drain, rinse under tepid water and drain again; set aside.

Cream the butter until fluffy and beat in the egg yolks one at a time. Very gradually add the sour cream and ham, blending thoroughly. Beat egg whites until stiff but not dry and fold into butter mixture with the *fleckerl.*

Butter a 1-1/2-quart (1.5 L) casserole and pour in the noodle mixture. Bake in a preheated 400°F (210°C) oven until top is nicely browned, about 25 minutes.

I particularly like serving this dish on a crisp autumn day with a green salad, cheeses and French bread. A light Riesling wine complements it nicely.
Makes 6 servings

NOODLES WITH SAUSAGES
Espagueti con Salchichas (Caribbean)

Noodle dough made with 1-3/4 cups (425 ml) flour
  and 2 eggs, page 28
2 tablespoons (30 ml) peanut oil
2 tablespoons (30 ml) finely diced salt pork
1 cup (250 ml) coarsely chopped baked ham
1 medium onion, coarsely chopped
3 large ripe tomatoes, peeled, seeded and coarsely
  chopped
1 green bell pepper, chopped
2 small fresh green chili peppers, seeded and
  chopped
10 pimiento-stuffed green olives, chopped
1 teaspoon (5 ml) capers in vinegar, drained
6 small garlic sausages or hot Italian sausages (about
  1 pound or 500 g), skinned and cut into small
  pieces
1 cup (250 ml) freshly grated Parmesan or dry
  Monterey Jack cheese

Make noodle dough according to directions in Master Recipe and cut into noodles approximately 5/8 inch (12 mm) wide with a fluted pastry cutter; set noodles aside.

In a heavy 4-quart (4 L) saucepan heat the peanut oil and sauté salt pork and ham until softened and lightly browned. Add onion, tomatoes, bell pepper, chili peppers, olives and capers and cook slowly for 15 minutes. Add the sausage and cook for 20 minutes, uncovered, until the sauce is thickened.

While the sauce is cooking, cook the noodles in boiling salted water until tender. Drain and put into a warmed serving bowl. Pour on sauce and serve immediately, with grated cheese on the side. Makes 4 to 6 servings

Note If you can get capers cured in salt (Italian or other Mediterranean markets), use an equivalent amount, soak them in several changes of water, then chop and use them as directed. They have much more flavor than the ones preserved in vinegar.

FRIED NOODLES WITH MIXED MEATS
Pancit Guisado (Philippines)

Noodle dough made with 1-3/4 cups (425 ml) flour
  and 2 eggs, page 28
3 to 4 tablespoons (45 to 60 ml) peanut oil
1/4 pound (125 g) pork butt, in 1 piece
1 whole chicken breast
6 garlic cloves, mashed
2 onions, thinly sliced
1 pound (500 g) shrimp, shelled and deveined
1/2 cup (125 ml) matchstick-cut smoked ham
2 cups (500 ml) shredded Napa cabbage
3 tablespoons (45 ml) light soy sauce
2 tablespoons (30 ml) white vinegar
Salt and freshly ground white pepper
Lemon wedges

Make noodle dough according to directions in Master Recipe and cut into noodles approximately 1/8 inch (3 mm) wide. Cook in boiling salted water until tender, drain and spread out on paper toweling to dry completely, about 20 to 30 minutes. Sprinkle about 1 tablespoon (15 ml) of the peanut oil over them evenly to prevent them from sticking together.

Simmer the pork butt in water to just cover until tender. Remove meat from water, reserving water, and cut into shreds. Simmer the chicken breast in water to just cover until tender. Remove from water, discard water, and bone, skin and shred the breast. Set pork and chicken aside.

Heat 1 tablespoon (15 ml) of the peanut oil in a wok or large skillet until very hot. Drop a handful of the noodles into the oil and stir fry until golden on all sides, adding more oil as needed. Remove from pan and repeat with remaining noodles until all are cooked.

Heat 1 tablespoon (15 ml) of the peanut oil in the pan and stir fry, *separately,* the garlic, onions, shrimp, chicken, pork and ham. As you remove each from the pan, reserve a small portion for garnish. You may combine the ingredients in a bowl, once they are removed from the pan.

Heat the pan and add the just cooked garlic, onions, shrimp, chicken, pork and ham along with the cabbage, soy sauce, vinegar, 1 cup (250 ml) of the reserved pork cooking water and salt and pepper to taste. Stir fry over high heat until almost all of the liquid has cooked away. Then add the noodles and stir fry, tossing well to mix, until heated through. Arrange on a warmed serving platter and garnish with the reserved ingredients and the lemon wedges.

Makes 6 servings

PORK AND PRAWNS WITH FRIED NOODLES
Mie Goreng (Indonesia)

1/2 pound (250 g) dried Oriental egg noodles
3 tablespoons (45 ml) peanut oil
1 onion, finely chopped
3 garlic cloves, finely chopped
2 fresh hot red chili peppers, seeded and sliced
1/2 teaspoon (3 ml) *trasi* (shrimp paste)
1/2 pound (250 g) pork butt, cut into small dice
1/2 pound (250 g) medium shrimp, shelled and deveined
1/2 small head Napa cabbage, shredded
3/4 teaspoon (4 ml) salt
1/2 teaspoon (2 ml) freshly ground black pepper
2 teaspoons (10 ml) light soy sauce
Finely slivered green onions
Cucumber slices

Place the noodles in warm water to cover about 10 minutes; drain. Cook the noodles in boiling water until tender; drain and set aside.

Heat the peanut oil in a wok or skillet and stir fry the onion, garlic and chili peppers until starting to color. Add the *trasi*, crushing it well; then add the pork and shrimp and stir fry until thoroughly cooked. Add the cabbage, salt and pepper and stir fry 1 minute. Put the noodles into the wok and stir gently until mixture is well blended and heated through. Add the soy sauce, mix well and mound on a warmed large platter. Sprinkle with green onions and garnish with cucumber slices.

Makes 4 servings

PASTA WITH BEEF AND VEAL

CONSOMMÉ WITH PORT WINE
Consomme a Porto Carne (Portugal)

The Portuguese use of port and sherry wine in cooking is very typical and unique to them. Not even the Spanish use them in quite the same way. The *acini di pepe* are *pasta* that look like grains of pepper.

3/4 pound (375 g) finely ground beef or veal
2 medium carrots, scraped and finely chopped
3 medium tomatoes, peeled and chopped
1 celery stalk with leaves, finely chopped
6 peppercorns
1/4 teaspoon (2 ml) whole cloves
6 egg whites
6 cups (1.5 L) chicken stock
1 cup (250 ml) *acini di pepe*
3/4 cup (175 ml) port

In a large saucepan combine meat, vegetables, peppercorns and cloves, mixing together thoroughly and breaking up meat. Beat egg whites lightly and stir into meat mixture. Stirring steadily, pour on the chicken stock and bring to a boil. Reduce heat so soup simmers gently and continue simmering, covered, for 2-1/2 hours. Just before serving, raise heat and bring to a boil. Drop in *pasta* and cook 3 to 4 minutes. Stir in port and serve immediately.

This can be served as a first dish before a large meal or as an entrée or main dish with good crusty bread and butter, a light salad with delicate dressing and fruits and cheeses for dessert. The wine should be chosen to go well with port, that is, a red wine, fruity without being sweet, or only very slightly sweet.
Makes 6 servings

VEAL WITH GINGER AND NOODLES
(an invention of the artist, Zev)

1-1/2 teaspoons (7 ml) ground ginger
1-1/2 teaspoons (7 ml) salt
1/2 teaspoon (2 ml) sugar
1/4 teaspoon (1 ml) freshly ground black pepper
3 pounds (1.5 kg) boneless veal, cut into large dice
2 tablespoons (30 ml) butter
1 cup (250 ml) chopped onions
2-1/2 cups (625 ml) chicken stock
Noodle dough made with 1-3/4 cups (425 ml) flour
    and 2 eggs, page 28
1 tablespoon (15 ml) cornstarch, mixed with
1 tablespoon (15 ml) water
Minced fresh parsley

Mix together ginger, salt, sugar and pepper. Dredge veal cubes in mixture and set aside for about 2 hours. In a large skillet melt the butter and brown the veal cubes, tossing to brown evenly. Add onions and cook until translucent. Add the chicken stock, cover and simmer gently for about 1-1/2 hours or until meat is tender.

While veal is cooking, make noodle dough according to directions in Master Recipe and cut into noodles approximately 1/4 inch (6 mm) wide. Cook the noodles in boiling salted water until tender. Drain and place on a warmed platter; keep warm.

Add cornstarch mixture to veal and cook until slightly thickened. Pour veal and its gravy over noodles and sprinkle with parsley.

If the veal is young enough, this dish is delightful and tender. A Gewürztraminer or similar dry white wine is splendid with it.
Makes 6 servings

Note Be sure the ground ginger is fresh. If you doubt it, get a new tin of it, or grate ginger root to the same amount.

LINQUINE WITH TOMATOES AND VEAL
Linguine alla Pizzaiola (Italy)

1 garlic clove, mashed
5 tablespoons (75 ml) olive oil
1 teaspoon (5 ml) crumbled dried oregano
1 teaspoon (5 ml) crumbled dried basil
1 teaspoon (5 ml) salt
Freshly ground black pepper to taste
1 pound (500 g) ripe tomatoes, peeled and sliced
4 slices veal (approximately 2 pounds or 1 kg)
Noodle dough made with 1-3/4 cups flour
    (425 ml) and 2 eggs, page 28

In a large saucepan combine the garlic, olive oil, oregano, basil, salt and pepper and put the tomato slices into it; let stand for 30 minutes. Add the veal slices and cook over low heat for 30 minutes.

While the sauce is cooking, make the noodle dough according to directions in Master Recipe. Roll out slightly thicker than usual and cut into noodles approximately 1/8 inch (3 mm) wide. Cook noodles in boiling salted water until tender. Drain and put into a warmed large shallow serving bowl. Remove the veal from the sauce and place on a warmed platter. Pour the sauce over the noodles and toss well. Serve the *linguine* with the veal.
Makes 4 servings

VEAL CHOPS WITH PARMESAN, MILAN STYLE
Côte de Veau Milanaise (France)

1 cup (250 ml) dry bread crumbs
1/2 cup (125 ml) freshly grated Parmesan cheese
6 veal chops
Salt and freshly ground black pepper
1 egg, lightly beaten
1 pound (500 g) small elbow macaroni
1/4 pound (125 g) clarified butter, page 57
1 tablespoon (15 ml) unsalted butter, melted
1 cup (250 ml) julienned boiled ham
1 cup (250 ml) sliced fresh mushrooms
1 tablespoon (15 ml) thinly sliced white truffles
   (optional)

Mix bread crumbs with half of the Parmesan cheese. Season veal chops with salt and pepper, dip in the beaten egg and dredge in bread crumb-cheese mixture.

Cook the macaroni in boiling salted water until tender. Drain and keep warm.

While macaroni is cooking, heat the clarified butter in a large skillet and brown the chops, turning only once.

Drizzle the unsalted butter on the macaroni and toss to separate. Season with salt and pepper and mix in ham, mushrooms and truffles. Toss very gently, and taste to correct seasoning.

Arrange the macaroni in a mound in the center of a warmed large round serving platter. Sprinkle with remaining Parmesan cheese and arrange veal chops around mound as a border.
Makes 6 servings

MACARONI WITH YOGURT SAUCE
Kiymali Makarna (Turkey)

3 tablespoons (45 ml) butter
1 medium onion, finely grated
1/2 pound (250 g) ground lean beef
2 medium ripe tomatoes, peeled and chopped
Salt and freshly ground black pepper to taste
1/2 pound (250 g) *farfalle* or *cravatte*

Yogurt Sauce
1 garlic clove
1/2 teaspoon (2 ml) salt
2 cups (500 ml) plain yogurt

In a saucepan melt the butter and sauté the onion until lightly browned, stirring constantly to prevent burning. Add the meat, breaking it up well with a fork, and continue to cook, stirring often, until browned. Add the tomatoes and cook 5 minutes longer. Season with salt and pepper.

While the meat is cooking, cook the *farfalle* in boiling salted water until tender. Drain and add to the meat. Heat gently until ready to serve.

To make the sauce, crush the garlic with the salt to a pastelike consistency. Place the yogurt in a bowl and add garlic-salt mixture. Beat until thoroughly blended.

Put beef and noodle mixture into a warmed serving bowl. Serve with yogurt sauce on the side.
Makes 4 servings

PASTA PIE, *CHEZ MOI*

Pie Shell
1 pound (500 g) *fusilli* or *capellini*
2 tablespoons (30 ml) unsalted butter
1/2 cup (125 ml) freshly grated Parmesan cheese
1 egg, beaten

Filling
2 cups (500 ml) Bolognese Meat Sauce,
    page 55
1 cup (250 ml) chopped green onions, including
    green tops
1 cup (250 ml) Mediterranean-type black olives,
    pitted and coarsely chopped
1 cup (250 ml) *Béchamel* Sauce, page 56
1/2 to 3/4 cup (125 ml to 175 ml) shredded
    mozzarella cheese

To make the pie shell, cook the noodles in boiling salted water until only barely tender. Drain well and mix in the butter. Mix together the cheese and egg and toss with the noodles, coating them thoroughly. Pour the mixture into a buttered 9-inch (23 cm) pie pan and let stand for 10 minutes to cool. Then place a second pie pan of the same size into the first and place a weight in it. (If you wish a thick crust, the second pie pan should be slightly smaller than the first.) Chill for at least 1 hour.

To assemble the pie, remove the weight and second pan from the pie shell. Spread the meat sauce over the bottom surface of the shell and sprinkle with the onions and olives. Pour the *Béchamel* Sauce in a circle in the center, leaving a rim of the meat sauce showing. Sprinkle the cheese over the top and bake in a preheated 375°F (190°C) oven for 25 to 30 minutes, or until cheese is melted and edges of pie are lightly browned. Cut into wedges to serve.
Makes 4 servings as a main course;
6 servings as a first course

GREEN *LASAGNE* WITH MEAT SAUCE
Lasagne Verde con Ragù (Italy)

1 recipe Green Noodle dough, page 40
1 recipe Bolognese Meat Sauce, page 55

Cheese Sauce
4 tablespoons (60 ml) butter
1 small onion, finely chopped
3 tablespoons (45 ml) unbleached all-purpose flour
2 cups (500 ml) milk, heated
3/4 cup (175 ml) freshly grated Parmesan cheese
Pinch of salt
Pinch of freshly grated nutmeg
3 egg yolks, beaten

Make noodle dough according to directions in recipe and cut into noodles approximately 3 to 4 inches (8 to 10 cm) wide with a fluted pastry cutter. Cook in a shallow pan of boiling salted water until tender. Drain and slip into a bowl of warm water to prevent them from sticking together; set aside.

To make the cheese sauce, melt the butter in a heavy saucepan and sauté the onion until tender; do not brown. Stir in the flour and cook for about 3 minutes, stirring constantly. Gradually add the milk, stirring constantly, until smooth. Add the Parmesan cheese, salt and nutmeg, continuing to stir constantly; cook until thickened. Beat a little of the hot sauce into the egg yolks and pour mixture back into the saucepan, beating vigorously. Set aside.

Butter a large shallow rectangular baking dish. Spread about one-fourth of the cheese sauce over the bottom, then one-third of the drained noodles, trying not to overlap them. Cover with one-third of the meat sauce. Repeat layers two more times and top with remaining cheese sauce. Bake in a preheated 325°F (160°C) oven for 20 minutes, then put dish in a preheated broiler until the top is golden brown. Let stand a few minutes and then cut into squares to serve. Serve very hot.

Makes 8 servings

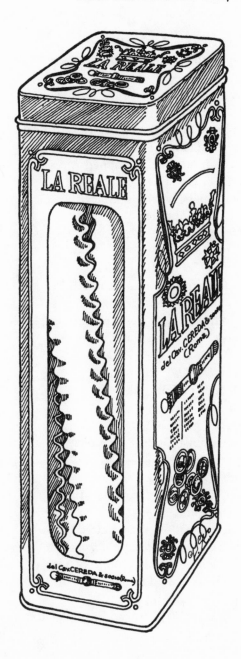

BOLOGNESE *LASAGNE*
Lasagne alla Bolognese (Bologna)

Meat Sauce
1/3 pound (150 g) coarsely ground beef
1/3 pound (150 g) coarsely ground pork
1/3 pound (150 g) coarsely ground veal
1 large onion, finely chopped
2 garlic cloves, finely minced
2 Italian parsley sprigs, minced
1 bay leaf, crumbled
1/4 teaspoon (1 to 2 ml) finely minced fresh
    rosemary
1/2 cup (125 ml) beef stock
2 medium ripe tomatoes, peeled, seeded and
    chopped
1/2 pound (250 g) fresh mushrooms, sliced
1/2 cup (125 ml) dry red wine

Noodle Dough
6-1/2 cups (1.5 L) unbleached all-purpose flour
Pinch of salt
6 eggs
2 tablespoons (30 ml) olive oil

Béchamel Sauce
2 cups (500 ml) half-and-half (light cream)
1 slice onion
2 tablespoons (30 ml) unsalted butter
2 tablespoons (30 ml) unbleached all-purpose flour
Pinch each of freshly ground pepper, salt and
    freshly grated nutmeg

1/4 pound (125 g) Italian Fontina cheese, cut
    into thin strips

To make the meat sauce, brown the beef, pork and veal in a large skillet, breaking them up well with a fork. Add the onion, garlic, parsley, bay leaf and rosemary and cook over moderate heat 10 minutes. Add the beef stock and tomatoes and cook for 10 minutes. Stir in mushrooms and cook for 5 minutes, then raise heat and add wine. Cook until the strong odor of the wine is gone and then reduce heat. Simmer very gently, uncovered, for about 2 hours, or until thickened.

To make the noodle dough, combine all ingredients as directed in Master Recipe, page 28, adding the salt to the flour and the olive oil to the eggs in the well. Roll out dough very thinly and cut into noodles approximately 1-1/2 inches (4 cm) wide with a fluted pastry cutter. Cook in a shallow pan in boiling salted water until tender. Drain and slip into a bowl of warm water to prevent them from sticking together; set aside.

To make the *béchamel* sauce, heat the half-and-half with the onion slice to the boiling point. Remove from heat and remove onion slice and discard; set half-and-half aside. In a heavy saucepan melt the butter and stir in the flour, pepper, salt and nutmeg until absorbed by the butter. Cook, stirring steadily, for about 3 minutes. Gradually add the half-and-half, stirring constantly. Cook until smooth, about 3 minutes. Remove from heat.

In a buttered large, deep, rectangular baking dish place a layer of drained noodles, just barely overlapping. Cover with about one-third of the meat sauce and then one-third of the *béchamel* sauce. Top with about one-fourth of the Fontina cheese strips. Repeat layers two more times. Top

with a layer of noodles and the remaining cheese strips. Bake in a preheated 350°F (170°C) oven for about 45 minutes, or until top is nicely browned. Remove from oven and let stand for a few minutes before cutting into squares to serve.
Makes 12 to 15 servings

BEEF MIROTON
(International)

This recipe is adapted from one in Elizabeth David's book, *Spices, Salt and Aromatics in the English Kitchen.* I quote from it: "Miroton is a dish primarily designed for using up the beef boiled for a *consommé* or in the *pot-au-feu,* from which you take some of the broth to complete the dish."

Noodle dough made with 1-3/4 cups (425 ml)
    flour and 2 eggs, page 28
1-1/2 pounds (750 g) cold cooked beef, in 1 piece
2 tablespoons (30 ml) butter or beef drippings
1 pound (500 g) onions, sliced paper thin
1 tablespoon (15 ml) unbleached all-purpose flour
2 cups (500 ml) clear beef broth, heated
1 teaspoon (5 ml) Dijon-style mustard
Butter
Minced fresh parsley
Freshly grated Parmesan cheese

Make noodle dough according to directions in Master Recipe and cut into noodles approximately 1/2 inch (12 mm) wide; set aside.

Slice the beef into 1/2-inch (12 mm) slices; set aside. Melt the butter in a wide, shallow saucepan and sauté the onions very slowly until soft and creamy; they must not brown. Slowly stir in the flour, and when the flour and butter are well blended, slowly stir in the broth and mustard. Simmer over very low heat, stirring from time to time. Taste and correct seasoning. If sauce is very thick, thin with a little more broth. Arrange the meat slices neatly in the pan, cover and continue cooking just until meat is heated through.

Cook the noodles in boiling salted water until tender. Drain and toss with butter. Place beef and sauce on a large flat serving platter and surround with buttered noodles. Sprinkle noodles with parsley and Parmesan cheese. You may also place a portion of noodles on each dinner plate, top with a few beef slices and finally some sauce. Sprinkle with parsley and serve.
Makes 4 servings

Note Should you object to such a generous use of onions in the sauce, use 1 small onion, thinly sliced, and substitute thinly sliced celery and thin strips of green bell pepper for the remainder.

MACARONI WITH MUSHROOMS
AND SWEETBREADS CASSEROLE
Pasticcio di Maccheroni all'Uso
di Romagna (Emilia-Romagna)

1 pound (500 g) macaroni
1/4 pound (125 g) veal sweetbreads
1 teaspoon (5 ml) fresh lemon juice
6 tablespoons (90 ml) unsalted butter
1/2 teaspoon (2 ml) salt
1/4 teaspoon (1 ml) freshly ground black pepper
1 recipe Neapolitan Style *Béchamel* Sauce, page 56
1 cup (250 ml) dried Italian mushrooms, soaked in
    water 30 minutes and drained
1/4 pound (125 g) prosciutto, cut into long
    narrow strips
1 black truffle, finely sliced (optional)
1/8 teaspoon (scant 1 ml) freshly grated nutmeg
1 cup (250 ml) freshly grated Parmesan cheese

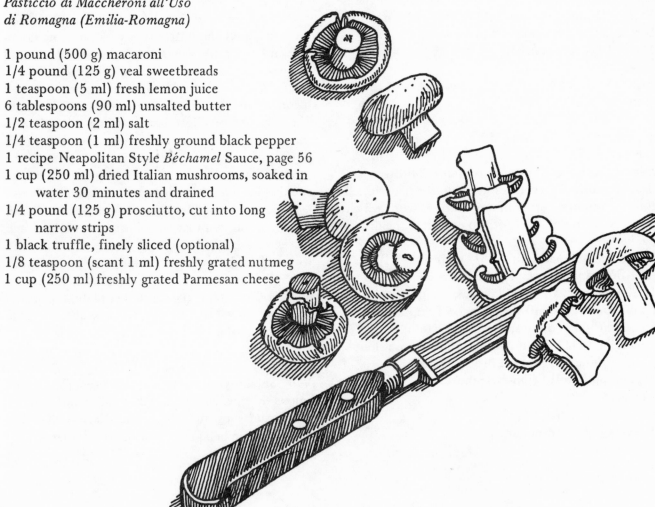

Cook the macaroni in boiling salted water until tender. Drain and set aside.

Put the sweetbreads and lemon juice in a small pot and add water to cover. Simmer 5 minutes and remove sweetbreads with a slotted spoon. Remove the membrane and any tough parts and chop coarsely; set aside.

In a large heavy skillet melt 4 tablespoons (60 ml) of the butter, and when it starts to color, stir in the sweetbreads. Add the salt and pepper and about half of the *béchamel* sauce and mix well. Then add the mushrooms, prosciutto, truffle and nutmeg and heat gently to blend flavors. Taste and correct seasoning.

Generously butter a 1-1/2-quart (1.5 L) *soufflé* dish or casserole and arrange one-third of the macaroni in the bottom. Cover with half of the sweetbreads mixture and then half of the remaining *béchamel* sauce. Dot with a third of the remaining butter. Repeat layers and end with macaroni. Sprinkle top with Parmesan cheese and dot with remaining butter. Bake in a preheated 350°F (170°C) oven for about 20 minutes. Serve from the baking dish.

Makes 4 to 6 servings

BEEF AND SQUASH SAUCE WITH NOODLES
Bassy (Ethiopia)

1-1/2 cups (375 ml) dried small white beans, soaked overnight in water to cover and drained
2 tablespoons (30 ml) peanut oil
2 medium onions, coarsely chopped
2 garlic cloves, finely minced
1 pound (500 g) boneless beef, cut into slivers or small cubes
3 tablespoons (45 ml) tomato paste
1 cup (250 ml) peanut butter or ground peanuts
Cayenne pepper to taste
3/4 pound (375 g) crookneck squash, thickly sliced
1/2 teaspoon (3 ml) salt
1/4 teaspoon (1 ml) freshly ground black pepper
1 pound (500 g) *fusilli*

Put the beans in a kettle with water to cover. Bring to a boil, reduce heat, cover and simmer until barely tender, about 45 minutes. Drain well and set aside.

In a heavy saucepan or kettle heat the peanut oil and sauté onions and garlic until lightly colored. Add the beef and cook only until raw redness is gone. Stir in the tomato paste, drained beans and water to cover. Simmer, uncovered, for about 40 minutes. If a large amount of sauce remains, raise heat and reduce to about 2 to 3 cups (500 to 750 ml).

Mix together peanut butter and cayenne pepper with a tablespoon (15 ml) or so of water until well blended. Stir into the sauce. Then stir in the squash, salt and black pepper and simmer for 15 minutes longer, or until beef is quite tender. Taste and correct seasoning with salt and black pepper.

While the sauce is finishing cooking, cook the *fusilli* in boiling salted water until tender. Drain and put into a warmed serving bowl. Pour on sauce and serve immediately.

Makes 4 to 6 servings

STEAK WITH APRICOTS ON FRIED *VERMICELLI*
(Egypt/North Africa)

In Egypt, this is usually eaten with the fingers. The meat is deftly mixed with a bit of yogurt and *vermicelli* into a small ball and swiftly popped in the mouth. Certainly it takes practice, but since fingers were invented before forks, *voilà*.

6 tablespoons (90 ml) olive oil
1 pound (500 g) fine *vermicelli*
2 pounds (1 kg) boneless lean beef, cut into
    1-inch (3 cm) cubes
1 small onion, finely minced
12 dried apricots, halved
1/4 cup (75 ml) water
1/2 cup (125 ml) seedless raisins
1/4 cup (50 ml) pine nuts
1/3 cup (75 ml) plain yogurt
1/2 cup (125 ml) chopped fresh parsley

Sauce
1 tablespoon (15 ml) butter
1 tablespoon (15 ml) unbleached all-purpose flour
1 cup (250 ml) milk
4 tablespoons (60 ml) tomato paste
Salt and freshly ground black pepper to taste

In a large heavy skillet heat 4 tablespoons (60 ml) of the olive oil and fry the *vermicelli,* tossing constantly, until lightly browned and crisp. Remove from skillet; set aside and keep warm. Wipe skillet of all bits of noodle, or they will burn and cause the meat to taste bitter. Heat the remaining olive oil in the same skillet and lightly brown the meat cubes and onion over medium heat, tossing occasionally to make sure meat is browned on all sides. Stir in the apricots and water, cover and cook over low heat 20 to 30 minutes, or until meat is tender.

While the meat is cooking, make the sauce. In a heavy medium-sized saucepan melt the butter and stir in the flour. Cook, stirring constantly, 2 to 3 minutes; do not brown. Add the milk all at once and cook over medium heat, stirring constantly, until sauce thickens. Add tomato paste and simmer over very low heat 6 to 8 minutes. Season with salt and pepper.

Add the sauce to the meat mixture and then stir in the raisins and pine nuts. Arrange a bed of the fried *vermicelli* on a wide, shallow serving plate and pour the meat mixture into the center, mounding it slightly. Make a well in the center of the mound and spoon in the yogurt. Garnish the mound with parsley and serve immediately.
Makes 4 to 6 servings

BEEF, SAUSAGE AND VEGETABLE STEW
Cocido (Argentina)

Cocido is a traditional Spanish dish and has a different version wherever Spanish-speaking people meet and cook. In Argentina, squash and corn are added, and the soup is served separately, with very fine noodles floated in it. The Spanish in early California had a tradition of serving *cocido*.

1 pound (500 g) dried chickpeas, soaked overnight in water to cover and drained
1 large chorizo sausage
1 large blood sausage
1-1/2 pounds (750 g) boneless beef, in 1 piece
1/2 pound (250 g) lean bacon, in 1 piece
3 large potatoes, peeled and quartered
1 small head cabbage, cut into 4 wedges
2 medium zucchini, thickly sliced
Kernels from 3 ears of corn
Salt and freshly ground black pepper
1/4 pound (125 g) very fine fresh egg noodles

In a large soup kettle combine the chickpeas, sausages, beef and bacon with water to cover by 1 inch (3 cm). Bring quickly to a boil, skim all froth from the surface, add about 1 cup (250 ml) cold water, then bring to boil again and skim again. Reduce heat, cover and simmer very gently for about 2 hours or until chickpeas and meat are tender. Add the potatoes and cabbage and cook for 25 minutes. Then add the zucchini and corn and cook for 8 to 10 minutes longer. Season with salt and pepper to taste.

Cook the noodles in boiling salted water until tender. Drain and put into a warmed deep soup tureen. Remove the meats and vegetables from the kettle with a slotted spoon and ladle the broth over the noodles in the tureen. Serve the broth and noodles as a first course. Serve the vegetables in a warmed deep platter and the meat, thinly sliced, on another warmed platter.
Makes 6 servings

BEEF, FISH AND VEGETABLES IN BROTH
Mizutaki (Japan)

This Japanese dish is "related" to the Mongolian hot pot, but is simpler and lighter. The dipping sauce is more delicate and less piquant.

Broth
2 quarts (2 L) chicken stock
Japanese soy sauce

Hot Pot
1/2 pound (250 g) tender beef, sliced paper thin
1/2 pound (250 g) white fish fillets, such as sea
    bass, snapper, cod, etc., sliced paper thin
2 squares fresh firm bean curd cakes, cut into
    1-inch (3 cm) cubes
8 large *shiitake* (dried mushrooms), soaked in
    warm water to soften for 20 minutes, drained
    and sliced
1 medium head Napa cabbage, shredded
8 green onions, slivered
1/2 pound (250 g) *shirataki* (noodles)

Dipping Sauce
1 small *daikon* (long white radish), grated
1/2 teaspoon (3 ml) *wasabi* (green horseradish
    powder)
1/2 cup (125 ml) Japanese soy sauce
1 teaspoon (5 ml) fresh lemon juice

Heat the chicken stock in an electric skillet or a flameproof casserole placed over a hot plate; season to taste with soy sauce.

Arrange all of the hot pot ingredients on a large platter in separate piles and set on the table within easy access of the diners. Provide each diner with a small bowl for some dipping sauce, a bowl and spoon for eating the broth and noodles, and chopsticks. Combine all of the ingredients for the dipping sauce, mixing well, and set on the table.

Each diner cooks his or her own food by holding it in the simmering broth with chopsticks. When all of the ingredients are eaten, add the noodles to the broth and heat through. Divide the soup and noodles among the diners.

Makes 6 to 8 servings

ORIENTAL NOODLE, BEEF AND VEGETABLE SALAD
(Chinese American)

Approximately 2 tablespoons (30 ml) peanut oil
2 pounds (1 kg) lean beef, cut into thin strips
2 garlic cloves, mashed
3 thin slices ginger root
Salt and freshly ground black pepper to taste
6 green onions, cut into thin strips on the diagonal
2 medium carrots, scraped and cut into thin strips
10 dried Chinese black mushrooms, soaked in
warm water to soften and thinly sliced
1/2 cup (125 ml) cloud ears (dried fungus),
soaked in warm water 30 minutes and cut
into thin strips
1 white onion, thinly sliced
1 cup (250 ml) thinly sliced bamboo shoots

6 ounces (168 g) bean thread noodles, soaked in
warm water to soften 10 minutes and drained
1/4 cup (75 ml) soy sauce
1 teaspoon (5 ml) Oriental sesame oil
1/4 pound (125 g) spinach leaves, cut into
thin strips
1 egg, beaten

In a wok or large skillet heat 1 tablespoon (15 ml) of the peanut oil and stir fry the beef, garlic, ginger root and salt and pepper over very high heat about 2 minutes. Remove to a small bowl and set aside.

In the same pan stir fry the green onions, carrots, mushrooms, cloud ears, white onion and bamboo shoots for 2 to 3 minutes, adding more oil if necessary. Remove from pan and set aside. Add 1/2 tablespoon (7 ml) of the peanut oil to the pan along with the sesame oil and place over high heat. Add the noodles and a little of the soy sauce and stir fry gently, gradually adding remaining soy sauce. Toss to distribute color evenly. Return meat and all the vegetables to the pan, including the spinach, and stir fry 1 minute. Remove to a platter and let cool to room temperature.

Lightly coat a small skillet with peanut oil and place over moderate heat. Pour in the egg and lift and tilt the skillet so the egg spreads evenly over the bottom of the pan; it should be very thin like a crêpe. Reduce heat and cook until surface of the egg is dry; do not let it brown. Turn egg pancake out onto a plate, fold in half and then in half again. Set aside to cool. Cut into very thin strips and scatter over the salad. Serve at room temperature.

Makes 8 servings

DUMPLINGS AND FILLED PASTA

SMALL DUMPLINGS
Nockerl (Hungary)

These dumplings are particularly adored by children, who like them with warm milk and brown sugar or syrup for a light supper.

2 eggs
2 cups (500 ml) sifted unbleached all-purpose flour
1 teaspoon (5 ml) salt
1/4 cup (50 ml) water
2 tablespoons (30 ml) butter, melted
Freshly grated Gruyère cheese

Break the eggs into a mixing bowl and beat lightly. Gradually add the flour and salt, stirring in well. As the dough thickens, add the water, little by little, to keep the dough malleable. Stir vigorously and steadily for about 10 minutes. Let dough rest about 10 minutes.

Bring a large saucepan of water to the boil and dip a teaspoon into it. With the teaspoon, scoop out a small quantity of the dough and let it slide off the spoon into the water, repeatedly dipping the spoon into the water before forming each one. Continue until all the dough is in the kettle and cook for 10 to 12 minutes longer. Taste the dumplings and if they have the slightest raw flavor, cook them a few minutes longer.

Lift out *nockerl* one at a time with a slotted spoon to a warmed buttered serving dish. Drizzle with melted butter and sprinkle with Gruyère cheese.

Makes 16 to 24 dumplings;
3 to 4 servings as a side dish

PUMPKIN DUMPLINGS
Gnocchi di Zucca Mantovani (Lombardy, Italy)

An autumnal dish, made when the pumpkin is ripe. It must be made with fresh pumpkin, for the canned variety is often too soft and mushy and has less flavor than it should.

1 pumpkin, approximately 3-1/2 to 4 pounds (1.5 to 2 kg)
Approximately 1-1/2 cups (375 ml) unbleached all-purpose flour
Pinch of salt
5 tablespoons (75 ml) unsalted butter, melted
1/2 cup (125 ml) freshly grated Parmesan cheese

Cut open the pumpkin and remove the seeds and "threads." Cut pulp away from skin in large pieces. Put the pulp in a saucepan with lightly salted water to just cover and simmer until tender. It is difficult to say how long it should cook, since pumpkins vary so, even within the area in which they were grown. Keep testing for doneness with the point of a sharp knife. When tender, remove the pumpkin pieces from the water promptly and drain well. Force through a large-holed strainer or put through a food mill. You should have 2 cups (500 ml) of pumpkin purée.

Put the pumpkin purée on a large floured working surface. Combine the flour and salt and gradually add it to the purée, working it in until a dough has formed. It is impossible to know exactly how much flour will be needed, again because pumpkins vary. Knead the dough very thoroughly until smooth and elastic, but still soft.

Pinch off pieces of dough, about 1-1/2 teaspoons (8 ml) in size, and press them against the curved back of fork tines to get the traditional rough surface and shape. As they are made, place them on a floured cloth and sprinkle lightly with more flour.

When all are made, cook them in a large kettle of boiling salted water, perhaps dropping in only 6 to 8 at a time to prevent them from sticking together. When they rise to the surface they are cooked. Remove them with a slotted spoon to a warmed serving bowl or individual serving dishes. Keep them warm until all are cooked. Drizzle with melted butter and sprinkle with Parmesan cheese. Serve very hot.
Makes 4 to 6 servings

SEMOLINA DUMPLINGS
WITH TOMATO SAUCE
Malloreddus (Sardinia)

These are a rather primitive type of *gnocchi* and are said to be "at least a thousand years old." It is suggested that they be made the day before they are to be served; they improve with standing.

Dough
2 cups (500 ml) semolina
Pinch of salt
Pinch of powdered saffron, dissolved in
1/4 cup (50 ml) or more warm water

Sauce
4 to 5 tablespoons (60 to 75 ml) olive oil
1 small onion, chopped
1 garlic clove, chopped
3 to 4 fresh basil leaves, shredded
6 large ripe tomatoes, peeled and chopped
Salt and freshly ground black pepper to taste

1/2 cup (125 ml) freshly grated Pecorino Sardo
   or Romano cheese

Make the dough according to directions in Master Recipe, page 28, combining the salt with the flour and adding the saffron water to the well. You may need to add more water to make a workable dough. Knead the dough on a lightly floured board for at least 20 minutes, or until smooth and elastic, but still firm. Cover and let rest for 30 minutes.

Roll out dough on a lightly floured board to a thickness of 1/2 inch (12 mm). Cut the dough into strips the thickness of your little finger and then cut the strips into 1/2-inch (12 mm) pieces. Press each small piece against the surface of a fine sieve or against the curved back of fork tines to get the traditional rough surface and shape. As they are made, lay them out on a floured cloth, sprinkle with more flour and let dry for a few hours, or a day or 2, if possible.

To make the sauce, heat the olive oil in a large skillet and sauté the onion, garlic and basil until onion is golden. Add the tomatoes and cook over moderate heat until thickened slightly. Season with salt and pepper, reduce heat and simmer gently until sauce is smooth and thickened, about 30 minutes.

Drop the dumplings, a few at a time, into a large kettle of boiling salted water. As soon as they rise to the surface, remove them with a slotted spoon to a warmed shallow serving bowl. When all are cooked, ladle them into individual shallow soup plates and pour a little of the sauce over them. Serve the Pecorino Sardo cheese on the side.
Makes 4 to 6 servings

Note This is how *malloreddus* are served in Sardinia, but for a richer dish, add chopped meat or crumbled sausage to the onion mixture for the sauce and brown it well before adding the tomatoes.

SWEET DUMPLINGS, VIENNESE STYLE
Noques (Austria)

Dough
1/4 pound (125 g) unsalted butter, softened
2 tablespoons (30 ml) sugar
5 egg yolks
Pinch of salt
3/4 cup (175 ml) sifted unbleached all-purpose
    flour
1 egg white, beaten until light and foamy
2 egg whites, unbeaten

Cooking Liquid
2 cups (500 ml) milk
2 tablespoons (30 ml) sugar
1 teaspoon (5 ml) vanilla extract

Custard Sauce
3 egg yolks
1/2 cup (125 ml) heavy cream
Sweetened milk from cooking *noques*

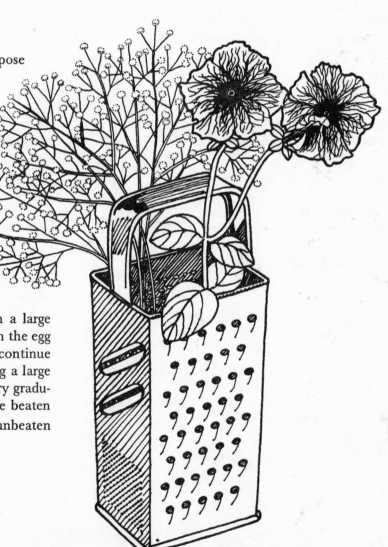

To make the dough, cream the butter in a large mixing bowl and work in the sugar. Beat in the egg yolks, one at a time. Add the salt and continue beating until mixture is quite fluffy. Using a large wire whisk, beat in the flour, adding it very gradually. When thoroughly mixed, blend in the beaten egg white; then mix in, one by one, the unbeaten whites. Set aside.

To make the cooking liquid, bring the milk just barely to a boil in a heavy enameled saucepan. Stir in the sugar and vanilla extract, and keep the liquid at just below the boiling point. This is important, because if the milk boils when the *noques* are cooking, they will become quite tough.

Using about 1 tablespoon (15 ml) of dough for each, form egg-shaped dumplings and drop them into the hot milk. Turn them with a spoon from time to time as they cook. When they feel firm to the touch, remove them with a slotted spoon to a warmed serving dish.

When all are cooked, make the custard sauce. Beat together the egg yolks and cream, and with a wire whisk, beat a little of the hot sweetened cooking milk into the egg mixture. Then add it to the milk in the saucepan and heat over very low heat, whisking steadily, until hot and thickened; do not let it boil. As soon as it is thickened, strain it through a fine sieve directly on to the *noques*. May be served hot or chilled.
Makes 4 to 6 servings

MATZO MEAL DUMPLINGS
Knaidlach (Jewish)

The traditional Sabbath eve and holiday dumplings. They may be served in a rich golden chicken broth, removed from the broth, mounded on a serving platter and drizzled with melted butter, or served as a side dish to roasts of meat or chicken. They should be fragrant, light and fluffy; sometimes they show veins of golden egg.

1 small onion, finely minced (optional)
1 tablespoon (15 ml) corn oil (optional)
3/4 cup (175 ml) fine matzo meal
2 eggs, lightly beaten
1/2 teaspoon (3 ml) salt
Generous pinch of freshly ground white pepper
1 tablespoon (15 ml) finely minced fresh
    parsley (optional)
1 tablespoon (15 ml) water
1-1/2 quarts (1.5 L) rich chicken broth

If including the onion, heat the corn oil in a small skillet and sauté the onion until lightly golden. Combine the matzo meal, eggs, salt, pepper, parsley, water and sautéed onion and blend well. Form into small balls about 1 to 1-1/2 inches (3 to 4 cm) in diameter.

Bring the broth to a boil and drop in the balls. Cook, uncovered, over medium heat for about 20 minutes. Serve immediately.
Makes 20 dumplings; 4 servings

Note The onion sautéed in oil and the parsley are optional in the sense that they are a variation on the original simple dumpling. The decision to add them or not comes down to the simple fact of whether one's mother or grandmother added them or not, for such is the nature of traditional dishes.

RAVIOLI, NICE STYLE
Ravioli à la Niçoise (Nice)

Dough
5 cups (1.25 L) sifted unbleached all-purpose flour
1-1/2 teaspoons (8 ml) salt
6 eggs

Filling
1 lamb brain
1/2 pound (250 g) raw lean ground beef or finely
    diced boiled or braised beef
1/2 pound (250 g) spinach
2 teaspoons (10 ml) butter
1 small onion, finely chopped
2 eggs, lightly beaten
Salt and freshly ground black pepper to taste
Pinch of freshly grated nutmeg

Tomato sauce or meat gravy of choice or butter
1 cup (250 ml) freshly grated Parmesan or
    Gruyère cheese
1/2 cup (125 ml) fine dry bread crumbs
Melted butter

Make the dough according to directions in Master Recipe, page 28, adding the salt to the flour. Form into a ball, cover and set aside.

To make the filling, poach the lamb brain in gently simmering salted water to cover for about 10 minutes. Remove from the water, let cool slightly and remove the outer membrane. Chop the brain very finely, put through a food mill or mash with a fork. Put into a large mixing bowl and mix in the beef. Discard stems and any imperfect spinach leaves, wash well and cook only in water clinging to leaves until just wilted. Drain, squeezing out all moisture and chop finely; add to the beef and lamb brain. Melt the butter in a medium-sized skillet and sauté the onion until translucent. Add the meat mixture and mix in well. Then stir in the eggs and cook over low heat, stirring steadily, until set. Season with salt, pepper and nutmeg, put in a mixing bowl and let cool.

Cut the ball of dough in half, keep one-half covered and roll out the other half on a lightly floured board into a rectangle as thin as possible. Put *small* mounds of filling at regular intervals on the sheet, about 2 inches (5 cm) apart, forming rows. Now roll out the second half of dough to an equal-sized sheet. Dampen the areas between the mounds of filling with a small brush dipped in water. Place the second sheet on top of the first and press it down between the mounds to make the 2 sheets of dough stick together. A ruler is very helpful for this, and it keeps the rows straight. Cut out the *ravioli* with a sharp knife or smooth or fluted pastry cutter. Sprinkle the *ravioli* very lightly with flour.

Bring a large kettle of salted water to a boil and drop in *ravioli*. Simmer for about 6 to 8 minutes; they float on the surface when ready. Drain in a colander and then place *ravioli* flat, well spaced, on a cloth.

Butter a large baking dish or *gratin* dish and arrange ravioli in it. Pour on a little sauce or gravy or dot with butter. Sprinkle on the Parmesan cheese and then the bread crumbs. Drizzle with melted butter and place in a preheated 425°F (220°C) oven for about 10 minutes or until nicely browned.
Makes 6 to 8 servings

RAVIOLI, LOMBARDY STYLE
Casônsèi (Lombardy, Italy)

Casônsèi are a specialty of the Lombardy region. Each town of the province makes these *ravioli*-like dumplings in a different way—different shapes, different fillings. *Casônsèi* are always served at wedding dinners and other festivities of the region.

Dough
2-3/4 cups (675 ml) all-purpose unbleached
    flour
Pinch of salt
3 eggs

Filling
1/4 pound (125 g) mild Italian sausage, skinned
1/4 cup (50 ml) freshly grated Parmesan
    cheese
3 tablespoons (45 ml) soft bread crumbs,
    soaked in milk to cover for 10 minutes

1/4 pound (125 g) unsalted butter
6 tablespoons (90 ml) freshly grated
    Parmesan cheese

Make the dough according to directions in Master Recipe, page 28, adding the salt to the flour. Form into a ball, cover and set aside.

To make the filling, crumble the sausage meat into a small skillet and cook in its own fat until lightly browned. Drain off fat, remove meat to a mixing bowl and mix in cheese. Squeeze the bread crumbs fairly dry and add them to the meat mixture. Work the mixture with your fingers until it forms a well-blended, firm mass.

Roll out the dough on a lightly floured board into a large rectangle as thin as possible. With a fluted pastry cutter, cut the dough sheet in rectangles approximately 3 inches by 5-1/2 inches (8 by 13 cm). Place a heaping teaspoonful of the filling on the center of each rectangle. Fold the rectangle in half lengthwise and press edges together very securely so the filling will not escape. Now working quickly so the dough does not dry out, form the dough packets into crescents: To form the outside (long) edge of the crescent, gently stretch the side where you pressed the edges together; then lightly pleat the inside edge to conform to the stretched top. As the crescents are made, set them on a lightly floured cloth and sprinkle them lightly with flour.

Bring a large kettle of salted water to a boil and drop in the dumplings a few at a time. Stir lightly and carefully from time to time so that they do not stick together. Simmer gently for about 6 to 8 minutes; they will float on the surface when ready. Remove with a slotted spoon and put on a warmed serving platter, keeping them warm until all are cooked.

When all are cooked, melt the butter and combine with the Parmesan cheese. Pour over the *casônsèi* and serve immediately.
Makes 6 servings

LENTEN *RAVIOLI*
Culingiones Sardi (Sardinia)

Dough
3-3/4 cups (925 ml) semolina
Pinch of salt
4 eggs

Filling
1 pound (450 g) spinach
2 tablespoons (30 ml) butter, softened
Pinch of freshly grated nutmeg
1/4 teaspoon (1 ml) salt
Freshly ground black pepper to taste
2 eggs
1-1/2 cups (375 ml) crumbled fresh (soft)
    Pecorino Sardo cheese
1 tablespoon (15 ml) unbleached all-purpose flour

2 cups (500 ml) Tomato Purée, page 54, heated to
    serving temperature
1/2 cup (125 ml) freshly grated dry (hard)
    Pecorino Sardo cheese

Make the dough according to directions in Master Recipe, page 28, adding the salt to the flour. Form into a ball, cover and set aside.

To make the filling, discard stems and any imperfect spinach leaves, wash well and cook only in water clinging to leaves, until just wilted. Drain, squeezing out all moisture, and chop finely. Put the spinach in a mixing bowl and add the butter, nutmeg, salt and pepper, mixing well. Then mix in the eggs, fresh Pecorino Sardo and the flour and work mixture together with a wooden spoon until smooth and firm.

Roll out the dough, make the *ravioli* and cook them in boiling salted water as described in *Ravioli, Nice Style,* preceding. After draining the *ravioli,* put them into a warmed deep serving dish and pour the Tomato Purée over them. Serve the grated Pecorino Sardo on the side.
Makes 6 servings

Note If you are unable to find the Pecorino Sardo cheeses, substitute any fresh piquant cheese, such as feta or Brindza for the fresh one, and Pecorino Romano for the dry one.

MANICOTTI WITH BOLOGNESE MEAT SAUCE
Manicotti al Ragù Bolognese (Italy)

Dough
2-1/2 cups (625 ml) unbleached all-purpose flour
3/4 teaspoon (4 ml) salt
3 eggs
1 tablespoon (15 ml) butter, melted and cooled
3 tablespoons (45 ml) lukewarm water

Filling
1/2 cup (125 ml) finely minced parsley
3 cups (750 ml) ricotta cheese
3/4 cup (175 ml) freshly grated Parmesan cheese
2 egg yolks
1/4 teaspoon (1 ml) freshly grated nutmeg
1/4 teaspoon (1 ml) salt

1 recipe Bolognese Meat Sauce, page 55
1 cup (250 ml) Cream Sauce, page 56
Freshly grated Parmesan cheese

To make the dough, combine the flour and salt and sift onto a pastry board or into a large mixing bowl. Make a well in the center and break in the eggs. Add butter and water to the well. Beat the liquids with a fork until well blended. With a fork or your fingers, gradually work the liquids into the flour until all the liquid has been absorbed by the flour. Knead on a lightly floured board until dough is smooth and elastic. Form into a ball, cover and let rest for 30 minutes.

To make the filling, combine the parsley, ricotta cheese, Parmesan cheese, egg yolks, nutmeg and salt; set aside.

Cut the ball of dough in half, leave half covered and roll out other half on a lightly floured board into a sheet as thin as possible. Cut into 4-by 6-inch (15 by 10 cm) rectangles, remove to a floured towel and let rest. Repeat with second half of dough. You should have 18 rectangles in all.

Cook the dough squares in boiling salted water until tender. Drain, rinse in warm water, drain again and lay out on a towel so they do not touch.

Pour a little of the meat sauce on the bottom of a buttered large shallow baking dish. Put about 1/4 cup (50 ml) of the cheese filling on each dough rectangle and roll up from the narrow end to form large rolls. Place the rolls, seam side down, in the baking dish. Cover with the remaining meat sauce and drizzle the Cream Sauce on top in a decorative fashion. Bake in a preheated 375°F (190°C) oven for 25 to 30 minutes. Serve with Parmesan cheese on the side.

Makes 8 or 9 servings

TORTELLINI OR CAPPELLETTI WITH MEAT AND CHEESE FILLING (Italy)

Since both these stuffed shapes can be filled with the same ingredients and differ only in the shape the dough is cut before filling and twisting into traditional forms, I have combined them in this recipe.

The square-cut ones come out looking like little peaked caps, which are *cappelletti* in Italian, while the *tortellini,* the round-cut ones, are "small twists." According to one legend, *tortellini* are made to look like "Venus' navel," and were first made by a Bolognese innkeeper who had slyly sneaked a look while the goddess was bathing in the woods. And indeed they do resemble a large, dimpled navel when well made.

Though in this recipe the *tortellini* and *cappelletti* are served in a tomato sauce, they are also delicious served with a cream sauce or cooked and served in rich broth.

Dough
4 cups (1 L) unbleached all-purpose flour
Generous pinch of salt
2 eggs
2 tablespoons (30 ml) olive oil
Approximately 3/4 cup (175 ml) water, boiling

Filling
2 tablespoons (30 ml) butter
1/4 pound (125 g) veal, cut into 1/2-inch (12 mm) dice
Salt and freshly ground black pepper to taste
1/4 pound (125 g) pork, cut into 1/2-inch (12 mm) dice
3 tablespoons (45 ml) finely minced prosciutto
1 cup (250 ml) ricotta cheese
1 egg yolk, beaten
1/2 cup (125 ml) freshly grated Parmesan cheese
1/4 teaspoon (1 ml) or less freshly grated nutmeg

1 recipe Tomato Sauce, page 53
1/2 cup (125 ml) freshly grated Parmesan cheese

To make the dough, combine the flour and salt in a large mixing bowl. Make a well in the center and break in the eggs and add the olive oil. Begin working the liquids into the flour, and little by little, add the boiling water, stirring with a long-handled wooden spoon, or your hands, to form a firm soft dough. (The amount of water is approximate, depending on the size of the eggs and freshness of the flour. It may take slightly more or less.) Knead dough vigorously on a lightly floured board for about 6 to 8 minutes, or until dough is smooth and shiny. Form into a ball, cover and let rest 30 minutes.

To make the filling, melt the butter in a skillet and sauté the veal, seasoning with salt and pepper, until lightly browned. Remove with a slotted spoon and set aside to cool. Add the pork to the same skillet, season with salt and pepper and brown lightly; then cook for 3 minutes, remove with a slotted spoon and set aside with the veal to cool. When cool enough to handle, finely chop the meats and put into a mixing bowl. Add the prosciutto, ricotta cheese, egg yolk, Parmesan cheese and nutmeg and mix well.

Cut ball of dough in half, keep one-half covered and roll out the other half as thinly as possible on a lightly floured board. Cut and form the dough as directed below, then repeat with the second half of dough.

Bring a large kettle of salted water to a boil. Drop in the *tortellini* or *cappelletti*, adding only enough so as not to crowd them. Simmer for about 5 minutes. They float on the surface when ready. Remove with a slotted spoon to a warmed serving bowl. When all are cooked, pour the Tomato Sauce over them, sprinkle with Parmesan cheese and serve immediately.

Makes approximately 200 dumplings;
8 to 10 servings

To Make Cappelletti

Cut the dough into 1-1/2 inch (4 cm) squares and put 1/2 teaspoon (2 ml) or less filling in the center of each square. Fold square diagonally across to form a triangle, pressing the edges together firmly. (If possible, try to form the triangle so the upper layer is a bit short of the lower one.) Now pick up the triangle by one of the base (long) ends and curl the triangle around your index finger, holding it firmly with the thumb. With the thumb and index finger of your other hand, pull together the ends of the base side and press together firmly. (It may be necessary to dampen the ends with a drop of water to make them adhere.) Pull the third corner toward you slightly, so that it stands up like the peak of a cap. As each one is made, set it on a towel and dust lightly with flour.

To Make Tortellini

Cut the dough into circles with a cookie cutter or the rim of a thin wineglass about 2 inches (5 cm) in diameter. Put 1/2 teaspoon (2 ml) or less filling in the center of each circle, then fold over the dough to form a half-moon shape, pressing the edges together firmly. Pick up the half moon by one end of the dough and curl it around your index finger, holding it firmly with the thumb. With the thumb and index finger of your other hand, pull together the corners by pressing one corner over the other. (It may be necessary to dampen the ends with a drop of water to make them adhere.) As each one is made, set it on a towel and dust lightly with flour.

Note If you have made these dumplings in the morning for evening use, turn them over every few hours so they do not dry out. If you wish to dry them for future use, turn more often until "leather dry." If kept in an open container in the refrigerator, they will continue to dry and will keep well for about 1 week. To freeze them, lay them out on a cookie sheet and freeze about 12 hours or more, then drop them into plastic bags and put them in the freezer.

KREPLACH
(Jewish European)

Dough
2 cups (500 ml) unbleached all-purpose flour
Generous pinch of salt
2 eggs
1 tablespoon (15 ml) water

Chicken stock (optional)
Butter and commercial sour cream (optional)

Make the dough according to directions in Master Recipe, page 28, adding the salt to the flour and the water to the eggs. Roll out as thinly as possible on a lightly floured board and cut into 3-inch (8 cm) squares. Prepare one of the following fillings and put 1 scant tablespoon (scant 15 ml) of it in the center of each square. Fold dough over to form a triangle, pinching edges together securely. It may be necessary to put a drop of water on edges of the triangle to make them adhere.

Drop the *kreplach* into boiling salted water or stock, adding only enough at a time so they are not crowded. Simmer for about 15 minutes, or until they rise to the surface.

If you have cooked the *kreplach* in stock, ladle the stock and *kreplach* into shallow soup plates. If you have cooked them in water, remove them with a slotted spoon, fry them in butter until lightly golden and serve with sour cream on the side.
Makes approximately 24 *kreplach;* 4 servings

Beef Filling
1 tablespoon (15 ml) rendered chicken fat or
    margarine
1/2 pound (250 g) ground lean beef
1 small onion, finely minced
Salt and freshly ground black pepper to taste

Heat the chicken fat in a heavy skillet and sauté the beef and onion over moderate heat for about 10 minutes, stirring often. Season with salt and pepper and set aside to cool before making *kreplach.*

Chicken Liver Filling
2 tablespoons (30 ml) rendered chicken fat
1/2 pound (250 g) chicken livers
1 small onion, finely minced
2 hard-cooked egg yolks
1/4 teaspoon (1 ml) salt
Pinch of freshly ground white pepper

Heat the chicken fat in a heavy skillet and sauté the chicken livers for 8 to 10 minutes, stirring often. Remove from heat and let cool slightly. In a meat grinder, food mill or food processor, grind together the livers, onion and egg yolks. Mix in salt and pepper, adding more if needed. Cool completely before making *kreplach.*

Chicken Filling
1 teaspoon (5 ml) rendered chicken fat
1/4 cup (50 ml) minced onion
1-1/2 cups (375 ml) ground cooked chicken
1 egg yolk
1 tablespoon (15 ml) minced fresh parsley

Heat the chicken fat in a small skillet and sauté the onion until translucent. Combine the onion with all remaining ingredients, mixing well. Let rest for 30 minutes before making *kreplach.*

CHEESE-FILLED DUMPLINGS
Vareniki (Russia)

Dough
3 cups (750 ml) unbleached all-purpose flour
1 teaspoon (5 ml) salt
3 eggs
2 tablespoons (30 ml) water

Filling
3/4 pound (375 g) baker's cheese or uncreamed
     cottage cheese
Salt
1 egg
2 teaspoons (10 ml) sugar
1 tablespoon (15 ml) butter, melted and cooled

1 tablespoon (15 ml) butter, melted
1 cup (250 ml) commercial sour cream, chilled

To make the dough, follow the directions in the Master Recipe, page 28, adding the salt to the flour and the water to the eggs in the well. Form the dough into a ball and cut in half. Keep half covered and roll out the other half on a lightly floured board into a very thin sheet. Cut into circles with a cookie cutter or the rim of a thin wineglass about 2 inches (5 cm) in diameter. Sprinkle the circles very lightly with flour. Repeat with second half.

To make the filling, force the cheese through a strainer to rid it of all lumps. Taste the cheese, and if it needs salt, add a little until it suits you. Add the egg, sugar and butter to the cheese and blend well.

Put about 1 teaspoon (5 ml) of the filling on each dough circle and then fold over the circle to form a half-moon shape, pinching edges together securely. (It may be necessary to put a drop of water on the edges of the circle to make them adhere.)

Bring salted water to a boil in a large saucepan and drop in the *vareniki,* adding only enough at a time so they are not crowded. Simmer for 10 to 15 minutes; they will float on the surface when ready. Remove with a slotted spoon to a warmed serving platter. When all are cooked, drizzle on the melted butter and serve with sour cream on the side.
Makes 4 to 6 servings

BEEF-FILLED DUMPLINGS
Pelmeni (Russia)

Pelmeni are served in a rich broth, simply boiled with melted butter drizzled over them, or fried and served with sour cream or, as in Siberia, with mustard and vinegar sauce.

Dough
2 cups (500 ml) unbleached all-purpose flour
Pinch of salt
1 egg
2 to 3 tablespoons (30 to 45 ml) water

Filling
3/4 pound (375 g) finely ground lean beef
1/4 teaspoon (1 ml) salt
Generous pinch of freshly ground black pepper
2 tablespoons (30 ml) water
1 tablespoon (15 ml) finely minced onion
      (optional)

1-1/2 quarts (1.5 L) rich chicken stock
Melted butter and minced fresh parsley, or
Melted butter and a mixture of distilled white
      vinegar and dry mustard, or
Butter, chilled commercial sour cream and minced
      fresh dill

To make the dough, combine the flour and salt and sift onto a pastry board or into a large mixing bowl. Make a well in the center and break in the egg. With a fork or your fingers, gradually work the egg into the flour to form a fairly stiff dough, adding a little of the water at a time. Knead on a lightly floured board until dough is smooth and elastic. Form into a ball, cover and set aside.

To make the filling, combine all the ingredients and mix together well.

Roll out the dough on a lightly floured board into a large, very thin sheet. Cut the dough into circles with a cookie cutter or the rim of a thin wineglass about 2 inches (5 cm) in diameter. Put about 1 teaspoon (5 ml) of filling on each circle. Fold circles in half to form a half-moon shape and pinch edges together. (If desired, you may join the 2 points of the half moon and pinch them together securely, putting a small drop of water on one of the corners to make them adhere firmly.) As you make the *pelmeni*, lay them on a lightly floured surface so they do not touch.

Bring the chicken stock to a boil in a large saucepan and drop in the *pelmeni*, adding only enough at a time so they will not be crowded. Simmer gently for 10 to 15 minutes. They will float on the surface when ready. Remove with a slotted spoon to a warmed buttered platter as each batch is cooked.

The *pelmeni* may be served in any of the following ways: drizzled with melted butter and garnished with minced fresh parsley; drizzled with melted butter and served with vinegar and mustard mixed to a sauce and passed separately; or fried in butter until nicely golden and served with sour cream and minced dill or parsley. You may also serve them simply in a little of the hot stock. Makes approximately 50 *pelmeni*; 4 to 6 servings

Variation Substitute ground lean pork for half of the beef in the filling.

LAMB-FILLED DUMPLINGS
Kyurza (Azerbaijan)

Noodle dough made with 1-3/4 cups (425 ml) flour
    and 2 eggs, page 28
Ground cinnamon
Plain yogurt

Filling
2 tablespoons (30 ml) butter
1 small onion, minced
3/4 pound (375 g) ground lean lamb
Salt and freshly ground black pepper to taste

Make noodle dough according to directions in Master Recipe. Form into a ball, cover and set aside.

    To make the filling, heat the butter in a skillet and sauté the onion until translucent. Add the lamb, breaking it up well, and sauté until lightly browned. Season with salt and pepper, remove from heat and let cool.

    Roll out the dough on a lightly floured board into a very thin sheet. Cut into circles with a cookie cutter or the rim of a thin wineglass about 2 inches (5 cm) in diameter. Put about 1 teaspoon (5 ml) of filling on one-half of each circle. Fold over other half to encase the filling and seal and pleat the edges together by pressing with the tines of a fork.

    Bring salted water to a boil in a large saucepan and drop in *kyurza,* adding only enough at a time so they are not crowded. Simmer for about 10 minutes; they will float on the surface when ready. Remove with a slotted spoon to a warmed serving dish. When they are all cooked, top with any remaining meat mixture and sprinkle with cinna-

mon. Serve immediately, with yogurt on the side. Makes 4 to 6 servings

Variations This dish exists in many other republics of the Soviet Union. It is sometimes made with meat mixtures of lamb and pork, beef and lamb and beef and pork, and sometimes an herb mixture is substituted for the meat in the filling. The circles are also often made larger, 4 to 5 inches (10 to 13 cm) in diameter, and stuffed with 2 to 3 teaspoons (10 to 15 ml) of the meat mixture. They are also served topped with a rather sour red berry jelly (cranberry jelly is a fairly good substitute) and clarified butter.

PASTA ROLL WITH SPINACH FILLING
Il Rotolo di Pasta (Italy)

This very attractive dish is quicker to make than many filled *pasta* forms.

Noodle dough made with 1-3/4 cups (425 ml)
    flour and 2 eggs, page 28
1 cup (250 ml) *Béchamel* Sauce, page 56
1/2 cup (125 ml) freshly grated Parmesan cheese
2 tablespoons (30 ml) unsalted butter

Tomato Sauce
1 pound (500 g) ripe tomatoes, halved
1 small onion, halved
Pinch of salt
Pinch of sugar

Filling
2 pounds (1 kg) spinach
1/4 pound (125 g) unsalted butter
2 tablespoons (30 ml) finely minced onion
4 slices prosciutto, finely minced
1 cup (250 ml) ricotta cheese
1 cup (250 ml) freshly grated Parmesan cheese
Pinch of freshly grated nutmeg
1 egg

To make the tomato sauce, put the tomatoes in a saucepan, cover and cook over moderate heat for 15 minutes. Force the tomatoes through a sieve or put them through a food mill and return them to the saucepan. Add the onion, salt and sugar and cook over very low heat for 1 hour. Remove from the heat and discard the onion.

While the tomato sauce is cooking, make the filling. Remove and discard spinach stems and any imperfect leaves. Wash remaining leaves thoroughly and cook only in water clinging to leaves, just until wilted. Drain well and squeeze out any excess moisture. Chop finely and set aside. In a medium-sized skillet melt the butter and sauté the onion until it is soft and starts to color. Add the prosciutto and cook for just a few seconds. Then add the spinach and cook for 3 to 4 minutes. Pour the mixture into a large bowl and stir in the ricotta cheese, Parmesan cheese, nutmeg and egg. Beat together until well blended; set aside.

Make noodle dough according to directions in Master Recipe. On a lightly floured board, roll dough out as thinly as possible into a large rectangular sheet. The exact size of the rectangle will depend on the cooking vessel you intend to use. Since you will end up with a long roll, a fish poacher or similar pan would be ideal. If you do not have a pan that will hold a very long roll, consider making 2 or 3 shorter rectangles.

Spread the ricotta mixture over the surface of the dough sheet, leaving a 1/4-inch (6 mm) border of dough on 3 sides and a slightly wider border on one of the long sides. Now fold the widest border over the filling and roll up the sheet until the roll is completed. Put a double thickness of cheesecloth, about 5 to 6 inches (13 to 15 cm) longer than the roll, on a flat surface. Place the roll on the cheesecloth and wrap the cheesecloth around it. Tie the "tails" of cheesecloth at either end of the roll with heavy string to prevent the filling from escaping.

Bring a generous amount of salted water to a boil in the pan you have chosen to cook your roll. Holding the cheesecloth tails, gently drop the roll into the water. When the water returns to the boil, reduce heat until the water remains at a gentle steady boil and cook for about 20 minutes. Using the long ends again, lift the roll from the water. (Use large slotted spatulas or spoons instead, if you fear the roll may break in the middle.) Set the roll on a flat surface and remove the cheesecloth while the roll is still hot. Let the roll cool, and with a very sharp knife, cut it into slices about 1 inch (3 cm) thick or slightly less.

Select a baking dish large enough to hold the slices in a single layer or slightly overlapping. Butter the dish generously. Combine the tomato sauce with the *Béchamel* Sauce and brush a small portion of it on the bottom and sides of the baking dish. Lay the slices in the baking dish and pour on the remaining sauce. Sprinkle the Parmesan cheese on the top and dot with butter. Bake in a preheated 375°F (190°C) oven for 20 minutes. Remove from the oven and let rest for about 10 minutes, then serve from the baking dish.

This dish may be assembled in the morning for baking and serving that evening. Set aside in a cool place until ready to bake.

Makes 6 servings

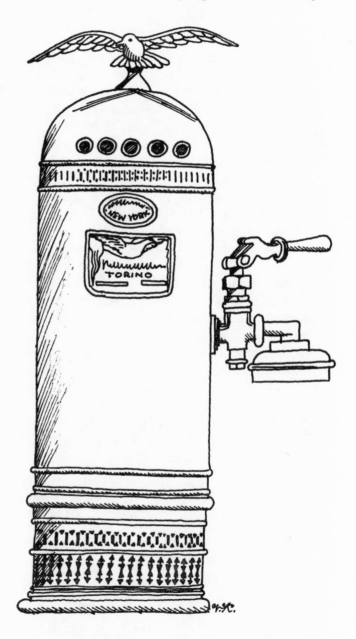

SHARON'S JEWEL BOX
Lo Scrigno de Sharon (Italy)

Another form of filled *pasta* is this "jewel box" of baked *pasta*. It is well known throughout Italy, though rarely seen in restaurants. It can best be described as finely cut green noodles with sauces, within a "box" made of rolled-out sheets of egg *pasta*. Cooks make a real attempt to outdo each other in making this dish as elaborate as they can. The most beautiful one I have ever seen is described in Marcella Hazan's book, *The Classic Italian Cookbook,* and which she calls *Lo Scrigno de Venere.* The following one is much simpler and more easily made, but still very pretty. When the upper crust is broken or lifted, it reveals the fine green *pasta* touched with bits of the sauces and is very appealing.

I dedicate my *scrigno* to my very patient editor, Sharon Silva, in a spirit of fond gratitude.

Noodle dough for the "box"
2 cups (500 ml) unbleached all-purpose flour
Pinch of salt
2 whole eggs
1 egg yolk

1 recipe Green Noodle dough, page 40

Meat Sauce
2 tablespoons (30 ml) unsalted butter
2 tablespoons (30 ml) olive oil
1 small onion, finely chopped
1 small carrot, finely chopped
1 celery stalk, finely chopped
1 pound (500 g) chopped lean beef
1/4 teaspoon (1 to 2 ml) salt
Pinch of freshly ground black pepper
1/4 cup (75 ml) dry white wine
1/4 pound (125 g) prosciutto, finely diced
1/4 pound (125 g) mozzarella cheese, shredded

1/4 pound (125 g) Gruyère cheese, cut into small dice
1/4 pound (125 g) Parmesan cheese, grated
1 recipe *Béchamel* Sauce, page 56, with a pinch of freshly ground white pepper

Make the noodle dough for the "box" according to directions in Master Recipe, page 28, adding the salt to the flour and the egg yolk to the well with the whole eggs. Form the dough into a ball, cover and set aside. Make the Green Noodle dough, form into a ball, cover and set aside.

To make the meat sauce, heat the butter and olive oil in a saucepan over moderate heat. Sauté the onion, carrot, celery and beef, breaking the meat up well, and cook until onion is soft and meat has lost its raw redness. Add the salt, pepper and wine, stirring in well. Bring to a boil, reduce heat and simmer gently for about 20 minutes.

While the meat sauce is cooking, roll out the

"box" dough on a lightly floured board into a large rectangular sheet. Cut into 12 squares approximately 5 inches (13 cm) to a side. Now roll out green dough as directed in recipe and cut into noodles as fine as possible.

Cook the dough squares in boiling salted water until tender. Lift out with a wide skimmer, lay out on a cloth so they do not touch and let cool. Cook the green noodles in the same water and drain; set aside.

Add the prosciutto and mozzarella cheese to the meat sauce and then stir in the green noodles. Remove from heat and toss well and quickly.

To assemble the "boxes," butter the insides of a 6 deep individual baking dishes (see note) and line each with a *pasta* square. Into each put approximately one-sixth of the green noodle mixture. Top with a little diced Gruyère and a little Parmesan cheese. Cover each with about one-sixth of the *Béchamel* Sauce and then top with another *pasta* square to form the "jewel box." Bake in a preheated 350°F (170°C) oven for 12 to 15 minutes. They should be heated through, but the top crust must not be browned.

Makes 6 servings

Note The size of your baking dishes will influence the number of "jewel boxes" you can make. The dishes should be fairly deep, round or square and of approximately 2-cup (500 ml) capacity. A smaller dish will give you 8 servings instead of 6. You may decorate the *scrigno* with sprigs of a preferred herb and a sprinkling of paprika, if desired.

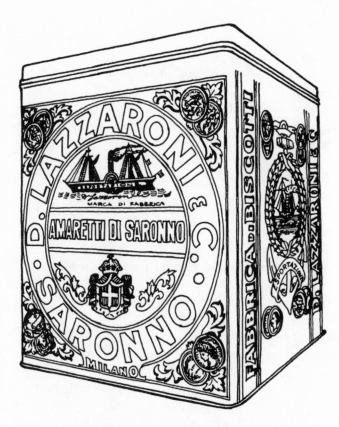

CANNELLONI WITH SWEETBREADS FILLING
Cannelloni al Forno (Italy)

Dough
3-3/4 cups (925 ml) unbleached all-purpose flour
Pinch of salt
4 eggs

Filling
1-1/2 pounds (750 g) veal sweetbreads
4 tablespoons (60 ml) olive oil
1 rosemary sprig
1 small onion, minced
1/2 pound (250 g) veal, cut into large dice
1/4 pound (125 g) bulk pork sausage
1/4 teaspoon (1 ml) salt
Generous pinch of freshly ground black pepper
6 tablespoons (90 ml) dry white wine
1 egg, beaten
1/3 cup (75 ml) freshly grated Parmesan cheese
Pinch of freshly grated nutmeg

2 tablespoons (30 ml) tomato paste, dissolved in
1/4 cup (50 ml) warm water
1/3 cup (75 ml) freshly grated Parmesan cheese,
    mixed with
1 tablespoon (15 ml) dry bread crumbs

Make the dough according to directions in Master Recipe, page 28, adding the salt to the flour. Form into a ball, cover and set aside.

To make the filling, put the sweetbreads in a saucepan with water to cover, bring to a boil, reduce heat and simmer 10 minutes. Drain the sweetbreads and remove their outer membrane; chop sweetbreads into small pieces and set aside. In a skillet heat the olive oil with the rosemary sprig. When the oil is hot, discard the sprig and add the onion, veal and sausage. Brown the meats and onion and season with salt and pepper. Raise the heat, pour in the wine and cook until the wine evaporates. Add the sweetbreads and cook, stirring, for 1 minute. Remove from heat and lift out meat mixture with a slotted spoon, reserving the juices in the pan. Put the meat mixture through a food mill, meat grinder or food processor and place in a large mixing bowl. Add the egg, Parmesan cheese and nutmeg and mix well; set aside.

Roll out the dough on a lightly floured board into a rectangle about 3/16 inch (9 mm) thick. Cut into rectangles approximately 4 by 6 inches (10 by 15 cm). Cook the rectangles, a few at a time, in boiling salted water until tender, but still quite firm. Remove with a slotted spoon and slip into cold water briefly, then lay out on a lightly dampened cloth to cool, being careful that the rectangles do not touch.

When the rectangles have cooled, divide the filling evenly among them, placing it on a narrow side of each rectangle and rolling them up to form a tube. Put the *cannelloni,* seam side down, in a single layer in a buttered shallow baking dish. Heat the reserved pan juices, add the tomato paste-water mixture, mixing well, and bring to a simmer. Pour the sauce over the *cannelloni* and sprinkle the Parmesan cheese-bread crumb mixture on top. Bake in a preheated 350°F (170°C) oven for 20 minutes, or until golden.
Makes 6 servings

SOUP WITH BEEF-FILLED DUMPLINGS
Adana Corbasi (Turkey)

This soup takes its name from the city of Adana in southern Turkey, famous for cotton production and this delectable dish.

Dough
2 cups (500 ml) unbleached all-purpose flour
Pinch of salt
1 whole egg
1 egg yolk
1 tablespoon (15 ml) olive oil

Filling
1 teaspoon (5 ml) olive oil
6 ounces (170 g) ground lean beef
1 small onion, finely minced
1 garlic clove, finely minced
2 tablespoons (30 ml) finely minced fresh
    parsley
1 tablespoon (15 ml) minced fresh thyme
Salt and freshly ground black pepper to taste

2 quarts (2 L) rich chicken or beef stock

To make the dough, combine the flour and salt and put on a pastry board or into a large mixing bowl. Make a well in the center and put the whole egg, egg yolk and olive oil into it. With a fork or your fingers, gradually work the liquid into the flour to form a fairly stiff dough, adding 1 tablespoon (15 ml) or so of water if needed to make the dough workable. Knead on a lightly floured board for about 10 minutes, or until dough is smooth and elastic. Form into a ball, cover with a lightly dampened cloth and let it rest for 1 hour.

To make the filling, heat the olive oil in a small skillet and sauté the beef, onion and garlic until onion is translucent and beef is browned. Remove from heat and mix in parsley, thyme, salt and pepper. Set aside to cool.

Roll out the dough on a lightly floured board into a large, very thin sheet. Cut the dough into circles with a cookie cutter or the rim of a thin wineglass about 2 inches (5 cm) or slightly larger in diameter. Put about 1 teaspoon (5 ml) of the filling on each circle. Fold circle in half to form a half-moon shape and pinch edges together. (It may be necessary to dampen the edges of the circle with a drop of water to make them adhere.)

Bring the stock to a boil and drop in the dumplings, adding only enough at a time so as not to crowd them. Simmer for about 10 to 15 minutes; they will float on the surface when ready. Remove to a warmed platter until all the dumplings are cooked, then return them to the soup to heat through.
Makes 6 servings

Variations These dumplings may also be cooked in boiling salted water, removed with a slotted spoon to a warmed serving platter and then drizzled with melted butter.

For additional flavor, yogurt is mixed with minced fresh mint, thyme and melted butter and dropped, in small amounts, into the soup just before serving. This same yogurt mixture can be served as a topping for the dumplings when they are not served in broth.

PORK AND SHRIMP *WON TON* IN SOUP
(China)

Filling
1-1/4 pounds (625 g) ground lean pork
1/4 pound (125 g) shrimp, shelled, deveined and
    coarsely chopped
6 dried Chinese black mushrooms, soaked in
    warm water to soften, drained and finely
    chopped
3/4 cup (175 ml) finely minced bamboo shoots
4 green onions, finely minced
1 tablespoon (15 ml) cornstarch
1-1/2 tablespoons (22 ml) light soy sauce
1 teaspoon (5 ml) Oriental sesame oil
1 egg, beaten

1 recipe square *Won Ton* Skins, page 46
Rich chicken stock, flavored with 1 or 2 slices
    ginger root
Chopped green onions

Combine all of the filling ingredients and mix together well. Put a scant teaspoon (5 ml) of filling
off center on each *won ton* skin and fold over, as
shown. Fold again and then bring the base (long)
ends together and pinch to seal securely, moisten-
ing edges with water if necessary. This last step is
most easily done by putting the triangle over your
index finger, so that the 2 ends hang below the
fingertip, and pressing the ends together with the
thumb and index finger of your other hand.

Drop the *won tons* in a large kettle of boiling
water, adding only enough at a time so as not to
crowd them. Simmer for about 10 minutes; they
will float on the surface when ready. Remove with
a slotted spoon and set on a cloth. When all are
cooked, bring the chicken stock just to a boil, add
the *won tons* and heat through. Ladle stock and
won tons into bowls and garnish with green onions.
Makes approximately 55 *won tons*

Fried Won Tons Make the *won tons* as directed
above, but do not boil. Heat peanut oil in a wok or
deep pan and deep fry the *won tons* until lightly
golden, about 1-1/2 to 2 minutes. Remove with a
slotted spoon, drain on paper toweling and serve
with Dipping Sauce, page 59.

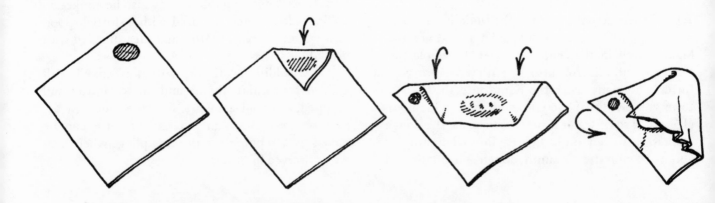

SOUP WITH VEGETABLE-MEAT DUMPLINGS
Mandoo (Korea)

Soup
4 pounds (2 kg) meaty beef bones
4 large slices ginger root
2-1/2 quarts (2.5 L) water
1 teaspoon (5 ml) salt
2 tablespoons (30 ml) light soy sauce or to taste

Dumplings
2 tablespoons (30 ml) peanut oil
1/4 pound (125 g) ground lean beef
1/4 pound (125 g) ground lean pork
3 tablespoons (45 ml) water
1/4 pound (125 g) bean sprouts
1/2 small head Napa cabbage
1/2 cup (125 ml) finely minced bamboo shoots
1 square *tofu* (Japanese-style bean curd), well
    drained and mashed
1/4 cup (50 ml) finely minced green onions
2 teaspoons (10 ml) crushed toasted sesame seeds
1/4 teaspoon (1 ml) minced garlic
Freshly ground black pepper to taste
30 to 36 square *Won Ton* Skins, page 46

Peanut oil
Chopped green onions
Chopped fresh coriander

To make the soup, put the bones, ginger and water in a large soup kettle. Bring to a boil and skim off any froth that forms on the surface. Reduce heat, cover and simmer for 2-1/2 to 3 hours. Strain stock and chill; remove any surface fat. Set aside.

To make the dumplings, heat the peanut oil in a skillet or saucepan and sauté the beef and pork until it loses its raw redness. Add the water and simmer gently until all of the liquid evaporates; set aside. Parboil the bean sprouts in lightly salted water for 2 minutes, then drain, chop finely and set aside. Parboil the cabbage in lightly salted water for 5 minutes, then drain and chop finely. Combine the cooked meats, chopped bean sprouts and cabbage, bamboo shoots, *tofu*, green onions, sesame seeds, garlic and pepper and mix well. Taste and correct seasoning, if necessary. Put a spoonful of filling in the center of each *won ton* skin, lightly dampen edges of skin with water and fold over to form a triangle, pressing edges together securely. As you make the dumplings, cover them with a towel to prevent them from drying out.

Return the soup to the kettle and bring to a boil. Add the salt and soy sauce. Taste and correct seasoning, if necessary. Drop the dumplings into the soup, adding only enough at a time so as not to crowd them. Simmer for about 10 minutes; they will float on the surface when ready. Remove with a slotted spoon to a warmed soup tureen. When all are done, drizzle a little peanut oil on them and then cover with the boiling soup. Garnish with green onions and coriander and serve.
Makes 6 servings

PORK AND SHRIMP DUMPLINGS
Shui Mai (China)

Filling
1/2 pound (250 g) ground lean pork butt
1/2 pound (250 g) shrimp, shelled, deveined
    and minced
1/3 cup (75 ml) finely minced water chestnuts
1 tablespoon (15 ml) Chinese rice wine or
    dry sherry
2 tablespoons (30 ml) cornstarch
1-1/2 tablespoons (22 ml) water
1/2 teaspoon (3 ml) sugar
1/2 teaspoon (3 ml) salt
1 tablespoon (15 ml) light soy sauce
1 teaspoon (5 ml) Oriental sesame oil

24 round *Won Ton* Skins, page 46
Fresh coriander leaves

Combine all of the filling ingredients and mix together well; set aside for about 15 minutes to let flavors blend. Put about 1 tablespoon (15 ml) of filling in the center of each *won ton* round. Place the round in the palm of your hand and bring up all the edges to envelope the sides of the filling, giving a "gathered" or "pleated" look to the sides and leaving the filling exposed at the top. Flatten the bottoms so the dumplings will stand up and place in a lightly oiled steamer pan or dish in a single layer. Put a small coriander leaf on top of each filling and steam over boiling water for about 20 minutes. Serve immediately.

Makes 24 *shui mai*

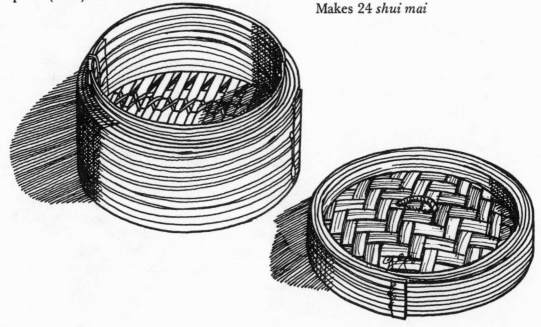

SHRIMP DUMPLINGS IN TRANSPARENT DOUGH
Har Gow (China)

Filling
1 pound (500 g) shrimp, shelled and deveined
2 tablespoons (30 ml) minced cooked ham
    (optional)
1 cup (250 ml) finely minced bamboo shoots or
    water chestnuts
2 green onions, finely chopped
1/2 teaspoon (2 ml) minced ginger root
1-1/2 tablespoons (22 ml) cornstarch
3/4 teaspoon (4 ml) Oriental sesame oil
1 tablespoon (15 ml) light soy sauce
1 tablespoon (15 ml) Chinese rice wine or
    dry sherry

1 recipe Wheat Starch Dough, page 48
Peanut oil

Make the dough, and while it is resting, combine all of the ingredients for the filling. Return to the dough and form into circles as directed.

To form the dumplings, pinch 4 little pleats into one side of each dough circle. Put 1 tablespoon (15 ml) of filling in the center of the circle, bring up the pleated side and the side opposite to cover the filling and pinch edges together at the top, decoratively, like the edge of a pie crust. When all of the dumplings have been made, place them in a lightly oiled steamer pan or dish in a single layer. Brush the dumplings with a little water to keep them from drying out and steam over boiling water for about 12 minutes.

Makes approximately 50 *har gow*

DESSERT *WON TON*
Jar Won Ton (China)

1/4 pound (125 g) pitted dates, finely chopped
3 tablespoons (45 ml) finely chopped walnuts or
    almonds
Grated peel of 1/2 lemon
Fresh orange juice, as needed
24 square *Won Ton* Skins, page 46
Peanut oil for deep frying
Powdered sugar

Combine the dates, nuts and lemon peel and enough orange juice to make the mixture hold together, about 2 teaspoons (10 ml). (The amount of orange juice needed will depend upon the moisture content of the dates.) Shape the mixture into 24 small cylinders about 3/4 to 1 inch (2 to 3 cm) long and 1/4 inch (6 mm) in diameter. Set a cylinder diagonally across each *won ton* square. Pick up a corner of the square, fold it over the cylinder and tuck the corner under the filling. Now roll up the square into a tubular shape, so that the filling is completely enclosed. Twist the ends of the tube and put your finger in each end to make it flare open. The *won ton* should look like a "popper" at a childrens' party.

When all are made, heat the peanut oil in a wok or deep pan and deep fry the *won ton* until lightly golden, cooking only 6 to 8 at a time. Lift out with a slotted spoon or chopsticks and drain on paper toweling. Let cool and then sprinkle with powdered sugar to serve.

Makes 24 *won tons*

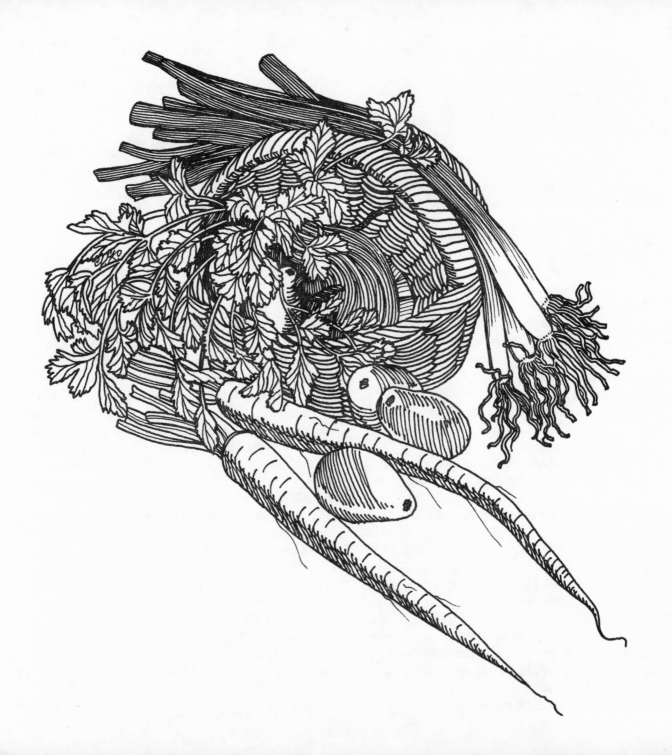

COUSCOUS

Though *couscous* is also found in Sicily, Brazil and southern France, all acknowledge its North African origin, where it dates from earliest times. Like many other *pasta* forms, *couscous* is usually made of semolina flour and water, but it differs from these forms in the manner the dough is manipulated into little "grains." Small pieces are pinched off a large ball of dough and then rubbed between the palms of the hands to form the "grains."

Couscous "grains" may be tiny or fairly large and coarse. The large grains, each one individually rolled, are called *mhammsa* and are, I believe, impossible to find in the United States. If you can find *couscous* sold loose and by weight rather than packaged, do by all means use it. The packaged kind is often precooked and will not stand up to the "working over" it should have, nor does it have the same texture and flavor. Each grain of *couscous* will, if properly cooked, be fluffy, separate and almost dry, with a chewiness characteristic of good *pasta*.

Like most national dishes, *couscous* is made differently by every North African cook and each swears his or her own is the only true *couscous*. I first ate *couscous* in Tangiers and was absolutely delighted with its delicacy and tenderness. Now I find I prefer the Moroccan *couscous* over others for this very reason. It is light and fluffy, and the stew (which can be made of almost any ingredient —pigeon, chicken, lamb, goat, fish, turnips, pumpkin, etc.) is never overcooked or concocted of so many ingredients they cannot be recognized.

Moreover, as you travel about North Africa, you find that *couscous* is known by many names— *seksu, sicook, scksu, siksu, kuskün*. In southern France it is called *couscous* with a singsong lilt; in Sicily, it is called *cùscusu*. Oddly enough it is also known in Brazil, where it is called *cuscuz*.

Years after I left Morocco, I met a young French architect, André Breton, living in Rome, who had been reared in Tunis. One day he told me how *couscous* was made in his mother's kitchen: A group of native girls (who worked in the house) sat in a circle around a huge circular basket. In the basket were large balls of dough they had made earlier in the day. The girls began by pinching off small pieces and rubbing them between the palms of their hands, letting them drop back into the basket. They sang and swayed rhythmically as they worked—picking up dough, rubbing it, dropping it into the basket, again and again until the *couscous* grains were the right size to please André's mother.

André asked his mother to send a batch of their homemade *couscous* to him. When she did, he and I prepared a Tunisian-style dinner for our friends. The main difference between the Tunisian *couscous* we made that day and the Moroccan *couscous* I had eaten years before was the incredible variety of ingredients the Tunisians tossed together for the stew and sauce. It seemed like we used every vegetable in the market. But it was nevertheless delicious, and I have included it here.

PREPARING *COUSCOUS*

When preparing *couscous,* you want to swell the grains with as much liquid as possible without reducing them to mush. *Couscous* must be free of lumps and each grain separate and almost, but not quite, dry.

The very first step is to wash the *couscous.* Put the *couscous* in a large bowl and pour on several cups of water. Quickly stir with your hands, then pour off the excess water by draining through a fine sieve. Pour the *couscous* back into the bowl and let it rest; the grains expand for about 20 minutes. Then, with both hands, fingers separated and "open," lift the grains lightly, sprinkling with more water if you feel it will absorb it. "Sift" the grains through your fingers, rubbing them together to undo lumps and "raking" the grains as you do soil in the garden.

Now dampen a long strip of muslin or a towel and twist it to fit around the top of a stock pot or bottom pan of a *couscoussière* (see information on *couscous* equipment, page 24). It will keep steam from escaping and force it up through the holes in the bottom of the top part of the *couscoussière.* Before putting on the top part, be sure that the stew or liquid in the lower part will not touch the *couscous* in the upper part.

With top in place, pour half the moistened *couscous* into the top part, and using your hand, form the *couscous* into a mound. Allow to steam for 5 minutes or so, then add remaining *couscous.* Steam, uncovered, for about 20 minutes over medium heat. Be sure the stew or steaming liquid does not boil, but simmers gently.

Now, return the *couscous* to the large bowl in which it was dampened and tossed. With a large wooden spoon or fork, spread the *couscous* flat. Add salt to a little water and sprinkle it over the *couscous.* Again, work the *couscous,* tossing and "raking" to break up lumps and distribute the water. The *couscous* should feel slightly moist and without lumps. Some prefer to work in a little butter or oil but that is a personal matter; it is not necessary. It can now stand for a few hours, covered with a cloth, if you have made it beforehand.

About 30 minutes before serving, again work through the *couscous* with your hands and again re-seal the section between top and bottom of the *couscoussière.* Again pour the *couscous* back into the top pan and steam as before, for about 20 minutes.

Whenever you make *couscous,* for any recipe, this is the procedure for preparing it, unless otherwise indicated.

BEEF AND LAMB COUSCOUS
(Tunis)

This is the recipe André and I used for our great feast.

Stew
Olive oil
1 large onion, cut in half
2 pounds (1 kg) beef stew meat, cut into large
　　pieces
2 pounds (1 kg) lamb stew meat, cut into large
　　pieces
2 large ripe tomatoes, peeled and quartered
1 turnip, quartered
4 celery stalks, cut into 1-inch (3 cm) pieces
3 zucchini, each cut into 4 pieces
6 small artichokes, quartered
1/4 cup (75 ml) tomato sauce
3 carrots, each cut into 4 pieces
1-1/2 teaspoons (7 ml) salt
Freshly ground black pepper
1 small white cabbage, quartered
2 large potatoes, peeled and quartered
1 small chicken, cut into serving pieces

Chickpeas
2 cups (500 ml) dried chickpeas, soaked overnight
　　in water to cover and drained, or
2 cans (16 ounce or 450 g each) cooked
　　chickpeas, drained
1 teaspoon (5 ml) ground cumin
Salt and freshly ground black pepper to taste

2 pounds (1 kg) *couscous*

To make the stew, heat about 1/4 inch (6 mm) olive oil in the bottom pan of a large *couscoussière* (or stock pot) placed over medium heat and add all the ingredients in the order given, except the potatoes and chicken. Stir frequently for the first 10 minutes of cooking. Then add water to cover and cook, covered, over low heat for 2 hours or until meat is tender. Add the potatoes and cook for 10 minutes. Add the chicken pieces and cook, covered, for another 30 minutes. Remove meats and keep warm.

While the stew is cooking, simmer the dried chickpeas with cumin in water to cover until tender; drain. Season with salt and pepper and add to stew. (If using canned chickpeas, simply drain, mix with seasoning and add to stew.)

To make the *couscous*, prepare it according to directions, preceding, steaming it over the stew as the stew cooks. (To be honest, André rubbed butter and warm water into the grains and then steamed them once, thoroughly, for about 45 minutes. This method does not, however, produce *couscous* that is as tender and fluffy as that produced by the double-steaming method.)

To serve, put the *couscous* on a large tray or platter and make a depression in the center. Pour on a few ladlefuls of the vegetables or broth (or both). Arrange the meats in one large bowl, vegetables in another. Serve broth in a separate bowl.
Makes 10 to 12 servings

COUSCOUS, TRAPANI STYLE
Cùscusu alla Trapanese (Sicily)

It is believed this ancient dish was introduced to southern Europe by the invading Moslems. When they were driven off, the Sicilians attempted to erase all marks of their hated overlords, but somehow *couscous,* or *cùscusu* as it is called in Sicily, persisted.

This recipe gives directions for making *cùscusu* from scratch. If you prefer the easy route, simply buy the largest and coarsest-grained *couscous* you can find and proceed to the fish stew.

Cùscusu
3 to 4 bay leaves
2/3 cup (150 ml) olive oil
1 pound (500 g) coarse semolina
Approximately 1 cup (250 ml) lightly salted water

Fish Stew
5 pounds (2.5 kg) assorted seafood, such as
    white fish, clams, mussels, squid, lobster,
    crayfish, shrimp, etc.
1-1/2 cups (375 ml) Tomato Sauce, page 53
1 large onion, chopped

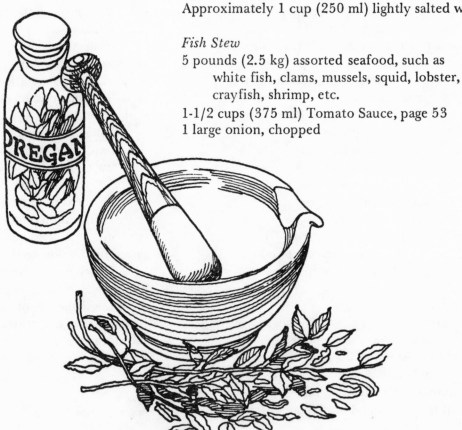

1 large celery stalk with leaves, chopped
1/2 cup (125 ml) chopped fresh parsley
1 garlic clove
1 bay leaf, crumbled
1 cup (250 ml) dry white wine
4 tablespoons (60 ml) olive oil
Salt and freshly ground black pepper to taste

Broth
Heads, tails and bones of filleted fish
Pinch of salt
1-1/2 quarts (1.5 L) water
1 parsley sprig
1/2 large onion
1 bay leaf

To make the *cùscusu,* first combine the bay leaves and olive oil in a small pitcher and let stand; the oil will absorb the aroma and flavor of the bay leaves while you make the *cùscusu.*

Pour the semolina into a large bowl about 1-1/2 inches (4 cm) deep and gradually sprinkle on the water. With both hands, work the water into the semolina to form a thick ball of paste (much like making any *pasta*). Since it is impossible to know just how much liquid the semolina will absorb, you may require more water or less, so add it very gradually or you will end up with a soggy mess. It is not easy to blend, since the semolina actually repels water, so prepare for hard work. Once you have made this ball of firm but soft paste, pinch off small pieces, and using fingers and palms of hands, break them into smaller and smaller pieces until you have "grains" *again.* They need not be round or even, but should be no larger than small round grains of rice.

Spread the grains of *cùscusu* out to dry and as you do this; check that they are quite separate and there are no lumps. The Sicilians do it out in the sun, of course, but you may have to use a large shallow basket or clean cloth spread over a large table. During the drying time (which is relative, depending on humidity, heat, etc.) return to the *cùscusu* from time to time and lift, toss and spread grains to keep them separate. When nicely dried, pour the *cùscusu* into a large wooden bowl and drizzle on a fine stream of the bay-scented olive oil, working it into the grains with your fingers. Set *cùscusu* aside.

Clean the shellfish for the fish stew and leave them in the shell or shell them as desired. Fillet the white fish, reserving heads, tails, bones and any trimmings for the broth. Set the seafood aside.

Now make the fish broth by combining the reserved fish heads, tails, etc. with all remaining ingredients in a saucepan. Bring to a boil, reduce heat, cover and simmer for about 30 minutes; strain.

Put the fish broth in the bottom of the *couscoussière* (or equivalent stock pot) and steam the *cùscusu* for the first time as directed on page 180. Remove the *cùscusu.* To the broth add all the stew ingredients, arranging the fish fillets and shellfish on top. Cover and cook over medium heat for about 20 minutes, or until the seafood is done. Carefully lift out the seafood and keep warm. Steam the *cùscusu* for the second time over the broth and vegetables.

When the *cùscusu* is done, mound it on a platter and arrange the seafood around it. Pour a little of the broth over the top and serve the remaining broth in a bowl on the side.
Makes 8 to 10 servings

COUSCOUS-STUFFED CHICKEN
Frakeh Ma'Amra (Morocco)

1/2 cup (125 ml) *couscous*
1/4 pound (125 g) unsalted butter
1/2 cup (125 ml) toasted blanched almonds
1/2 cup (125 ml) tightly packed seedless raisins
Ground cinnamon
Powdered saffron
3 tablespoons (45 ml) dark aromatic honey
2 fresh hot chili peppers, finely minced, or
1-1/2 teaspoons (7 ml) or less cayenne pepper
1 large roasting chicken
Salt and freshly ground black pepper
1 small onion, grated
2 cups (500 ml) water

Steam the *couscous* over water as directed on page 180, doing only a single steaming for about 20 minutes, then spread the *couscous* out and let it dry for 20 minutes. Return the *couscous* to the top of the *couscoussière* and steam over water for 15 minutes. Now put the *couscous* into a large bowl and toss with 2 tablespoons (30 ml) of the butter. Stir in the almonds, raisins, and a pinch each of cinnamon, black pepper and saffron. Toss well to blend flavors, then stir in 2 tablespoons (30 ml) of the honey and the chili peppers. Using two forks, toss well. Taste and correct seasoning, if necessary.

Rub the cavities of the chicken with salt and black pepper; stuff them loosely with the *couscous* mixture. Sew or skewer the openings closed. Mix about 2 tablespoons (30 ml) of the butter with a pinch each of saffron, salt and black pepper and rub on the outside of the chicken. Cover the bottom of a large flameproof casserole with the grated onion and set the chicken on top, breast side up. Pour the water into the casserole and dot chicken with remaining butter.

Place the casserole over moderately high heat and bring the liquid to a boil. Reduce heat, cover tightly and simmer gently for about 30 minutes, basting from time to time. Uncover casserole and carefully turn the chicken over. Continue cooking, covered, until the chicken is tender. Test for doneness by piercing the thigh with a fork; when juices are no longer pink the chicken is cooked.

Remove the chicken from the casserole and keep warm. Turn heat up to high and boil the juices, reducing them to about 1 cup (250 ml). Stir in remaining honey and a generous pinch of cinnamon. Return the chicken to the casserole on top of the now-thickened sauce and gently turn it in the sauce several times to glaze the skin; try to avoid breaking the skin. Then transfer the chicken to a heated serving dish and remove sewing threads or skewers. Taste sauce and correct seasoning, if necessary, adding a little more butter, if desired. Pour sauce over and around the chicken and serve immediately.
Makes 6 servings

Note This amount of stuffing and sauce will also be adequate for 6 Cornish game hens or squabs. A very young turkey of no more than 6 to 6-1/2 pounds (approximately 3 kg) will also fill nicely.

SWEET *COUSCOUS*
(North Africa)

A sweetened form of *couscous* can be found in all of the countries along the northern coast of Africa. It differs somewhat in each country and each is, of course, known by a different name. All are, however, overwhelmingly sweet to my taste, so I have, in adapting the recipe, adjusted it to suit Western tastes.

2 cups (500 ml) fruit juice, such as tamarind, orange, etc., or a combination
1 tablespoon (15 ml) rosewater
1 cup (250 ml) medium grain *couscous*
1/4 pound (125 g) *smen* (clarified butter, page 57), melted and cooled
1/4 cup (75 ml) finely ground pistachio nuts
1/2 cup (125 ml) superfine sugar, mixed with
1-1/2 tablespoons (22 ml) ground cinnamon
1/4 cup (75 ml) coarsely chopped pistachio nuts
1/2 cup (125 ml) candied almonds (sometimes called Jordan almonds)
Additional 1/2 teaspoon (2 ml) rosewater
1/2 cup (125 ml) pomegranate seeds or pitted dates, rolled in superfine sugar then broken up into small bits

Combine the fruit juice and 1 tablespoon (15 ml) rosewater, sprinkle a little over the *couscous* in a large bowl and separate the grains well. Then steam the *couscous* over the remaining fruit juice as directed on page 180. After the first steaming, return the *couscous* to the bowl and work 3 to 4 tablespoons (45 to 60 ml) of the *smen* and the ground pistachios into it. Be sure to eliminate all lumps, then steam a second time over the fruit juice and work in remaining *smen*. The *couscous* should be light and fluffy and free of lumps.

On a large serving tray mound the *couscous* and sprinkle on the cinnamon-sugar mixture in a decorative pattern. Then sprinkle on the coarsely chopped pistachios and arrange the candied almonds around the edge as a border. Sprinkle on the 1/2 teaspoon (2 ml) rosewater and the pomegranate seeds.
Makes 6 servings

INDEX

GERTRUDE HARRIS was first introduced to *pasta* in the kitchen of her parents, Russian Jews who had emigrated to New York. Here she helped her mother prepare the *kreplach* or *varnishkes* of Eastern Europe. Later, during the 11 years she and her husband, the painter-sculptor Zev, lived in Paris and Rome, and during the many years she has lived in California, Ms. Harris came to admire and acquire the *pasta* recipes of many cuisines. These recipes—some from friends, some from restaurants and some from her own experimentation—comprise this book.

Pasta International is Gertrude Harris' third book for 101 Productions. *Pots & Pans, Etc.,* a critical guide to cookware, was published in 1971, and hailed by M.F.K. Fisher as "a jewel"; a British edition is being published by Penguin in England. In 1972, her second book, *Foods of the Frontier,* was published to equally high critical acclaim. Writing in *California Today,* Mary Gottschalk stated that *Foods of the Frontier* "is one of the best cookbooks ever published and should be on the shelf of every cook. . . ."

But Gertrude Harris' creativity extends beyond the kitchen. She not only cooks, but paints and writes poetry as well. She received a bachelor's degree in art education from New York University and has directed galleries of contemporary art in New York City, Rome and Monterey, California. Her art reviews have appeared in various journals in the United States and abroad, and her poetry has been published in several anthologies, including *53 American Poets,* edited by Ruth Witt-Diamant and published by Kenkyusha, Japan.

Gertrude Harris is also an authority on herbs. She raises many varieties in the garden of her home in Point Richmond, California, and has conducted lectures and herb taste-ins throughout the San Francisco Bay Area.

VERNON KOSKI describes himself as a painter by avocation and an illustrator by vocation. He studied at the Art Center College of Design in Los Angeles and later received a bachelor of fine arts degree from the University of Oregon. For 11 years he worked as a commercial artist in New York and presently lives in Sausalito, California, where he paints and does free-lance illustration and design. His work has been reproduced on many posters, magazine and record album covers.